China, the United States, and the Global Economy

EDITED BY

SHUXUN CHEN

AND

CHARLES WOLF, JR.

RAND

Library of Congress Cataloging-in-Publication Data

China, the United States, and the global economy / edited by Shuxun Chen and Charles Wolf, Jr.

p. cm.

"MR-1300-RC."

ISBN 0-8330-2963-0

1. China—Economic conditions—1976– 2. China—Foreign economic relations—United States. 3. United States—Foreign economic relations—China. I. Chen, Shuxun. II. Wolf, Charles, 1924– III. Rand Corporation. IV. Rand–CRF Conference (1999 : Santa Monica, Calif.).

HC427.92 .C464449 2001
330.951—dc21

00-068329

Published 2001 by RAND
1700 Main Street, P.O. Box 2138, Santa Monica, CA 90407-2138
1200 South Hayes Street, Arlington, VA 22202-5050
RAND URL: http://www.rand.org/
To order RAND documents or to obtain additional information, contact Distribution Services: Telephone: (310) 451-7002; Fax: (310) 451-6915; Internet: order@rand.org

FOREWORD

This book contains the edited papers presented by Chinese and American scholars and practitioners at the second of four annual conferences organized by RAND in Santa Monica, and the China Reform Forum (CRF) in Beijing. The second conference was held at RAND on November 9–10, 1999, with about 30 participants including the authors and their discussants. The list of participants appears at the end of this volume.

The second CRF–RAND conference and the editing and other requisites for readying the original papers for publication could not have been accomplished without the generous support of several organizations and individuals. These include—besides the China Reform Forum and RAND—the Committee of 100 and Henry Tang, the Hoover Institution and John Raisian, the Capital Group Companies and Gina Despres, Lombard Investments and Joseph Chulick, the UCLA Center for International Studies and Richard Rosecrance, the Zhejiang Gateway International Investment Company and James Bitonti, and the Overland Group and Fred Liao.

It is a pleasure to acknowledge and express our appreciation for their support. It goes without saying that none of these organizations or individuals bears any responsibility for the content of the wide-ranging views and policy suggestions presented in the book.

Charles Wolf, Jr.
Santa Monica, California

CONTENTS

Foreword iii

Acronyms xi

Chapter One
CHINA, THE UNITED STATES, AND THE GLOBAL ECONOMY: INTRODUCTION AND OVERVIEW
Shuxun Chen, China Reform Forum, and Charles Wolf, Jr., RAND 1

Part I: Outlook for the Global Economy

Chapter Two
TRENDS AND PROSPECTS IN THE GLOBAL ECONOMY
Gary Hufbauer, Institute for International Economics 11

Chapter Three
WORLD ECONOMIC RESTRUCTURING AND CHINA'S ECONOMIC TRANSFORMATION
Yuanzheng Cao, BOC International Holdings Ltd. . . . 25
Discussant: Benjamin Zycher, RAND 45

Part II: Outlook for the U.S. Economy

Chapter Four
CAN THE UNITED STATES' ECONOMIC SUCCESS CONTINUE?
Gail Fosler, The Conference Board 49

Part III: Trends and Prospects in the Chinese Economy

Chapter Five
CHINA'S ECONOMIC GROWTH: RECENT TRENDS AND PROSPECTS
K. C. Yeh, RAND 69

Chapter Six
THE CHINESE ECONOMY IN PROSPECT
Angang Hu, Chinese Academy of Sciences 99

Chapter Seven
THE ROLE OF FOREIGN-INVESTED ENTERPRISES IN THE CHINESE ECONOMY: AN INSTITUTIONAL FOUNDATION APPROACH
Yasheng Huang, Harvard Business School 147

Chapter Eight
CHINA'S MACROECONOMY: EXPANDING DOMESTIC DEMAND AND INTERIM REFORMS
Xiaomin Shi, China Society for Research on Economic System Reform 193
Discussant: Alice Young 205

Part IV: U.S.-China Economic and Security Relations

Chapter Nine
CHINA AND THE WORLD ECONOMY: THE SHORT MARCH FROM ISOLATION TO MAJOR PLAYER
Harry S. Rowen, Asia Pacific Research Center, and Hoover Institution 211

Chapter Ten
AMERICAN INTERESTS IN AND CONCERNS WITH CHINA
John Despres, Private Consultant 227
Discussant: Shuxun Chen 233

Chapter Eleven
SINO-U.S. ECONOMIC AND TRADE RELATIONS
Xianquan Xu, MOFTEC 237
Discussant: Hang-Sheng Cheng 253

Chapter Twelve
U.S.-CHINA: BONDS AND TENSIONS
Hui Wang, First China Capital 257

Conference Agenda 289

List of Participants. 291

Biographical Summaries of Chapter Authors 295

ACRONYMS

BEA	Bureau of Economic Analysis
COEs	Collectively owned enterprises
CPE	Centrally Planned Economies
CPI	Consumer Price Index
CTOEC	China Tianjing Otis Elevatory Company
FAW	First Automotive Work
FDI	Foreign direct investment
FIEs	Foreign-invested enterprises
FSU	Former Soviet Union
GDP	Gross domestic product
GNP	Gross national product
ICI	Investment Company Institute
IO	Industrial organization
IPF	Institutional and policy factors
IT	Information technology
LEI	Leading economic indicators
MNCs	Multinational corporations
MOFTEC	Ministry of Foreign Trade and Economic Cooperation

NAFTA	North American Fair Trade Association
NIEs	Newly industrialized economies
OECD	Organization for Economic Cooperation and Development
P/Es	Price earnings ratios
PPI	Producer Price Index
PPP	Purchasing power parity
RMB	Renminbi (yuan)
S&P	Standard and Poor's
SAIC	Shanghai Automotive Industrial Corporation
SEZs	Special Economic Zones
SOEs	State-owned enterprises
SPC	State Planning Commission
SSB	State Statistical Bureau
TEC	Tianjing Elevatory Company
TFP	Total factor productivity
TVEs	Township and village enterprises

Chapter One

CHINA, THE UNITED STATES, AND THE GLOBAL ECONOMY: INTRODUCTION AND OVERVIEW

Shuxun Chen and Charles Wolf, Jr.

ABOUT THIS BOOK

From 1998 through 2000, the China Reform Forum (CRF) in Beijing and RAND in Santa Monica have jointly organized an annual conference of experts from China and the United States, focusing on economic and security subjects of mutual concern. Venues of the three conferences alternated between Beijing and Santa Monica, and conference participants included practitioners as well as scholars from both countries.

This book contains the papers delivered at the 1999 conference in Santa Monica, California, whose theme, "China, the United States, and the Global Economy," provides the book's title.[1] The conference agenda and list of participants appear at the end of this volume.

The broad theme was deliberately chosen to provide ample scope to address both economic and security interests and concerns of the United States and China. While the theme was overly ambitious, it allowed participants to address both quantitative and qualitative aspects of the subject: quantitative data relating to trade and investment, both bilaterally between China and the United States, and multilaterally between them and the rest of the world; and qualitative considerations such as those relating to China's (and Taiwan's)

[1]The subject of the conference held November 16–17, 2000, in Beijing was "The Challenges of Globalization."

membership in the World Trade Organization (WTO), as well as the convergent and divergent security interests of China and the United States.

The principal objective of the 1999 CRF–RAND conference was to compare analysis and judgments from both sides about the economic outlook for each of the three entities referred to in the conference title—China, the United States, and the Global Economy. Associated with but subsidiary to this aim, the conference papers and accompanying discussions considered the extent to which the economic outlook in each of the three entities is dependent on, or independent of, that for the other two.

OVERVIEW OF THE CHAPTERS

In Chapter Two, Dr. Gary Hufbauer examines the outlook for the global economy. He projects relatively rapid growth in some countries and regions, but not in others. These differences he ascribes to four principal "drivers": macroeconomic stability, the rule of law, privatization and the market economy, and international trade and investment. Hufbauer's "bottom-line" assessment is that East Asia is likely to be the world's most rapidly growing region, while the rich Organization for Economic Cooperation and Development (OECD) countries will sustain reasonably good rates of growth, (about 1.8 percent per capita per year). He concludes that "one thing that will not happen . . . is a blissful convergence between rich and poor countries." Some of the poorer countries in East Asia will move toward convergence, but most will not.

It is no surprise that Dr. Hufbauer finds that sustained growth and prosperity in the American economy will redound to China's benefit through its stimulus to China's exports to the United States. However, he also suggests that China's economic development will be more affected by factors other than the buoyancy of the American economy: for example, by streamlining and genuinely privatizing China's state-owned enterprises (SOEs), extending the rule of law, and enforcing property rights and contracts. In turn, the economic outlook in the United States is likely to depend much more on domestic factors—for example, sustained productivity improvements, stable monetary and fiscal policy, and high employment rates—than on developments in China. Most economists would also assert what

Dr. Hufbauer's balanced evaluation only implies: China's economic prospects are much more likely to be influenced by the U.S. economy than is the U.S. economy to be influenced by that in China.

Dr. Cao's contribution in Chapter Three on "World Economic Restructuring and China's Economic Transformation" envisages three principal challenges facing China's economy: rural industrialization, modernization and restructuring of urban industry, and "developing its knowledge economy." His chapter is principally concerned with how these challenges will be affected by, and may in turn affect, the global economy. His discussion anticipates increased "globalization" and opening of China's economy, its exposure to intensified international competition, the effects of these trends on the restructuring and reform of China's economy, and its comparative advantages in international trade.

In Chapter Four, Dr. Gail Fosler, poses a critical question: "Can the United States' Economic Status Continue"? Her answer is strongly affirmative. Although acknowledging "these very optimistic conclusions may appear to be Panglossian," she grounds them in the buoyancy of consumer incomes and consumption demand, rather than in the enhanced technology and productivity of the high-tech economic sectors in the United States.

In Chapter Five, Dr. Yeh reviews "China's Economic Growth: Recent Trends and Prospects." He notes and dissects the myriad problems and puzzles presented by China's economic statistics. He concludes from this analysis that, while the aggregate size of China's economy has been underestimated, its economic growth has probably been overestimated by at least 2–3 percent! Dr. Yeh contends that China's problem of sustaining an adjusted economic growth rate of 6–8 percent is likely to be an "arduous challenge." He concludes that the long-term growth rate is in fact likely to be somewhat lower: "How much lower will depend largely on the pace, direction, and effectiveness of economic reforms."

Professor Angang Hu's Chapter Six, "The Chinese Economy in Prospect," assesses China's near-term and longer-term growth prospects. In the near-term, he emphasizes the importance of anti-deflationary policies in the economy to offset the deflationary tendencies engendered by the downsizing of SOEs and the accompanying increases in urban unemployment and the losses of pension, health care, and other social benefits that typically have been provided by the SOEs to their employees. For the longer-term, Professor Hu's package of recommended policies is far-reaching, dramatic, and daunting. The package of reforms includes reducing the burden of taxes and fees on investors, canceling direct and indirect subsidies to the SOEs, building an efficient "social safety net," establishing transparent competitive bidding procedures for production and procurement contracts, reducing or canceling tariffs and nontariff barriers, and repealing current policies and practices that discriminate against or in favor of foreign investment.

If President Jiang Zemin and Premier Zhu Rongji were to give these policies the explicit imprimatur of China's government, such negative consequences as might ensue from them in the short-run would be swamped in the medium to longer-term by the gains for China, the United States, and the global economy.

In Chapter Seven, Professor Yasheng Huang presents a provocative analysis of "The Role of Foreign-Invested Enterprises in the Chinese Economy," employing what he refers to as an Institutional and Policy Factors Approach (IPF). He acknowledges the importance of foreign direct investment (FDI), and the relatively rapid growth of foreign-invested enterprises (FIEs) as sources of both gross national product growth and of real investment in fixed assets, compared with the contributions of the SOEs. Addressing the question of why FDI and FIEs are ascribed special importance in China's economic growth, Professor Huang devotes about equal attention to two issues: rebutting the standard explanations and advocating his own novel explanation. In the first category, he finds the conventional explanations—enhanced productivity, export performance, bridging savings-investment gaps, and importing technology and improved management techniques—to be unconvincing.

In the second category, Professor Huang describes a new approach to explaining the FDI/FIE phenomenon in China—an approach that places principal emphasis on institutional and policy factors. In brief, IPF focus on the imperfections and inefficiencies in China's domestic product and financial markets. These inefficiencies, he argues, result from China's slowly changing legacy of central planning, and of non-market-based mechanisms for resource allocation: for example, the favoritism still accorded to SOEs in access to capital and their protection from import competition. The result is discrimination against domestic start-ups and competitive markets. The institutional and policy factors approach also includes China's jurisdictional decentralization, which inhibits those Chinese provinces that are short of savings access to capital in other provinces that have excess savings.

In Chapter Eight, Dr. Xiaomin Shi considers "China's Macroeconomy: Expanding Domestic Demand and Interim Reforms," focusing on the "structural contradictions" that inhibit China's growth and modernization. He emphasizes the "contradiction" between the efforts of financial and central ministerial management, on the one hand, and the operation of market mechanisms in allocating resources, on the other. To reduce if not remove these contradictions, Dr. Shi urges that the division between government and market responsibilities should be more rigorously defined. Government should retreat "from areas in which government interference is improper," while increasing its "presence" in areas where Dr. Shi believes the market does not function well. He envisages a concentration of government efforts to "promote and perfect market mechanisms," while supervising the behavior of market players to prevent monopoly and abuse.

In Chapter Nine, Professor Henry Rowen elaborates China's "Short March from Isolation to Major Player." He charts the "march" in terms of China's growing shares of international trade and global foreign investment, according particular attention to the important facilitating role of Hong Kong and prospectively of China's accession to WTO.

John Despres presents in Chapter Ten a broad overview of "American Interests In and Concerns with China." Among the main U.S. interests that he cites are preventing wars in Asia, ensuring that China's relations with Taiwan remain peaceful, and sustaining growth in both the Chinese and American economies. More specifically, he notes China's economic growth is of importance to the United States—"not just to large multinational firms like Boeing, Microsoft and Motorola," but to American workers, farmers, and small businesses, as well. The importance of these interests will expand as China's markets open further as a result of WTO membership.

He points out that China also registers as a U.S. security concern in connection with Taiwan's peaceful future, and in China's evolving relations with "nuclear-armed South Asia." In Mr. Despres' view, U.S. concerns also extend to China's "one-party dictatorship," and the constraints it imposes on human rights, noting that "openly criticizing such strict constraints . . . will continue to be an essential expression of American ideals."

Dr. Xianquan Xu addresses "Sino-U.S. Economic and Trade Relations" in Chapter Eleven, concentrating on two key issues: the U.S. bilateral trade deficit with China and China's accession to WTO. Concerning the first of these issues, he contends that U.S. estimates of the bilateral trade deficit are based on erroneous data and, in any event, "the United States should not view its trade deficits with China as a serious problem." It might be noted in passing that while many American economists would demur on the statistical part of this contention, most would concur with Dr. Xu's quoted conclusions about trade deficits and especially the bilateral U.S. trade deficit with China.

Turning to China's accession to WTO, he suggests this will propel economic reform, enhance China's economic openness, and strengthen the rule of law in the economy and society at large.

Finally, in Chapter Twelve, Dr. Hui Wang provides a broad overview of U.S.-China relations—bonds and tensions. Among the "bonds" he cites regional security and prosperity, "business ties," bilateral trade, and preservation of the global environment. Among the "tensions," he emphasizes the status and future of Taiwan—citing "the contradictions," as he sees them, in U.S. policies toward Taiwan, as well as the bilateral trade imbalance and ideological divisions (including human rights in China). Dr. Wang concludes with the admonition that emphasis on the bonds in the U.S.-China relationship, rather than the tensions, is plainly advisable because "if the United States treats China as a friend, China is likely to act like one."

So much, then, for a brief overview of the diverse contributions to the 1999 conference between RAND and the China Reform Forum included in this volume. Particularly noteworthy is the diversity among the papers presented by senior Chinese scholars and members of the bureaucracy. Notwithstanding their diversity, several common themes emerge. These include, for example, the multiplicity of developments in the global economy encompassed by the term "globalization," including especially the frequent attention in several of the chapters to global capital flows, the importance of foreign direct investment, technology transfer, and enhancement of economic openness. Underlying these themes is agreement among both Chinese and American authors concerning the substantial benefits to be realized by China from these developments.

Indeed, these common themes were in large measure responsible for our decision to focus the third annual CRF–RAND conference in Beijing in November 2000 on "The Challenges of Globalization."

THE CHALLENGES OF GLOBALIZATION: COMMENTS ON THE BEIJING CONFERENCE IN 2000

While the emphasis accorded in both the American and Chinese papers to globalization is important to note, the term's precise meaning as reflected in the various chapters that use it is ambiguous. The millions of words and the dozens of books that purport to describe and define "globalization" recall the observation of an 18th century American philosopher, Benjamin Franklin: "A flood of words, and a drop of reason," as well as those of an anonymous 17th century poet: "Where words most abound, much sense beneath is rarely found"!

At a simple, nontechnical level, globalization may be defined as "the act, process, or policy of making something worldwide in scope or application."

A narrower definition focusing on economic openness, might be expressed in these terms: "globalization represents the increased speed, frequency, and magnitude of access to *national* markets by *nonnational* competitors." Moreover, this definition is intended to cover *all* markets including social, cultural, recreational, intellectual property, literature, film, music, and sports as well as those for merchandise and commercial services.

Globalization has struck all the countries of the world like a turbulent wave, capturing attention by politicians, scholars, entrepreneurs, workers, farmers, and voters around the globe. Some see it as a good fortune for global economic development, and some consider it a dangerous threat, if not a disaster. In any event, the issue is important. People from different countries with differing points of view should seek to strengthen mutual understanding.

The 2000 conference in Beijing on "The Challenges of Globalization" addressed the following aspects of globalization:

1. Meaning and measurement of globalization.
2. Experience, lessons, and implications of globalization across countries and historically since the mid-19th century.
3. Issues facing the United States and China in relation to globalization including issues of the recent trends of the U.S. economy, the recent explosive development in the information technology industry and the role of innovation, and empirical examination and implications of economic integration across the Taiwan Strait.

The annual CRF–RAND conferences offer scholars and practitioners a forum to demonstrate and exchange views and ideas from their broad and diverse backgrounds. It provides a platform for scholars and officials to explore and explain current and future issues and policies—in the process enhancing mutual appreciation and understanding.

Part I

OUTLOOK FOR THE GLOBAL ECONOMY

Chapter Two

TRENDS AND PROSPECTS IN THE GLOBAL ECONOMY

Gary Hufbauer

The global economy is a big subject, with numerous dimensions and conflicting currents. My observations are addressed to long-term scenarios—change over the next 20 years. The longer the time horizon, the greater the spectrum of possibilities. Rather than present an array of outcomes, my scenarios are ones that I regard as most likely. More optimistic perspectives on the world economy over the next 20 years can be found in the 1997 Organization for Economic Cooperation and Development (OECD) publication, *The World in 2020: Towards a New Global Age.*

LONG-TERM GROWTH: A BACKWARD VIEW

For those of us near the end of our careers, the year 1980 seems remarkably close and the year 2020 seems awfully distant. But the two years are equally spaced from this conference. Before speculating on unknown prospects in the murky future, it may be useful to underscore familiar trends in the clearer past.

Since 1980, two regions in the world economy have performed well: the rich OECD nations, which on average had good growth, and East Asia (including China, but excluding Japan), which had spectacular growth. Between 1980 and 2000, per-capita gross domestic product (GDP) in the rich OECD area (excluding Mexico and Korea) grew by about 1.4 percent annually, reaching $28,000 (at year 2000 prices in purchasing-power terms).[1] Per-capita GDP in East Asia grew by about 5.8 percent annually, reaching $4,600 (again in purchasing power). The world population in 2000 is about 6.1 billion, of which 0.9 billion live in rich OECD countries and 1.8 billion live in East Asia. For these 2.7 billion, the last two decades have, on the whole, been good years.

The same is not true elsewhere in the world. After a terrible decade in the 1980s, Latin America was struggling with modest growth in the 1990s. Over the past two decades, per-capita GDP has grown about 0.9 percent annually, reaching $7,200. India has gained ground, with annual per-capita GDP growth of about 3.1 percent. But in absolute terms, India remains very poor, with per-capita GDP of about $1,900.

Most of Africa, Russia, much of the former Soviet Union (FSU), Iraq, Iran, Afghanistan, Pakistan, Bangladesh, and Burma have endured disaster after disaster. All told, the population of these troubled countries numbers 1.9 billion. They have a wide range of per-capita GDP figures, but the average is probably around $2,800. Average per-capita GDP figures do not convey the extent of grinding poverty. In many countries, more than half the population exists on less than $2 per person per day. One out of three Russians lives on $1 per person per day.

Underlying the disparate trends in the world economy are four broad themes, or economic "drivers," that distinguish between winners and losers.

Macroeconomic Stability

A necessary condition for satisfactory long-term economic performance is macroeconomic stability. This means low inflation (under 10 percent per year); modest fiscal deficits (under 4 percent of GDP) or even fiscal surpluses; and an exchange rate that does not fluctuate wildly (average absolute real appreciation or real depreciation of more than 20 percent annually qualifies as "wild"). Nearly all the OECD countries and East Asia observed these conditions. During the

---

[1] All dollar amounts are in 2000 prices in purchasing-power terms unless otherwise noted.

1980s, these conditions were violated in most of Latin America; in the 1990s, they have been missing in Russia and many countries of the FSU; and for the last two decades, they have been absent in most of Africa and parts of the Middle East.

Once a country has experienced five or ten years of macroeconomic instability, it is hard to restore order. By that time, powerful interests (such as the military, industrial oligarchs, or strong unions) have acquired a grip on public spending and central bank credit, and it is terribly difficult to curtail their demands. Only with a social revolution were these forces defeated in Latin America. They still dominate in Russia, most of the FSU, most of Africa, and many other impoverished countries.

By the same token, after five or ten years of macroeconomic stability, powerful interests spring up to defend the *status quo*—a combination of pensioners, civil servants, others on fixed incomes, salaried employees, and most financial institutions. These forces are evident in Japan and the European Union—regions that value low inflation and fiscal prudence, even though their economies endured subpar performance in the 1990s.

Rule of Law

A contributing condition to satisfactory economic performance is the rule of law, especially as it applies to commercial dealings: property rights, contract rights, and honest administrative and judicial systems. The conceptual opposite to the rule of law is the rule of power. Under the rule of power, the person, company, or ministry with the upper hand appropriates most of the economic gain. In its crudest form, the rule of power is simply the rule of the military, as in the Congo, where the ownership of mines shifts with the fortunes of battle. In more subtle forms, the rule of power revolves around the minister who dispenses valuable licenses and permits, as in Indonesia.

Most countries lie along the spectrum between the rule of law and rule of power. The writing of economic laws (e.g., regulation, taxation, bankruptcy, etc.) is usually an exercise in political power rather than dispassionate public policy. Even in the "law-abiding" United Kingdom, the administration of justice reflects power in the sense that court litigation is expensive and the loser must bear the entire cost of both parties. While the role of power can never be abolished, economic performance is better favored by the rule of law. There are two reasons for this proposition.

First, societies that prize the rule of power devote substantial resources to the acquisition and defense of power—money for armies and police, money for political position, money for bribes. From a social standpoint, these resources are wasted, but from a private standpoint, the payoff can be enormous. In extreme forms—as in Russia, Congo, Afghanistan, Burma, and Cambodia—resources devoted to the acquisition of power literally devour the nation's economic base.

Second, societies that prize the rule of power erode the incentive to save and invest. Why should anyone build up a business when it may be taken away (by the police), taxed away (through bribe payments), or regulated away (through permits denied)? This question is especially acute for a small or medium firm, or a foreign firm without much political power. Weaknesses in the rule of law help explain why large conglomerates have thrived—at the expense of small and medium firms—in such countries as Korea and the Philippines. In these environments, even a lucky firm that escapes direct predators will suffer, because its capitalized value will be low, reflecting the uncertainties facing any prospective new owner.

In extreme forms, a weak rule of law takes a heavy toll on human capital. Why should a family invest long years and heavy expense in educating a child to become an accountant, chemist, or engineer when society's prizes are awarded to military officers and politicians? These distortions help explain the weak technical education of elite students in such countries as Vietnam and Venezuela. They also explain why talented and trained individuals head for the United States, Canada, or Europe.

Privatization and the Market Economy

Countries that have done well in the past two decades have turned their productive sectors over to private firms. These countries observe the basic tenets of a market economy; hence price controls and quota requirements are infrequent. In addition, successful countries generally expose their firms to competition, both domestically and internationally, thereby curtailing the power of private monopolies and oligopolies. A few countries permit an active market for corporate control, both through friendly mergers and acquisitions and through hostile takeovers.

Privatization and free markets mean that vast swaths of the economy are no longer subject to the power of public officials. This represents a major break, because public companies can award jobs to political supporters, and regulated markets can favor key constituencies. Moreover, once open competition is allowed, in corporate control as well as product markets, upstart companies can overthrow established business firms.

To sitting officeholders, the "costs" of privatization, deregulation, and a market economy are substantial; but to the economy, the payoff in terms of growth is ample. A functioning market economy invests scarce capital more rationally between competing uses. The result is to lift the return to capital economywide. For example, two economies may both save and invest 15 percent of GDP annually. In the economy with large elements of public control, the annual return to investment may be as low as 5 percent; in an economy with functioning markets, the annual return may be as a high as 15 percent. The difference in returns translates into gains of 1.5 percent of GDP annually. This is not a fanciful calculation. Recent econometric work suggests that the growth difference between a country with a closed and monopolistic financial system to an open and competitive financial system is 1.3 percent to 1.5 percent annually.

International Trade and Investment

Successful countries have, for the most part, opened their economies to international trade in goods and services and to international direct and portfolio investment. An economy that is open to international trade enjoys the "static" benefits of aligning its productive structure to prices prevailing in world markets: It imports goods and services that it produces less efficiently, and exports goods and services that it produces more efficiently. Beyond these static benefits, an economy that is open to international trade experiences the "dynamic" benefits that accrue when the market power of local monopolies is weakened and local firms are spurred to adopt best-practice management and technology. The combination of static and dynamic benefits increases GDP growth (for countries that start with a closed economy) by up to 2.0 percent per year.

A country that takes the further step of allowing international direct and portfolio investment in a wide range of productive sectors can do even better. Direct investment usually brings the fastest application of best-practice management and technology. Portfolio investment—if accompanied by strict regulation and surveillance of financial institutions—can serve to narrow the gap between domestic and international interest rates and introduce new forms of financial innovation to the domestic economy. Plausible estimates suggest that foreign direct investment (FDI) can add up to 0.8 percent to annual GDP growth, and financial innovation can add another 0.2 percent.

Postscript: Savings and Investment; Innovation and Diffusion

My list of economic "drivers" does not include *savings and investment* nor *innovation and diffusion*. These elements are critically important. However, in modern times, they are more the result than the cause of a successful political and economic environment.

Macroeconomic stability and the rule of law are the drivers that foster high rates of personal savings and investment. Personal savings usually take the form of education, housing, and retirement plans (especially for advanced industrial countries, and for emerging countries that have followed the Chilean example of reforming their social security systems). When properly measured, personal savings rates should include both retained corporate earnings (hence corporate investment) and the acquisition of human capital through better education. Higher savings rates promote higher GDP growth rates. When savings rise by 5 percent of GDP, the GDP growth rate is probably boosted by 0.5 percent annually. However, there is little a government can do through targeted measures (such as tax incentives or public campaigns) to increase private savings and investment. Instead, the government enhances private savings and investment largely by implementing sustained macroeconomic stability and the rule of law.

Much the same is true of innovation and diffusion. Here, the key drivers are privatization and the market economy, together with international trade and investment. At the frontier of basic research, government funding can sponsor pioneering innovations. Advanced discoveries in genetics and disease, computers, the Internet, new materials, and much else have sprung from public laboratories. Most innovations, however, emerge from industrial research and development, driven by the possibility of private profit. Nearly all diffusion occurs in response to market competition, both domestic and international. Laggard firms that lose markets are driven to embrace new technology and management practices.

LONG-TERM GROWTH: A FORWARD VIEW

If my list correctly identifies the four drivers of long-term growth, then my forecasting task has been simplified. The question for each region is the extent to which it will embrace the four drivers over the next two decades. For convenience, I have organized my exposition in terms of six regions: the rich OECD countries (excluding Mexico and Korea), East Asia (including China but excluding Japan), Latin America (including Mexico and the Caribbean), India, and finally Africa, Russia, and other troubled countries.

In terms of population, the rich OECD countries may grow by 100 million persons over the next two decades, to reach about 1.0 billion in 2020. The East Asian nations may grow by 300 million to reach 2.1 billion. Latin America may grow by 100 million to reach 0.6 billion. India may grow by 300 million to reach 1.3 billion. The poor and desperate countries in Africa, Russia, and elsewhere may grow by 800 million to reach 2.7 billion. All told, in 2020, world population may reach 7.7 billion (or somewhat more), a population growth of 1.6 billion in 20 years. Nearly 95 percent of the population growth will take place outside the affluent OECD nations.

Rich OECD Countries

The rich OECD countries have, with some exceptions, incorporated the four drivers in their political and economic systems. As a consequence, the next 20 years should be good, with average GDP percapita growth of about 2.0 percent per year, a faster rate than the past twenty years. At this rate, per-capita GDP will reach $42,000 in 2020. Flaws in the four drivers are more interesting than the overall optimistic trend.

The biggest threat to macroeconomic stability is the rising fiscal burden of health care and social security benefits associated with aging populations. In 2020, more than 40 percent of the population in continental Europe and Japan will be 65 years of age or older. The number of grandparents will exceed the number of grandchildren. Grandparents are expensive in terms of health care and pensions. Moreover, they vote.

The threat to macroeconomic stability is greater in continental Europe than Japan, because Europe has a longer and deeper commitment to public pensions and health care. Unless Europe and Japan find politically acceptable means of curtailing pension and health expenditures, or raising taxes (which are already very high in Europe), per-capita GDP growth could be depressed by 0.5 percent per year.

Both continental Europe and Japan must change to acquire "full" market economies in the Anglo-Saxon sense. In particular, they must foster markets for corporate control—both voluntary mergers and hostile takeovers. Europe is well on the way, with the annual volume of corporate mergers, acquisitions, and takeovers in Europe now about the same as in the United States. Japan is far behind, but change is on its way. With freer markets for corporate control, many benefits will ensue: restructuring, better management practices, adoption of new technology, and more efficient use of the workforce.

The biggest threat to international trade and investment is the antiglobalization, especially strong in the United States but evident throughout the OECD. The backlash camp will not succeed in erecting new barriers to world markets. But it may succeed in slowing down or blocking new liberalization initiatives. This would retard international economic integration, but for the OECD countries the worst-case toll on per-capita GDP growth would probably be less than 0.2 percent annually. Trade and investment restrictions such as tariffs, quotas, and reserved sectors are generally low. Integration over the next 20 years will thus be driven by market forces already at play: linked capital markets (where barriers hardly exist), sharply falling telecommunications and computing costs, and lower transportation charges (especially air cargo).

If the backlash forces secure a political foothold in the United States and Europe, the real losers will be emerging countries that are beginning to adopt the international growth drivers. First, they will loose because historic U.S. and EU barriers to exports from developing countries will endure that much longer – exports of textiles and apparel, specialty agriculture, light manufactures and processed foods are all at risk. Second they will lose as "me-too" resistance to liberalization takes hold within developing nations.

East Asia

My scenario calls for 5.0 percent annual per capita GDP growth in East Asia over the next two decades, somewhat less than since 1980, but still the best in the world. At this rate, East Asian per-capita GDP will reach $12,000 in 2020. This is an optimistic figure, and entails much greater policy transformation in East Asia than in the rich OECD area.

East Asia currently has full command over only one of the drivers: macroeconomic stability. The V-shaped recovery now under way in the aftermath of the 1997/98 financial crisis largely reflects good macroeconomics. The principal macroeconomic weakness in East Asia is China's large central budget deficit. When correctly measured to include subsidies to state-owned firms and the annual interest lost on nonperforming loans held by state banks, the figure probably amounts to 9 percent of GDP annually. This is much too high.

The other macroeconomic weakness in East Asia is the long habit of pegging currencies to the U.S. dollar, or to a basket of currencies heavily weighted by the U.S. dollar. In the wake of the crisis, most countries (excluding China) have sensibly abandoned their pegs in favor of a free float. Over the next 20 years, if East Asian countries are prepared to build very large foreign exchange reserves, and to reform their financial systems dramatically, a return to dollar pegs may prove feasible. Alternatively, East Asia could create its own regional money, but to survive the new currency would need even stronger disciplines.

East Asia has partially installed two of the other economic growth drivers: privatization and the market economy, and international trade and investment. High per-capita GDP growth critically depends on fully embracing these two drivers over the next 20 years. In some East Asian countries (for example, China and Vietnam), large segments of the economy remain to be privatized. In many East Asian countries, monopoly and oligopoly firms dominate the economy, and effectively limit external as well as internal trade and investment. This is widespread in Korea and Indonesia, but also characterizes segments of the economy in Thailand, the Philippines, and China. Equally important, the market for corporate control barely exists throughout East Asia. An optimistic, high-growth scenario depends on extensive mergers, acquisitions, and takeovers.

Over the past 20 years, East Asian countries have generally liberalized their trade and investment regimes, both unilaterally and in the context of multilateral negotiations. But barriers still exceed OECD levels by a wide margin. East Asian bound tariff rates are often above 20 percent, even though applied tariff rates are usually in the range of 10 to 15 percent. While inward investment has been liberalized, many countries still require formal or informal consent before allowing foreign firms to establish operations. In the next 20 years, East Asian nations will necessarily rely more on their own unilateral and regional initiatives, and less on multilateral World Trade Organization negotiations, to acquire open trade and investment systems. There are two reasons for this proposition: The OECD countries are less enthusiastic about policy-driven liberalization, and they have fewer reciprocal concessions to offer.

East Asia's greatest weakness is in the rule of law. This was painfully illustrated by financial malfeasance that set the stage for the 1997/98 crisis and continues to play out in the prolonged resolution of insolvent banks and bankrupt corporations. Elevating the rule of law means diminishing the rule of power. My optimistic outlook for East Asia is based on the assumption that, over the next 20 years, a succession of reform leaders will look beyond the personal benefits that could accrue from exploiting their office and instead build institutions that create a rule of law.

Latin America

My scenario calls for Latin American per-capita GDP to grow 3.0 percent annually over the next two decades, reaching $13,000 in 2020. For Latin America, this is a highly ambitious figure and will require major reforms.

Latin America has a recent and somewhat fragile commitment to macroeconomic stability. Until the early 1990s, high inflation, large fiscal deficits, and wild exchange rates wracked most Latin American countries. In the 1980s, Chile started the parade toward macroeconomic stability, followed a decade later by Argentina. Other countries later joined the stability camp, most importantly Brazil. While stability has brought prosperity to the top 20 percent of employees, most workers have seen little improvement over two decades. Hence fragility, especially in the Andean countries and parts of Central America. Yet with each passing year the stability coalition gains political power. Over the next two decades, most Latin American nations will likely follow the Argentine example, anchoring their currencies to the U.S. dollar and backing their anchors with prudent fiscal and monetary policies.

The rule of law is making headway in Latin America. The region has a tradition of civil codes, covering all aspects of commercial life. The problem has been honest implementation. But the courts and regulators are improving. The biggest threat is the flood of drug money, bringing with it urban violence, rural guerrillas, and corruption of politicians, police, and judges. These side effects deter foreign investment specifically and economic progress generally. The Andean countries, together with parts of Central America and the Caribbean, are blighted and could miss out on economic growth.

Apart from a few sectors (e.g., petroleum and electric power), Latin America has embraced privatization and the market economy. It is pursuing integration with world trade and capital markets. Chile has unilaterally opened its economy. As a North American Free Trade Association (NAFTA) member, Mexico has instituted a regime of open trade and investment. Over the next decade, most of Central America and the Caribbean will become *de facto* associates of NAFTA. Brazil still has extensive protection, but barriers are rapidly coming down in the Mercosur context. Continued economic liberalization is critical for Latin America to achieve sustained per-capita GDP growth of 3.0 percent.

India

My long-term scenario calls for Indian per-capita GDP to grow by 3.5 percent annually, only a slight improvement over the past 20 years. At a 3.5 percent growth rate, Indian per capita GDP will reach $3,800 in 2020. India is so poor that, with modest reforms, it should achieve that rate. The wrenching reforms achieved in China, Chile and a few other countries seem out of reach for the Indian political and social structure. Instead, modest reforms look like an upside limit.

Macroeconomic stability in India (as in Brazil) is threatened by the claims of civil servants, pensioners, and assertive states. It is further threatened by extensive reliance on foreign exchange controls, rather than monetary discipline, as a means of regulating the exchange rate.

These foreign exchange controls, buttressed by extensive tariff and nontariff barriers, insulate India from international trade and investment. Much of the economy is either state-regulated or dominated by large firms that are intertwined with political parties. In formal terms, India is governed by the rule of law, but the administrative and judicial machinery is notoriously slow and corrupt. All this is changing, but even reform governments seem constrained to move at a slow pace.

Africa, Russia, the FSU, Iran, Pakistan, etc.

The outlook for these countries is bleak, both in economic and social terms. In Africa, AIDS is rampant. In desperate Russia, male life expectancy has dropped to 58 years. These countries will be lucky if per-capita GDP grows at 1.5 percent per year, reaching an average of $3,800 in 2020. Two decades ago, many of these countries were richer than India. Two decades hence, they will be lucky to keep up with India. Prospects are so bad among these troubled nations that the World Bank, the IMF and the OECD search for the smallest rays of hope. But in fact none of the growth drivers are evident. Macroeconomic policy is in shambles and trade barriers are extreme.

Production and distribution are controlled either by the state or by crony capitalists. The rule of law is a farce.

As everyone knows, but is too polite to say, these economies are run on predatory principles. Economies based on predatory principles have been with us throughout history. Predatory principles inspired feudal wars in Europe during the Middle Ages. In the colonial era, the principles were exported to Latin America, Asia and Africa. The surprise is not the persistence of predatory principles, but their occasional displacement by growth drivers.

These days we hope that the World Bank and International Monetary Fund will displace predatory principles in afflicted countries. But at most these institutions can bring macroeconomic stability. They can do little to create a true market economy in the face of kleptocratic leaders and criminal enterprises. They cannot create a benign colonial corps of police, regulators, and judges.

Nor can the troubled nations rely on larger flows of official assistance. As a share of GDP in the rich OECD countries, official assistance is headed towards the vanishing point. Moreover, the politics of international institutions and major OECD donor countries ensure that official assistance largely goes to countries with strategic importance, and the rest is spread thinly across the spectrum of claimants. Hence it is difficult to reward, with official support, those few countries that spontaneously replace predatory principles with growth drivers.

Despite the hostile internal and external environment facing this group, some countries will manage to break from the predatory mold. Which ones? Egypt? Ghana? Uganda? Ukraine? Kazakhstan? Pakistan? Bangladesh? The few countries that escape will first grow their economies at home and then find support in the private international economy. New trade opportunities will emerge and investment will begin to arrive.

SUMMING UP

Enormous changes will characterize the next 20 years. The population profile in rich OECD countries will become older. The relative importance of non-OECD countries will increase, both in economic and strategic terms. Countries will abandon their national currencies (in fact if not in name) and anchor to the dollar, the euro, the yen—or a weighted combination of the major currencies. Capital markets will become highly integrated. Large firms will equate labor productivity and compensation across many regions of the world. E-commerce will blossom. A huge proportion of services trade will be conducted over the Internet. Retail firms will supply whole regions, through Internet orders, not just metropolitan areas.

But one thing that will not happen, according to my scenario, is a blissful convergence between rich and poor countries. In the year 2000, the ratio between per-capita GDP in the OECD and the per-capita GDP in the bleakest group of countries is about 10 to 1, \$28,000 to \$2,800. In the year 2020, the ratio will probably increase to about 13 to 1, \$40,000 to \$3,000—an absolute difference of \$38,200 per person per year. *Absolute* differences in real per capita income are already enormous and they will become even more staggering. To be sure, the gap between OECD and East Asia will close. But on the whole, *absolute* income differences 20 years hence will widen, and relative income ratios will not narrow.

Chapter Three

WORLD ECONOMIC RESTRUCTURING AND CHINA'S ECONOMIC TRANSFORMATION

Yuanzheng Cao

Since 1978, China's economic system has undergone a 20-year-plus market-oriented reform. Over that period, economic evolution and structural transformation were mostly driven by domestic factors; now however, they are increasingly influenced by economic globalization and worldwide industrial progress. For the 21st century, it is likely that Chinese economic development will be increasingly influenced by the world economy, especially the economies of other Asian nations. The Chinese economy will rest on China's strategy for involvement in this process. It is an interactive process. Understanding this process will help in creating a better world economic structure. This chapter provides a brief analysis of economic globalization and worldwide economic structural improvements, an analysis and illustration of challenges and choices facing China, and focuses on possible Chinese economic developments.

INTEGRATION AND RESTRUCTURING OF THE WORLD ECONOMY

Compared with the past, new factors are influencing the structure of the world economy. The driving forces are transformation of former centrally controlled economies into market economies; transformation of import substitution in developing economies into export-oriented development; use of transnational management strategies and global expansion of large corporations in developed countries; flows of commodities, services, personnel, and capital increased by modern science and information technology advances; and a stable political environment brought about by détente that encourages international capital flows.

These new factors interact with each other, making the world market develop at a rapid speed and promoting the integration of national economies. This integration is manifested as growth of international trade in excess of that of domestic production, growth of international investment in excess of that of international trade, and growth of short-term capital in excess of long-term capital among various forms of international capital flows (see Figure 3.1).

Rapid integration of financial markets is particularly remarkable. Transaction volume per day in foreign exchange markets is as high as $1.5 trillion, 100-odd times over world trade volume. This amount is higher than the sum of foreign exchange reserves in all countries. Therefore, several strong economies joining forces would not be able

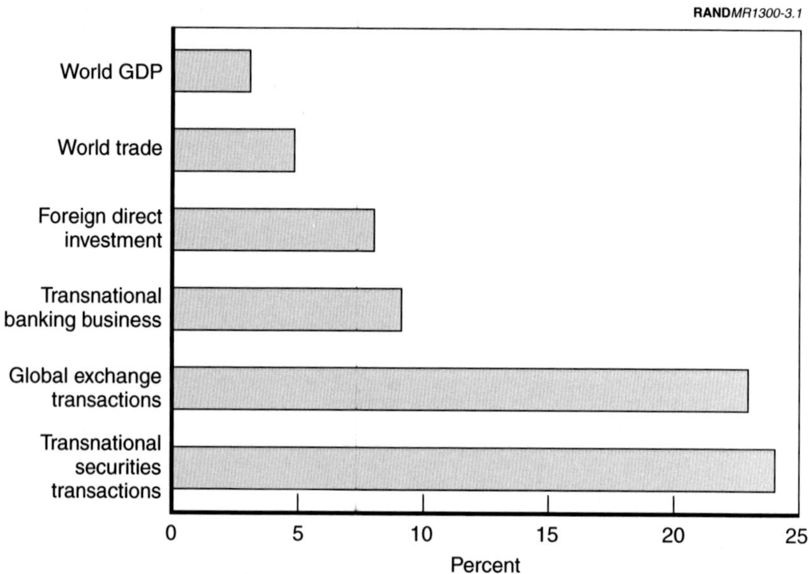

SOURCES: Author, China Reform Forum.

Figure 3.1—Indices of Economic Globalization: Rates of Growth in 1996

to interfere with exchange rates. In 1980, international security transactions by American investors were only 9 percent of the GDP; however, it rose to 135 percent in 1993, and the growth rates in Germany, Britain, and some other countries were even higher. According to some estimates, global financial market capitalization will reach $83 trillion in 2000, three times that of the GDP of OECD countries.

Economic globalization helps perpetuate the integration of national economies. Therefore, each country's economy is a link in the chain of the global economy. Accordingly, the efficiency of traditional and independent economic policy is waning, which is mainly reflected in "independent" monetary policies, freedom of capital accounts, and pegged exchange systems being harder to balance simultaneously. Thus it is necessary to form a common view of the international political and economic order and then build a framework for international political and economic order based on this common view.

Economic globalization translates into fierce competition. In parallel with economic globalization are dramatic changes in the economic order backed by industrial restructuring and modernization and extensive use of new technologies, primarily information technology (IT). World economic restructuring and industrial modernization require that human capital related to knowledge and technology become increasingly important in economic performance. According to estimates, high-tech industries contributed 27 percent to the increased GDP from 1993 to 1996, far higher than the 14 percent from the construction industry and 4 percent from the auto-making industry. In addition, American enterprises and residents spend more on IT hardware than for new houses, new cars, and auto parts.

An internationalization of labor division, driven by globalization, has created a worldwide production chain from knowledge-intensive industry to capital-intensive industry to labor-intensive industry. Restructuring and transnational industrial transfer are accelerated, creating unique features in the world economy.

TRADITIONAL INDUSTRIES ARE FACING THE PROBLEM OF OVERCAPACITY WORLDWIDE

Great changes took place in economic and technological bases in the 1990s. IT development is expanding and concluding the third industrial revolution. The life cycle of technology and products is shorter—many new technologies enter standardized scale production soon after they come out. The expanding speed of new product generation is greater than that of their markets. So overproduction, especially overproduction in traditional industries, is more serious than at any other time in history. In the past, overproduction was caused by high prices, but, since it is now caused by rapid product generation, it is a comprehensive problem. In fact, some industries have no economic value, because their price elasticity tends to be zero. This problem is spreading to other industries. For example, in the auto industry production capability in 1996 was 68 million vehicles, but actual production was only 50 million vehicles. By 2000, global auto production capability is expected to reach 80 million vehicles, but the actual demand will be less than 60 million vehicles. Of course, not only the auto industry—including leading industries in the first industrial revolution such as textiles, but also signal industries in the second and third industrial revolutions such as steel, chemicals, and television manufacturers—are confronting the same problem. Large-scale overcapacity results in fierce market competition. Against this background, a new round of transnational mergers spread across the whole world, involving almost all traditional industries. The scale of these mergers is growing. Heated worldwide competition is forcing enterprises to take measures to cut costs in order to increase production efficiency. These measures sacrifice employment for market share in the face of weakened global consumption, resulting in global market deflation.

SERVICE INDUSTRIES HAVE BECOME A MAJOR SOURCE OF ECONOMIC GROWTH

Science and technology progress has considerably improved production efficiency, expanding production capability in excess of market consumption, causing marketing and market expansion to become the focus of competition. In the future, industries will find more profitability in after-sale services, and the products' importance will diminish, becoming a lure for customers to enjoy after-sale services. Thus, a combination of high value-added products and services will become a new economic growth engine, drawing purchasing power and employment opportunities to these sectors. In America, the production value of service sectors accounted for 75 percent of its GDP in 1996, and employment opportunities were 80 percent of the total.

Rapid development of service sectors has promoted upgrading of industrial structures, including unidimensional growth of the total volume economic indicator and transformation of traditional economic cycles. Agriculture is the leading industry of agricultural societies, with the main cause of economic fluctuation being good or poor harvests. Mechanical mass production in capitalistic societies results in the separation of production and consumption, making economic fluctuation inescapable. However, in service industry–based economies, in which production and consumption occur simultaneously, the usual characteristics of economic fluctuation are changing. In America, for example, 1999 was the ninth consecutive year of American economic growth. The boom has lasted longer than any of America's booms after World War II and will likely outlast the booms of the "Japanese miracle" and the "German miracle" following World War II. The economic academic community uses the term "new economy" to explain why U.S. corporations have been very profitable and the reasons behind recent favorable inflation experience.

REDEFINITION OF LEADING INDUSTRIES IS LEADING TO DRAMATIC CHANGES IN THE WORLD ECONOMIC ORDER

A country's leading industry has two interrelated features: first, the industry plays an important role in the country's industrial structure; second, the industry is in line with the future direction of the world economy. Currently, the candidates for lead industries are those related to high-tech fields, i.e., computer (software, hardware, and service), telecommunications, and information (including publishing and entertainment). At present, most countries are pursuing scientific and technology advances, in addition to industrial adjustments, to stay firm in the fierce competition among leading industries. It appears that the United States has taken the lead in the competition, outpacing Japan, Western Europe, and other countries.

Recently, American economic growth has been characterized by rapid development in high-tech industries. The United States has a clear advantage in the raw materials market for computers and semiconductors, while maintaining a good reach in key components and software development. It also has the leading edge in technology-intensive industries, including electronics, telecommunications, optical instruments, aviation and space flight, and new technologies. Since the 1980s, American enterprises have invested more than $100 billion per year in IT and related fields. Generally speaking, the United States has reversed the declining trend of its competitiveness, compared with Japan and Western Europe, and regained its competitive edge in international markets.

With the backdrop of globalization and dramatic adjustment and improvement of the world economic industrial structure, we may gain a deeper understanding of the Japanese economic decline following the evaporation of its bubble economy and of the Asian economic crisis in 1997. Viewed with this deeper understanding of the global overcapacity of traditional industries, the Asian financial crisis reveals itself to be essentially the result of industrial restructuring that has lagged far behind the world economy.

The East-Asian economic model features placement of technological introduction before technological development, use of comparative advantage, and adoption of export-oriented strategies to promote economic growth. Historically, these approaches made sense and were greatly successful. However, if a nation does not emphasize technology development after reaching a reasonable degree of economic development, then it will not be able to raise its status in the international division of labor—likely getting locked into the lower echelons of the international production chain and being subject to economic shocks during global industrial restructuring and modernization. For example, Japan's technological export volume relative to its import volume was 0.007 in 1953, 0.13 in 1970, and only 0.38 in 1989, far lower than the U.S. ratio of 5.26 and the British ratio 0.92 in 1987. In addition, from 1950 to 1996, the Japanese received only four Nobel Prizes in physiology, physics, chemistry, and economics, while Americans received 178, and the British 46. These differences show Japanese weakness in basic research. In the 1990s, this weakness has lead to its failure to succeed in high-tech industry. A similar example can be seen in South Korea, which maintains an image as a high-tech producer, yet the country's actual production capability remains low. The top-selling and well-known Hundai, likely the most famous export product of South Korea, is an imitation of an Italian body design, and its motor is designed and manufactured by the Japanese Mitsubishi Corporation. In addition, 85 percent of South Korea's color TV parts are manufactured in Japan. And, although South Korea is the fifth largest PC exporter, it actually manufactures only computer disks. High dependence on foreign capital, markets, and technology leaves the rest of the Southeast Asian economy in a very vulnerable position. Southeast Asian nations depend on cheap land resources and cheap labor, but if either is lost, foreign capital and even domestic businesses will leave these countries. Also, if foreign capital or technology markets levy restrictions on these countries, they will lose their basis of survival and development.

Since industrial modernization of Asian countries has lagged behind that of other nations, Asian industries have no competitive advantage in the world economy. Thus, to maintain and expand their quota of the market, they must reduce their prices, which in turn tends to cause Asian currencies to depreciate. Other developed nations adopt industrial modernization quickly, making their competitive advantage more evident compared with that of Asian nations, and the currencies of these countries tend to appreciate. As mentioned above, since currencies of Asian countries are softening, while European and American currencies are hardening, the pegged exchange system of many Asian nations is hard to maintain, and financial crisis is inevitable.

CHALLENGES FOR THE CHINESE ECONOMY

Based on the preceding text, it appears that the most prominent conclusion to be drawn is that the only way for emerging Asian economies to adapt themselves to economic globalization is to speed their economic and industrial restructuring, which has proven to be a severe challenge.

However, the challenge of industrial modernization is more severe for China.

Since the founding of the People's Republic of China, especially since 1978, China's transformation from a traditional agricultural society to a modern industrial society has been accelerated by industrial restructuring. China's industrial structure evolved around the objective of industrialization; therefore, the proportion of primary (agricultural) industries in China has steeply declined, the proportion of secondary (manufacturing) industries has continually ascended, and the proportion of tertiary (service) industries has only marginally increased (see Table 3.1).

The trends shown in Table 3.1 generally accord with the industrial structure transformation of all countries during the industrializing process. However, China's industry structure is still in an interim development phase, compared with the development of other industrialized countries. Three attributes confirm this level of industrialization. To begin, the proportion of primary industries in China dropped from 50.50 percent in 1952 to 18.39 percent in 1998; also, the proportion of secondary and tertiary industries increased from 49.50 percent in 1952 to 81.61 percent in 1998. Nonagricultural industries, including service industries, have become the pillar of China's economy. In addition, the end products of some important industries in China have become number one sellers across the globe. Such pillar industries as auto making and housing have developed by leaps and bounds, showing that China's industrial system is being perfected and tends to be mature. Lastly, China's most important export products are machinery and electrical appliances, and its most important import products are raw materials. Thus, China is purchasing raw materials from around the world and shipping its industrial products across the world (see Table 3.2).

Although China's industrial structure has followed the regular patterns of industrialization for other countries, the differences, as

Table 3.1

China's Industrial Structure (1952–1998)
(in percentage)

Industries	1952	1965	1978	1985	1989	1992	1995	1997	1998
Primary Industry	50.50	37.94	28.10	28.35	25.00	21.77	20.51	19.09	18.39
Secondary Industry	20.88	35.09	48.16	43.13	43.13	43.92	48.80	49.99	48.73
Tertiary Industry	28.62	26.97	23.74	28.52	31.95	34.31	30.69	30.93	32.88

SOURCE: *China Statistical Yearbook*, 1999.

Table 3.2

Structure of China's Foreign Trade (in percentage)

	1985	1990	1995	1997	1998
Structure of exports					
Primary goods	50.6	25.6	14.4	13.1	11.2
Manufactured goods	49.4	74.4	85.6	86.9	88.8
Structure of imports					
Primary goods	12.5	18.5	18.5	20.1	16.4
Manufactured goods	87.5	81.5	81.5	79.9	83.6

SOURCE: *China Statistical Yearbook,* 1999.

compared with the patterns of industrialization of other countries, are obvious.

First, urbanization lags far behind industrialization. While nonagricultural industries are a mainstay of the national economy, the agricultural sector still employs a large proportion of the labor force—disproportional to its output (see Table 3.3).

In 1998, the proportion of employees in primary industries was 49.8 percent, but their output was only 18.4 percent of the national economy. The secondary industrial sector employed only 23.5 percent of the labor force, but its output accounts for 48.7 percent of GDP. The relative labor productivity of the former was 0.37 (only 18.7 percent

Table 3.3

Employment of China's Population Compared with the Sector's Proportion of the National Economy (in percentage)

Industries	1985	1990	1995	1996	1997	1998
Primary						
Employment	62.4	60.1	52.2	50.5	49.9	49.8
Proportion of the national economy	28.4	27.1	20.5	20.4	18.7	18.4
Secondary						
Employment	20.9	21.4	23	23.5	23.7	23.5
Proportion of the national economy	43.1	41.6	48.8	49.5	49.2	48.7
Tertiary						
Employment	16.7	18.5	24.8	26	26.4	26.7
Proportion of the national economy	28.5	31.3	30.7	30.1	32.1	32.9

SOURCES: *China Statistical Yearbook,* 1999, and *A Statistical Survey of China,* 1999.

of the latter) and was also far less than 1.23 of the tertiary industry sector. These percentages reveal the dualistic nature of China's economic structure. Vast differences between productivity and income of all industry sectors, as described by Simon Kuznets, are a result of excessive labor supplies to nonmodern sectors and impeded productivity rises of these sectors. If this situation lasts persists, the process of further industrialization will be blocked and social stability will be threatened.

Therefore, China's nonagricultural industries' value amounts compared with the main body of the national economy, but proportion of employees in the first class dominated the worker forces at present and will do in the future. The conflict of a dual economic structure will likely remain into the future. It will be reflected in the enlarged income gap between industry and agriculture, rising from 2.12 in 1991 to 5.25 in 1995, and estimated to reach 5.62 in 2005 (see Table 3.4).

Second, while primary industrialization still requires a further boost, the trend of heavy industrialization is making remarkable strides.

The process of industrialization is usually characterized by a gradual shift from labor-intensive light industries to capital- and technology-

Table 3.4

China's Industrial Structure Compared with a Forecast for 2005 (in percentage)

	Primary Industry	Secondary Industry	Tertiary Industry
Proportion of value of output in 1991	26.6	46.1	27.3
Proportion of labor force	51.8	21.4	18.9
Income gap between industry and agriculture primary industry	2.12		
Proportion of value of output 1995	20.0	48.9	31.1
Proportion of labor	50.5	23.5	26.0
Income gap between industry and agriculture primary industry	5.25		
Proportion of value of output 2005	15.5	52.0	33.5
Proportion of labor	42.5	25.32	33.18
Income gap between industry and agriculture primary industry	5.62		

SOURCES: *China Statistical Yearbook*, related years.

intensive heavy industries. Since light industries are labor intensive, they easily absorb redundant labor from primary industries, but heavy industries are not as capable in absorbing redundant labor. In China, however, the proportion of heavy manufacturing industries' output has risen from 35.5 percent shortly after the founding of Peoples' Republic of China to 50.7 percent in 1998 (see Table 3.5). Although development of heavy industries is difficult in late stages of industrialization, it will be doubly hard on the Chinese labor force, which has a large number of rural laborers that may be left behind in a surge toward rapid growth of heavy industries.

Third, although China's industrial structure has a high level of manufacturing, it is far from what it ideally should be.

Since 1978, the proportion of low-level manufacturing sectors' output (in light industry with agricultural products as raw materials and in mining sectors of heavy industry) has greatly decreased. However, low-level expansion and repetitive construction in some of these industries and sectors are causing serious economic problems. Product quality lags demand, leading to the national economy's dependence on imports of high-level manufactured goods (see Table 3.6). Horizontal expansion of low-level manufacturing industries has increased domestic competition in these sectors, including high consumption of energy and raw materials. This in turn has caused inflated demand for energy and raw materials and has further delayed modernization of industrial structures (see Table 3.7).

In general, the Chinese industrial system relies on low-level technology, and high-tech industries are still in the seedling phase. This status is evident in major industrial sectors, which use low-level tech-

Table 3.5

Proportion of Light and Heavy Industries in China

	1952	1957	1978	1980	1985	1990	1995	1998
Heavy industries	35.5	45.0	56.9	52.8	52.9	50.6	52.7	50.7
Light industries	64.5	55.0	43.1	47.2	47.1	49.4	47.3	49.3

SOURCE: *China Statistical Yearbook*, 1999.

Table 3.6

Proportion of Heavy Chemical Industries and Light Industries in China

	1985	1990	1995	1998
Light industry				
Using farm products as raw materials	70.83	69.72	68.40	63.27
Using non-farm products as raw materials	29.17	30.28	31.57	36.73
Heavy industry				
Mining and quarrying	12.57	12.11	10.75	10.46
Raw materials industry	37.70	41.59	41.39	39.12
Manufacturing industry	49.73	46.31	47.88	50.42

SOURCES: *China Statistical Yearbook*, related years.

Table 3.7

Proportion of Raw Materials Industries and Manufacturing Industries in China

	Value Added (year)		
Five countries[a]	17.9 (1989)		
United States	13.7 (1990)	21.0 (1980)	28.8 (1965)
Japan	16.7 (1989)	26.6 (1965)	32 (1953)
South Korea	17.9 (1988)	24.1 (1979)	29.1 (1971)
Brazil	31.5 (1989)	34.5 (1974)	39.6 (1961)
China	35.6 (1993)		

SOURCE: Adapted from "Reflection on China's Industrial Structure in New Era," *Management World,* February 1997.

NOTE: Raw materials industries include chemicals, quarry products, glass products, nonmetal mineral products, nonferrous metals, and steel.

[a]The five countries are the United States, Japan, France, Germany, and the United Kingdom.

nologies and are unable to supply their own equipment. Large-scale IC (integrated circuit) chips account for only 40 percent of all IC chips made in China, and foreign enterprises supply 80 percent of the telecommunications equipment needs in China. The average life span for more than 2,000 leading products from China is 10.5 years, 3.5 times greater than that of the same products made in America. The other evidence is that, back in 1967, 45 percent of American workers were employed in information sectors (the economic information index was 242), while by 1994, only 9.9 percent of Chinese workers were employed in information sectors (the economic information index was only 84) (see Table 3.8). Thus, there is much room

Table 3.8

Information Technology Development of Several Countries

Country (year)	Economic Information Index	Value-added About Info. Sector (% GDP)	Employees in Info. Sector (% of total workers)
America (1967)	242	48.5	45.0
Japan (1979)	100	35.4	38.0
South Korea (1980)		39.0	14.3
China (1994)	84	24.68	9.9

SOURCE: First Conference on China's Information Problem, Beijing, 1994.

for further development of technology-related industries in China, particularly high-tech industries.

There are many causes behind the differences between information technology development of the countries shown in Table 3.8, including historical, international, domestic, developmental, and structural reasons. However, the following two reasons are especially important:

1. There is no one system that provides reliable support for economic development.
2. In a global marketplace, industrial development is more sensitive to international competition.

Choosing a System for Economic Development

Experience in the world economy shows that markets are the driving force behind industrial evolution. Each country's industrial structure develops largely as a result of market choices. Governmental involvement should be limited to rectifying market failures and providing a stable environment for industrial evolution.

However, for a long time, China's economic planning system has been highly centralized. The system wields the state's power to mobilize all possible resources to realize industrialization quickly, shaping a state industrialization pattern, not a market-oriented one. Objectively, this pattern places barriers between industry and agriculture and between the city and the countryside, sharpening conflicts in this dualistic economy. In addition, bureaucratic resource allocation is rigid and inefficient, distorting prices and causing malformed industrial development and redundant construction.

The rationale for system reform lies in the bureaucratic and economic abuses detailed above. In its favor, China has, since 1978, been attempting economic system reform through development of a market-oriented economy; however, China's economic system remains in protracted transition—a market-oriented economic system suitable to economic development has not been established, and system abuses continue.

Presently, the administrative bureaucracy perpetuates conflicts between good market decisions and maintaining the status quo: The scale of enterprise investment remains small, expansion of wise market-share distribution is blocked, and non-state-owned enterprises remain difficult to grow.

In addition, no clear relationship exists between industrial capital and financial capital. Financial institutions remain the major funding source for Chinese production enterprises, providing only relatively simple low-risk loans, leaving the capital market incomplete. Lack of funding sources is the major reason for high asset liability ratios and low momentum for enterprises to compete in a market-oriented economy, especially the state-owned large- and medium-sized enterprises. Moreover, no proper high-risk financial channels exist to support high-tech industries in China.

Furthermore, the lag of state-owned enterprise reform also affects industrial restructuring. Barriers against transfer of state-owned enterprises continue to exist, causing restructuring to be formidable. These barriers are political and social in nature. Politics mixes with enterprise management because of the long-term role the government has played in the care of state-owned enterprises. Thereby no one entity takes true responsibility for these enterprises leaving them little reason to change and adjust to a market-oriented economy. Industrial sector restructuring, therefore, faces strong "administrative barriers." On the social front, an incomplete social safety net may create great social hardships when state-owned enterprises transfer to the private sector.

Industrial Development in the Face of International Competition

International economic experience has shown that opening an economy to international trade is an important component of industrialization strategy for developing countries. Over the past 20 years, opening China's economy has gone a long way toward promoting China's economic development.

However, international trade, while breaking China's isolation, has also lead China to become overly dependent on it: More than 80 percent of China's total trade volume is the import and export of industrial products. With a high growth rate, foreign trade has become the major driving force behind industry and even the entire economy. The growth rate of manufactured goods' export (8.6 percent) is higher than that of the total volume of foreign trade, which shows the good commodity structure of Chinese foreign trade and that the machining industry's main impulse is toward the development of foreign trade (see Table 3.9).

Of special note is that since the mid-1990s, the foreign-market orientation of China's industry has accelerated, as shown by the marked improvement in the export structure of manufactured goods (see Table 3.10). Machinery and transport equipment took the lead

Table 3.9

Growth of Industry and Foreign Trade

	1995	1996	1997	1998	Growth Rate (%)
GNP (in 100 millions of yuan)	57494.9	66850.5	73142.7	78017.8	10.7
Total exports and imports (in 100 millions of USD)	2808.6	2898.8	3250.6	3239.3	4.9
Value-added of industry (in 100 millions of yuan)	24718.3	29082.6	32310.8	33541	10.7
Value of imports by manufactured goods (in 100 millions of USD)	1076.67	1133.92	1137.5	1172.14	2.9
Proportion in value of imports	81.51%	81.68%	79.90%	83.63%	
Value of exports by manufactured goods (in 100 millions of USD)	1272.95	1291.23	1588.39	1631.57	8.6
Proportion in value of exports	85.56%	85.48%	86.90%	88.79%	

SOURCES: *China Statistical Yearbook*, related years.

NOTE: USD is U.S. dollars.

Table 3.10

Export Structure of Manufactured Goods (in percentage)

	1995		1996		1997		1998	
	Exports	Imports	Exports	Imports	Exports	Imports	Exports	Imports
Manufactured products	100	100	100	100	100	100	100	100
Chemical and related products	7.14	16.07	6.87	15.97	6.44	16.96	6.32	17.20
Light and textile industrial products	25.33	26.72	22.07	27.68	21.68	28.33	26.51	19.85
Machinery and transport equipment	24.67	48.89	27.35	48.30	27.52	46.39	48.43	30.79
Miscellaneous products	42.85	7.67	43.70	7.48	44.36	7.52	43.04	7.21
Products not otherwise classified	0.00	0.64	0.01	0.57	0.00	80	0.00	0.64

SOURCES: *China Statistical Yearbook*, related years.

among exports, amounting to $50.23 billion in 1998 (48.43 percent of all exports), which is much higher than the proportion of light and textile industrial products (26.51 percent). In addition, the export structure of machinery and transport equipment has been changing for the better: The proportion of more technology-intensive products is going up, and that of more labor-intensive products is going down. The structure of such traditional exports as light and textile industrial products also changed for the better. Resource and labor-intensive, low value-added, low-technology products decreased in percentage and less labor-intensive high-technology high-value-added products made a marked increase.

Since industries in China are oriented toward competition on the international market, Chinese industrial development is increasingly influenced by international economic changes. On the international market, Chinese competitive strength is relatively weak because Chinese industries remain in the middle and lower echelons of the international division of labor and because technology in China is relatively lower than in other nations. On the one hand, exporting has become increasingly difficult, with declining export prices; on the other hand, China has increased its market share of foreign products and foreign-invested enterprises' products. These two factors increase the difficulties of production and of the transfer of state-owned enterprises in particular. In addition, the textile and other light industries slowed their growth around 1985; after 1989, the production capability of durable consumption goods dropped; and from the mid-1990s onward, bottleneck sectors such as steel, oil, and raw materials began to fall because of market saturation. All of these developments were related to international competition.

THE FUTURE OF THE CHINESE ECONOMY

As discussed above, the rapid international development of information technologies and high-tech industries are quickly leaving China behind in international competition, causing yet greater challenges for China in modernizing its industrial structure. China will simultaneously face rural industrialization, urban industrial structural modernization, and development of its high-tech industries. These will prove to be formidable tasks. To achieve these economic goals, China must dismantle its dualistic economic structure, absorb rural laborers into nonagricultural sectors, and continue to develop labor-intensive industries. However, economic globalization and worldwide overcapacity in traditional industries leave less room for development of labor-intensive industries, which will also impede rural industrialization and urbanization in China. In addition, there are some contradictions between industrialization and an information-technology-based economy. Developing a knowledge-based economy requires development of China's physical economy. However, industry is already a mature sector, with a worldwide division of labor that has created strong access barriers. Also, because of high-tech industry development, mainstream industries, in decline internationally, can no longer provide lasting momentum to economic development.

Thus, with the backdrop of economic globalization, the available choices for Chinese economic development are limited, requiring thought and caution. Generally, any new economic development strategy should accurately employ China's resource endowment, increase China's international competitive power through comparative advantage, and accelerate capital accumulation, swapping comparative advantages when necessary and stimulating rapid industrial structural modernization.

To begin, China's main comparative advantage lies in its physical capital. Labor-intensive industries need to continuously absorb and employ new technologies, IT in particular, and to reinvent themselves, reduce costs, and improve competitive power. Through capital accumulation brought about by improved competitive power, capital-intensive manufacturing industries can be developed gradually, especially high-tech-related manufacturing industries. In the field of heavy industries, energy- and material-saving technologies need to be used to reduce costs through waste reduction.

In addition, development of high-tech industry is closely related to human resource accumulation. According to Roemer and Lucas economic growth theory, human capital is an important element in the long-lasting growth of per-capita income and it helps explain economic differences from nation to nation. Countries that are able to convert their economies to dependence on alternative resources—human capital resources—do better in the global economy. Therefore, science, technology, and education, which are major sources of social development—contribute to the flexibility of a nation's human capital. In contrast with developed countries, China is short of human capital. By cultivating human capital, through science, technology, and education, China can find a more economically practical balance among its labor- and capital-intensive industries and high-tech industries.

Lastly, flexible and innovative administrative and judicial systems must be established to enhance economic development. These systems should support fair legislation and law enforcement, protection of intellectual property rights, independent and effective contract arbitrage, a perfected financial systems, transparent capital markets, a social security system, and a perfected public finance and expense system. At present, state-owned enterprise reform and financial system reform should be priorities.

It is noteworthy that the Chinese government is aware of the challenges facing the Chinese economy in the 21st century, made a positive policy response, and put forward a strategy of rejuvenating China through science and education. China is attempting to advance state-owned enterprises reform and financial system reform, speeding up economic restructuring and expanding the policy to open the nation to trade in order to achieve sustainable development. The above reform measures are producing positive effects. The Chinese economy is growing rapidly and deflation has relaxed. We have every reason to believe that the Chinese economy will show a better performance with above measures.

China's population is 1.3 billion. As such, it has an important effect on the world economy, especially the economies of Asian nations. For example, during the Asian economic crisis in 1997, China maintained its currency valuation, which avoided further currency depreciation in other Asian countries. China's behavior during that crisis garnered world praise.

On the worldwide front, China negotiated trade agreements with the United States and more than ten other countries. China's entry into the World Trade Organization is expected soon. Just as the international economy affects China's economy, so too China's economy has an effect on the international economy. A symbiotic relationship exists whereby without the success of China's economic transformation, restructuring of the world economy will be hindered.

When China realizes its goals of rural industrialization, urban industrial structural modernization, and development of a knowledge-based economy, it will not only promote development of its domestic economy but also the world economy. Thereby, world economic restructuring and the redefinition of leading industries will favor China's using its comparative advantage and will benefit China's economy.

COMMENTS ON YUANZHENG CAO CHAPTER

Benjamin Zycher

This chapter is a useful and interesting treatment of the dilemmas facing Chinese economic reform. In particular, the emphasis is upon the effect of relative prices in world markets; those relative prices are seen as constraints that are likely to hinder the transformation of the Chinese economy into a "high-tech" leader able to compete effectively in an increasingly "globalized" world economy. Many other discussions of the broad Chinese economic reform problem have tended to emphasize such shorter term problems as that of the unemployment likely to follow privatization of the state-owned enterprises, or to follow a sharp reduction in the degree to which they are subsidized. Accordingly, Dr. Cao's discussion is particularly useful in that it emphasizes a broader and longer-term perspective on the reform problem.

The chapter ought to be expanded in the following dimensions.

First, the definition of "high-tech" industries or sectors needs to be clarified. This is a problem common across a broad range of economic discussions, but it is important nonetheless. One reason that the problem is so widespread is that a useful definition of "high-tech" industries is surprisingly difficult to formulate. It simply is not enough merely to mention computers and microprocessors and lasers as a sort of compendium of "high-tech" characteristics. Were we to visit a modern plant producing potato chips we would be struck by the very high-tech nature of the operation. There would be very few workers; and the production process would be highly automated, modern, computer-controlled, and efficient. In a phrase, it would be highly "high-tech", but no one includes potato chip production in their list of "high-tech" industries.

That point is more fundamental than may appear to be the case at first glance. Economists, businessmen, and policymakers tend to fall into the trap of deciding that an economy must become more "high-tech" in some loose sense, and then delineating precisely which sectors, industries, and products ought to be favored. And that leads to a second suggestion: The chapter emphasizes particular sectors too heavily, and economic institutions that can be predicted to yield true reform and growth too little. In other works, Dr. Cao's chapter ought to emphasize the issue of comparative advantage in global specialization far more heavily than it does, and therefore, the sorts of economic institutions that would allocate resources in more productive ways.

Third, the chapter needs a fuller treatment of what can be called the political economy of reform. The current state of the Chinese economy and the obstacles and pressure facing the reform process, in substantial part, are the result of choices made among conflicting economic and political goals. More fundamentally, past choices among economic institutions reflect precisely those trade-offs, and future choices will continue to do so. Dr. Cao seems to argue that the major constraint weighing upon the Chinese reform process is the likely evolution of relative prices in world markets, which will make the transformation path difficult. I would argue that the major constraint is the Chinese leadership's perceived set of political costs attendant upon the choice of institutions that would lead the Chinese economy naturally to pursue its comparative advantage in global markets. That discussion is difficult politically for Chinese nationals, but it is crucial in any serious examination of alternative paths in pursuit of greater growth for the Chinese economy.

Finally, there are additional quibbles of the sort that emerge in the reading of any material. The emphasis in the chapter on political "stability" is misplaced in that there are many "stable" political systems with severely counterproductive economic institutions and thus poor economic performance. "Export-oriented" development strategies are seriously to be questioned in terms of their longer-run contribution to growth and competitiveness. There is little reason to believe that service sectors are less prone to economic cycles than, say, manufacturing sectors in the relevant context of long-run returns to investment. In short: The chapter is interesting and useful and ought to be expanded.

Part II

OUTLOOK FOR THE U.S. ECONOMY

Chapter Four

CAN THE UNITED STATES' ECONOMIC SUCCESS CONTINUE?

Gail Fosler

OVERVIEW

The U.S. economy will continue to advance at about 4.0 percent in 1999 and 3.5 to 4 percent in 2000—despite rising interest rates. Both consumer and investment spending are likely to maintain or accelerate past their recent pace, with the manufacturing sector further aided by a pickup in exports.

The structural depth of this growth cycle suggests that the economy will continue to grow relatively quickly, even in the face of Federal Reserve restraint. Indeed, the risks to this updated outlook are not so much that the U.S. economy will slow of its own accord, but that a delayed and relatively cautious Federal Reserve policy will permit growth to accelerate further, requiring larger and potentially more destabilizing interest rate increases at some later date. The following discussion reviews the strength of the American consumer, the state of the U.S. business cycle as evidenced by the Conference Board's leading economic indicators, and examines the outlook for inflation and for Federal Reserve action in the coming months. A concluding section discusses the difficult issue of U.S. stock prices: outlook and implications.

TRACKING THE U.S. ECONOMY

While the early stages of the current economic cycle were powered by investment spending, the U.S. consumer has now taken the lead, accounting for almost 70 percent of U.S. market growth in 1998 and 1999. Thus, business investment, although continuing to account for 18 percent of U.S. growth, has recently been overshadowed by the U.S. consumer. Figure 4.1 shows the relative contributions to growth among the key sectors for the past several years and projections for 1999 and 2000.

The robust U.S. consumer sector is not an illusion based on high confidence and high stock prices. Consumer income gains have been among the strongest and most persistent in a generation. Real disposable income has consistently accelerated since 1993, reaching a peak of 3.5 percent per year. While not as rapid as in the 1960s, con-

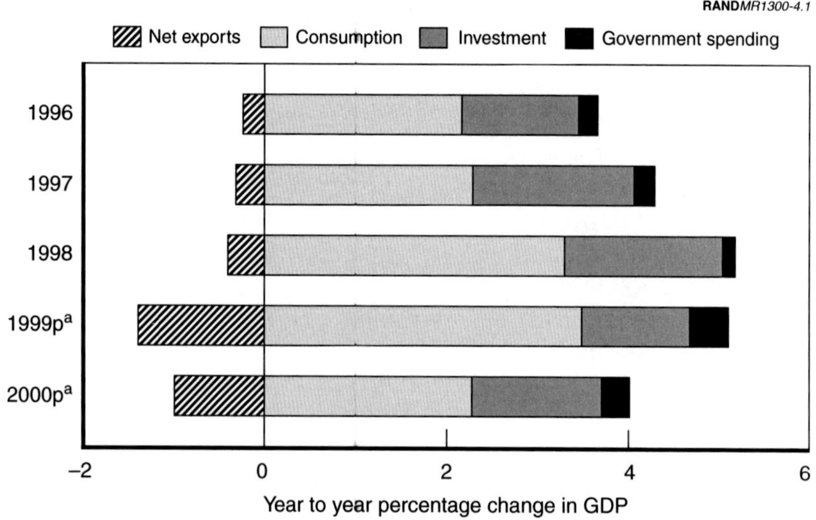

Figure 4.1—The U.S. Consumer Continues to Drive Economic Growth

sumer incomes have been advancing steadily for the past seven years (see Figure 4.2). There is some evidence from recent government revisions that these income estimates are understated.

Moreover, the acceleration in consumer incomes is rooted in an acceleration in total wage and salary income to more than 6 to 7 percent annually through September 1999. Although consumers have many sources of income, wages and salaries are the foundation of their spending base. The rise in total wages and salaries is considerably faster than the pace of wage gains indicated by other wage series such as average hourly earnings, because total wages factor in both hours and employment gains as well as pay increases (see Figure 4.3). Thus, not only is consumer real income growth rising overall, but the core component, from a spending perspective, is accelerating even faster. It's no surprise, then, that the Conference Board's consumer confidence index continues at near-record levels (see Figure 4.4).

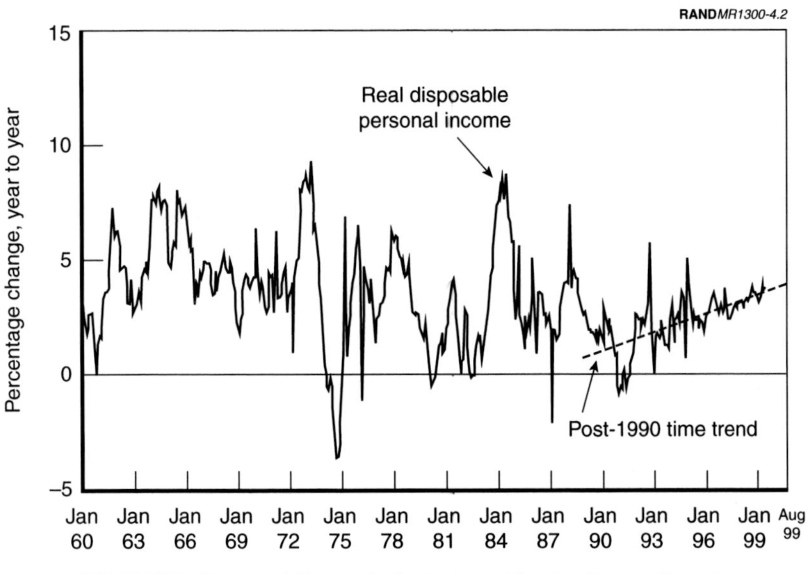

Figure 4.2—Consumer Incomes Have Been Advancing Steadily

Figure 4.3—Growth in Wage and Salary Income Remains High

Recent economic concerns regarding consumers have focused not on income growth but on the savings rate. The conventionally reported consumer savings rate is a poor gauge of consumer spending power for several reasons. First, consumer spending is itself overstated when spending on big-ticket items like cars and furniture rises, because the full purchase price is accounted for in the quarter the item is purchased. Second, disposable income is understated because although capital gains are deducted from income, tax payments used to calculate disposable income include taxes on capital gains—a discrepancy that accounts for 2 to 3 percentage points of disposable income. Finally, consumers are inclined to spend more of this income when asset markets are adding to their net worth. In other words, consumers can achieve their balance sheet goals without supplementing their net worth with savings. A better measure of the savings rate, such as the one published by the Federal Reserve, has also declined but not as dramatically (see Figure 4.5). Thus, con-

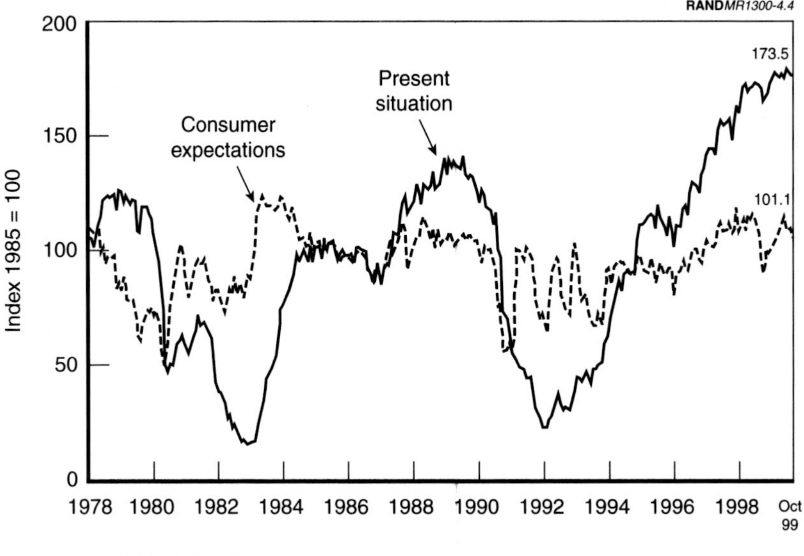

Figure 4.4—Present Situation Is Close to Historic Highs, But Expectations Have Softened

sumers are not so much spending their financial gains directly, but spending a larger share of their incomes because they are confident in their long-term financial welfare.

In short, the U.S. consumer is enjoying excellent income gains, high levels of confidence, and enormous gains in terms of real wealth. Given the recent financial market advance, consumers' net worth is close to double the levels of the beginning of the decade. These gains in both income and wealth are reinforced by the demographics of the U.S. market, where more than 57 percent of all households are in the 45 to 65 age group. (This share will swell to 79 percent by 2010.) These households are in their peak earning years, accounting for 40 percent of all household income and 80 percent of income growth. With these demographics and good income and asset growth, the U.S. consumer market is enjoying considerable momentum that will not be easily reversed.

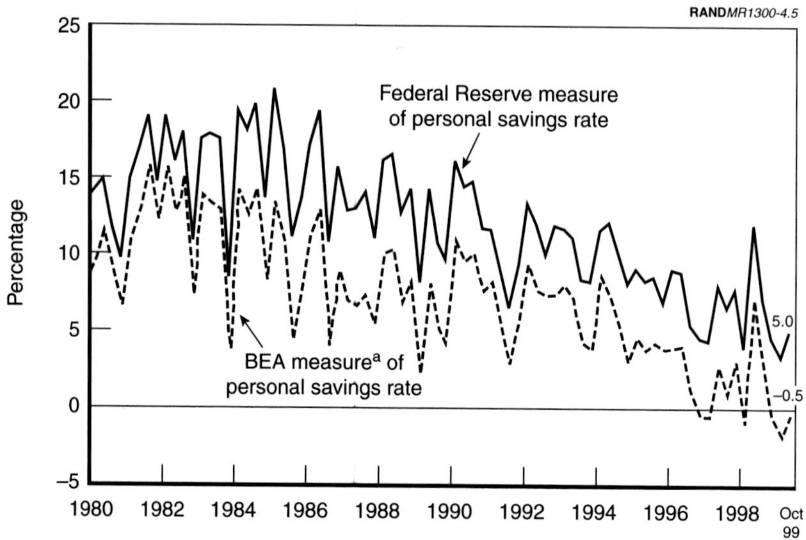

[a]Calculated using flow-of-funds data.

SOURCES: Bureau of Economic Analysis, the Federal Reserve, and the Conference Board.

Figure 4.5—Federal Reserve Savings Rate Takes Account of Investment Nature of Consumer Durable Purchases

WHAT DO THE LEADING ECONOMIC INDICATORS TELL US?

The Conference Board's leading economic indicators (LEI) also do not point to a slowdown. Although the pace has slowed after several months of sharp advances, the underlying structure continues to point to growth. Figure 4.6 shows the LEI itself, and Figure 4.7 illustrates key subcomponents. The financial indicators (i.e., stock prices, money growth, and the yield curve) remain overwhelmingly positive—even considering the recent pullback in stock prices. Although the household and manufacturing indicators (i.e., confidence and new orders for consumer goods) are less dramatic, they are also edging up. The labor sector, having reached full employment, is generally neutral.

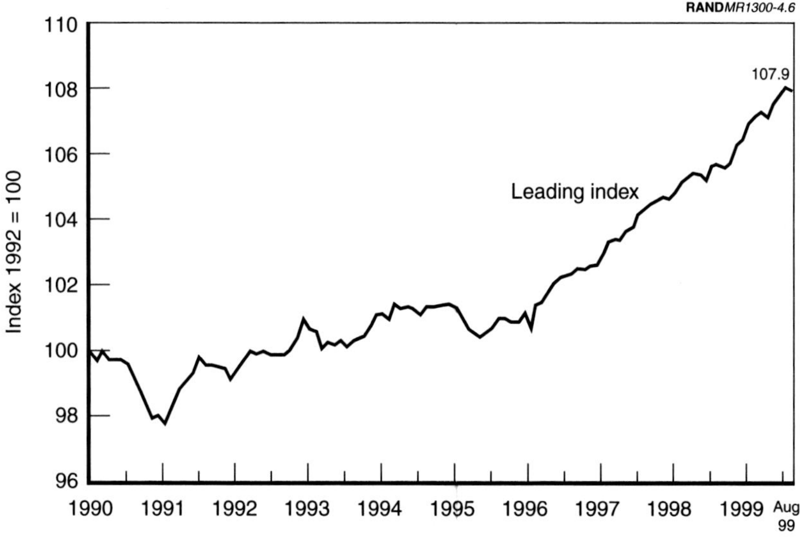

Figure 4.6—Leading Index Points to Continued Growth

The central role of the financial indicators in driving the leading index underscores the choices the Federal Reserve faces. If the Federal Reserve really wants to slow the economy, it will have to raise short-term interest rates enough to cause the yield curve to flatten (i.e., long-term rates to fall) and money growth and stock prices to decline sharply in some combination. The policy of gradually adjusting short-term interest rates in small increments, which the Federal Reserve has pursued in recent years, will likely have little effect—especially in an economy with considerable momentum and few imbalances. Incremental policies will yield incremental results that can be overridden by strong economic fundamentals. Under such policies, the U.S. economy is therefore likely to continue to grow faster than expected—rather than slow of its own accord—and see gradually rising short- and long-term interest rates. The year 2000 economic forecast has been revised upward to reflect this outcome (see Table 4.1).

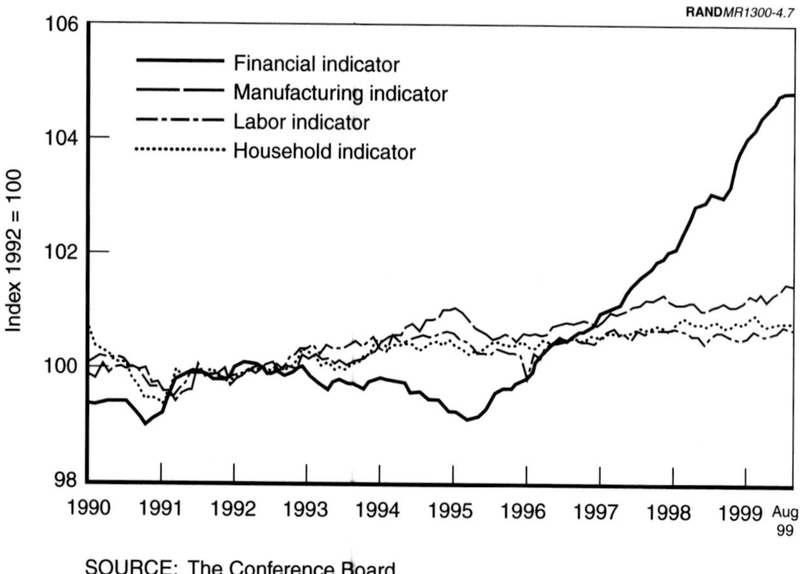

Figure 4.7—Financial Component Remains Overwhelmingly Positive

REKINDLING INFLATION

The September 1999 rise in the Producer Price Index (PPI) and the subsequent hike in the Consumer Price Index (CPI) reinforced the notion that, along with U.S. growth, inflation is also on the rise. Aside from a rebound in energy prices, and certain seasonal problems, however, there is little in either commodity prices or core goods and services prices to suggest a serious inflation threat.

First, although commodity prices are turning up, relatively modest growth in the developing world (i.e., 3 to 5 percent) compared with the growth in the mid-1990s will keep a lid on prices. Second, advances in manufacturing capacity will keep utilization rates below levels required for significant price increases, even with the pickup in manufacturing activity. Third, competition of all sorts, including from cheap imports, will continue to keep a lid on prices. Only in a few domestic services, such as health, education, and personal care, will inflation rise in the 3 to 5 percent range.

Nevertheless, even in this relatively quiescent environment, the core CPI—now running at a 2.2 to 2.3 percent annual rate—will move up to a 2.5 to 2.7 percent rate and possibly 3.0 percent in 2000. This acceleration will not be sufficiently rapid or consistent enough to provoke a substantial cyclical tightening by the Federal Reserve.

POSSIBILITIES AND PROBABILITIES

All of this adds up to a particularly favorable business environment with rapid growth, moderate pricing capacity, and gradually—indeed, very gradually—rising interest rates. The Federal Reserve has established the principle of moving against inflation risks and/or outright inflation signals themselves, but not higher-than-expected growth. How deeply the Federal Reserve believes in the "new economy" notion is unclear. Nevertheless, the Federal Reserve appears willing to let economic growth run its course no matter what the rate, as long as outright inflation performance remains benign. Ongoing Conference Board research suggests that the sustainable growth rate in U.S. GDP may be as high as 3.5 percent. While it is possible that the Federal Reserve would raise rates significantly and in rapid succession, the probable outlook shows a very gradual rise in short-term rates over the next year, with corresponding increases in long-term rates. Indeed, to the extent that the incipient Asian recovery falters, or Brazil and Argentina weaken further, the Federal Reserve may be even further constrained in its efforts to raise interest rates.

ARE HIGH STOCK PRICES A BURDEN?

A critical concern in the U.S. outlook arises not from the underlying economy nor even from traditional Federal Reserve policy. Rather, the heady level of U.S. stock prices constitutes a serious risk to the U.S. economy as a whole.

Table 4.1

The Conference Board's Economic Outlook, 1999–2001, Percentage Change, Seasonally Adjusted Annual Rates (except where noted)

	(Actual) 1999 2nd Quarter	3rd Quarter	4th Quarter	2000 1st Quarter	2nd Quarter	3rd Quarter	4th Quarter	2001 1st Quarter	1999 Annual	2000 Annual	2001 Annual
Real GDP	1.6	5.1	5.6	4.0	0.8	5.1	4.2	2.3	4.1	3.8	3.2
Gross domestic purchases	3.3	4.4	6.0	4.9	-1.2	5.6	4.5	2.1	5.1	3.8	3.2
CPI[a] inflation	3.4	2.9	2.4	2.4	2.4	2.6	2.6	2.3	2.2	2.6	2.5
Real consumer spending	4.8	4.1	4.0	2.7	2.9	3.1	2.6	3.1	5.2	3.3	2.9
Light vehicle sales (mil. units)	16.73	16.95	16.64	15.93	15.78	15.78	15.58	15.68	16.6	15.8	15.50
Housing starts (mil. units)	1.61	1.65	1.59	1.56	1.5	1.47	1.45	1.41	1.66	1.50	1.42
Real capital spending	10.8	7.7	7.5	12.9	-2.2	9.3	6.6	2.8	8.9	7.3	4.7
Inventory change (bil. '92$)	7.4	22.3	60.5	73.1	6.4	38.1	61.5	34.6	32.3	44.8	37.4
Real government purchases	-1.9	1.8	2.6	2.5	1.4	3.2	3.0	3.2	2.1	2.0	2.9
Federal	-3.6	-3.1	-0.1	1.1	-1.0	4.1	2.9	3.1	0.0	0.1	2.4
State and local	-1.1	4.5	4.1	3.2	2.6	2.8	3.0	3.2	3.2	3.0	3.2

Table 4.1—continued

	(Actual) 1999 2nd Quarter	3rd Quarter	4th Quarter	2000 1st Quarter	2nd Quarter	3rd Quarter	4th Quarter	2001 1st Quarter	1999 Annual	2000 Annual	2001 Annual
Net exports (bil. '92$)	338.0	328.4	341.7	362.8	320.7	334.5	344.8	342.8	328.0	340.7	349.5
Exports	4.9	7.6	7.4	7.0	7.6	7.8	8.8	7.2	3.5	7.3	7.5
Imports	15.1	2.7	9.7	11.8	-6.2	10.1	9.8	4.9	10.2	6.5	6.3
Pre-Tax operating profits (bil.*)	859	887	900	907	932	942	961	956	879	936	935
Industrial production	4.0	4.9	4.5	4.1	4.1	4.4	3.7	3.7	2.6	4.3	3.7
Unemployment rate (%)	4.3	4.2	3.8	3.6	3.7	3.6	3.5	3.6	4.2	3.6	3.8
90-day T-Bills (%)	4.45	4.65	4.87	5.07	5.24	5.44	5.50	5.56	4.60	5.31	5.61
10-yr Treas Bonds (%)	5.54	5.89	6.09	6.29	6.46	6.46	6.46	6.46	5.63	6.42	6.46
30-yr Treas Bonds (%)	5.80	6.04	6.35	6.55	6.72	6.72	6.72	6.72	5.89	6.68	6.72
Exchange rates											
$/EURO	1.06	1.05	1.07	1.09	1.13	1.14	1.20	1.16	1.08	1.14	1.10
Yen/$	121	105	105	105	100	95	90	90	111.75	97.5	90

*Current $ Level with inventory adjustment and capital consumption adjustment.

[a]Consumer Price Index.

1. Are investors taking rational risks in investing in the U.S. stock market?
2. Is the market vulnerable to a sizable correction that could destabilize the U.S. economy?

The respective answers are "yes" and "no." Although the stock market has backed off from its highs, stock values still reflect significant earnings gains in the future. Indeed, with the turn of the century, the market will likely decline further as investors become increasingly risk averse. However, the Conference Board forecast suggests the year 2000 overall is likely to be a good economic year and a good year for earnings.

In addition, a sizable correction (i.e., a 20 percent year-on-year decline in stock prices) also seems highly unlikely. In contrast to the "random walk" hypothesis, investors appear to be taking advantage of the reduced volatility in U.S. stocks over the last 40 years—in particular, the relatively rare incidence of a major decline—and are investing for the "long term." The market has turned in a 20 percent annual decline or greater only ten times in the last 128 years—all but one of which occurred before 1950. The only major market correction during the post–World War II period occurred in 1974–75, when recession, oil price increases, and political crisis combined to drag the market down by 43 percent.

The decrease in the volatility of stock prices since 1960 is complemented by a sharp rise in the mean annual return. In contrast to a mean annual market return of 6 percent historically, the mean yearly gain in the stock market rose to 9 percent in the post-1960 period and 16 percent post-1990. If we look at the total return of stocks, which reflects monthly price changes plus the reinvestment of monthly dividends and the compounding effect of dividends paid on reinvested dividends, the annualized one-year rate of return has been close to 20 percent during the 1990s. In short, U.S. stocks have been a remarkably good investment vehicle.

The decline in volatility and the increase in returns in recent years should not be a surprise. The U.S. stock market has grown dramatically in depth and breadth, with the number of publicly traded stocks rising from 6,600 in 1988 to almost 9,000 in 1997. Correspondingly, market capitalization rose from $2.8 trillion, or 57 percent of U.S. GDP, to $11.2 trillion, or 150 percent of U.S. GDP. Pension funds and 401k investments dominate the market, accounting for half of total outstanding equity. In addition, the regulatory and institutional structure surrounding the stock market has become more sophisticated, as witnessed by the creation of a number of industry-based self-regulating bodies like the Investment Company Institute (ICI), which sets standards for the mutual fund industry, as well as by increasingly stringent corporate governance practices. The growth in the futures markets and other derivatives offers effective hedges against risk, and the Federal Reserve has assumed an effective role as lender of last resort, especially recently. Equally important is the rise in corporate earnings—even after adjustment for inflation. Real earnings per share have risen tenfold since 1960 and have more than doubled since 1991 (see Figure 4.8).

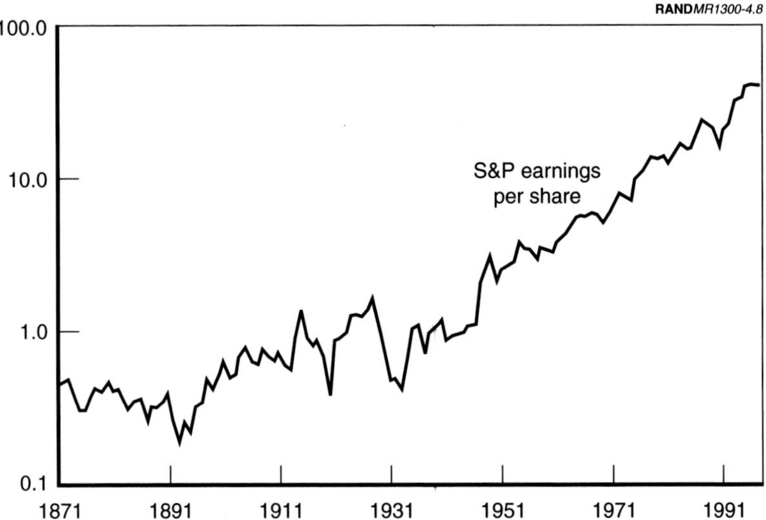

SOURCES: Standard and Poor's and the Conference Board.

Figure 4.8—Post-1990 Period Represents Most Impressive Earnings Gains in History

In the end, the answers to these issues will be found not in the past but in the future. The comfort of historical probabilities notwithstanding, there is much about the future that is simply unknown. Just as average stock market returns have improved in the last 30 or 40 years, perhaps the present surge is another "great leap forward" and is a symbol of a new "golden" age. History does not occur in three- or five-year increments, and such extended periods have happened in the past. Nevertheless, for such bold conclusions to be true, the stock market and the private business sector will have to overcome the law of diminishing returns and continue to reinvest future earnings at comparable or higher rates of return than have been achieved in recent years. In so doing, some of the laws of human nature itself and its political and economic institutions will have to be rewritten.

IS THE PAST A PROLOGUE?

It is almost impossible to find an historical precedent for today's stock market. Does that mean it is too high? Is the future simply a series of calculable probabilities based on past experience or are there other ways to test the reasonableness of what is going on today in the context of the future?

One way to answer these questions is to examine what price earnings ratios (P/Es) indicate about stock market valuations. Price earnings ratios presumably combine earnings growth expectations with the prevailing discount rate. When interest rates (i.e., the discount rate) fall, price earnings ratios should rise because lower interest rates raise the present value of a company's future earnings. When earnings expectations rise, P/Es should also rise. Figure 4.9 shows the actual P/E ratios for the Standard and Poor's (S&P) 500 and the P/Es implied by the six-month prime commercial paper rate since 1988. Until 1996, actual P/Es bore a striking resemblance to what might have been expected given the decline in interest rates over this period. In other words, the stock market fully capitalized the decline in interest rates but was relatively agnostic about future earnings growth.

However, since 1996, P/Es have surged. The present P/Es for the S&P are 31 times earnings. It would take a decline in interest rates to around 3 percent to justify P/Es at these levels. More realistically,

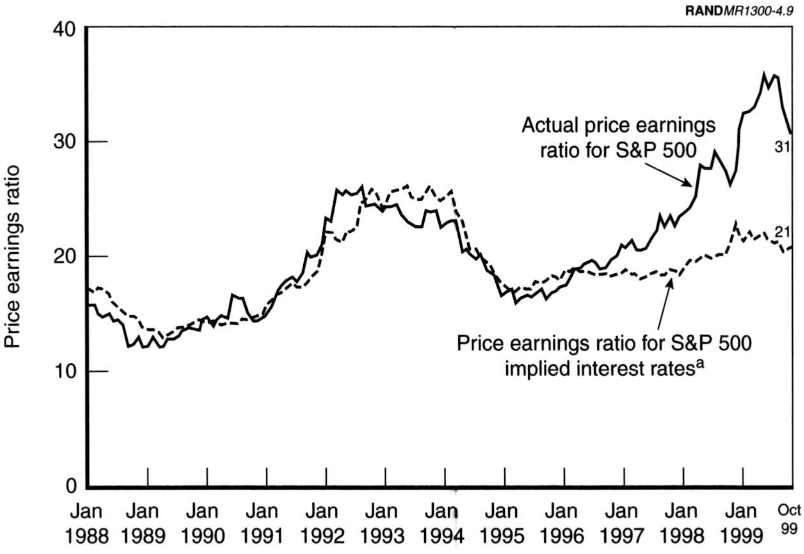

Figure 4.9—Interest Rates Do Not Justify Current Price Earnings Ratios

these P/Es probably imply an expected surge in corporate earnings. Still, earnings would have to rise by close to 50 percent for the P/Es of the S&P 500 to return to the level of 20 or so that is consistent with the likely trend in interest rates. While the relatively favorable economic outlook for 1999 and 2000 is likely to keep earnings rising at double digit rates, current stock prices appear to capitalize very large earnings gains several years into the future. Today's investor is willing to buy high on the assumption that future earnings will drive stock prices still higher.

A related question is just how representative these market P/Es are. If the appreciation in the S&P has become increasingly concentrated in a few stocks, the current high-market P/Es might signal that portions of the market, but not the whole market, are "overvalued." Unfortunately, the distribution of P/Es in the S&P 500 suggests that the apparent optimism implied by the average P/E is increasingly representative of the whole market. Only 15 percent of the stocks in the S&P 500 have P/Es below 20 P/E, with 25 representing the median. Alternatively, 80 stocks, or close to 20 percent of the index, have P/Es over 50. Since 1996, not only have P/Es surged for the market as a whole, but the entire P/E distribution in the S&P 500 has shifted to higher and higher valuations. Thus, the caution apparent in overall stock prices today reflects a reappraisal of these high PIEs—for the moment.

From almost every perspective, today's stock market suggests substantial optimism about the future. In the above example, a 25 to 40 percent gain over two and a half years would be achievable given the historical averages. Nevertheless, the U.S. stock market, as measured by the S&P 500, was becoming increasingly expensive. More declines appear likely in the near term. Whether the market will continue to rise depends upon the ability of the U.S. economy to both continue to improve productivity performance above its historical average and to translate that productivity growth into real returns for investors. Some economists assert that certain product markets, especially technology, will enjoy increasing returns. But human nature and the law of diminishing returns are not to be dispensed with lightly. The future may be bright, but our insistence on capitalizing on opportunities in current market values raises the bar on future performance and increases the risk imbedded in current stock price levels.

CONCLUSION

For the U.S. stock market, the balance of the risks argues for little gain for the next year or so—as long as U.S. interest rates are rising. Nevertheless, it is difficult to make the case that the market has a lot of downside—since corporate earnings will continue to grow moderately. The U.S. economy is in the midst of a major technological shift, which is most often discussed under the "new economy" label to explain the favorable inflation experience of the last few years, as well as why U.S. corporations have been so profitable. The new technical capacities are creating cost-saving opportunities on the input side, and new product opportunities on the output side—while competitive U.S. capital and project markets create the pressures to turn these opportunities into earnings and higher stock values.

Can the U.S. consumer survive a prolonged period with little increase in stock values—even a significant drop of say 10 percent or so from current values? Absolutely! As mentioned earlier, U.S. consumer spending does not depend on a rising stock market but on continued strong earnings gains supported by favorable demographics and significant wealth gains. These wealth gains increasingly come from appreciating home prices as well as the stock market. Indeed, these wealth gains influence consumers to spend more from current income because their long-term wealth objectives are being achieved through asset appreciation.

These very optimistic conclusions may appear to be Panglossian, but are nonetheless real. The U.S. economy is in a "golden period" at the moment—a relatively favorable circumstance for the rest of the world as well. The risks to this success come not from the traditional economists' view of imbalances (i.e., the trade deficit) but rather whether the political system is strong enough and far sighted enough to use the resources created by these good times to reinforce future growth or whether decisions made today, especially with respect to expanding government entitlements, will absorb resources unduly and undermine growth in the longer term.

Part III

TRENDS AND PROSPECTS IN THE CHINESE ECONOMY

Chapter Five

CHINA'S ECONOMIC GROWTH: RECENT TRENDS AND PROSPECTS

K. C. Yeh

China's economic growth in the last two decades has been phenomenal. Is such rapid growth sustainable? Assessments of various observers differ widely. Some, like the economists at the World Bank (1997a), believe that the prospects are bright. Others, like Lardy (1998), have doubts, fearing that a financial crisis looms (see also Restall, 1999). Still others, like Segal (1999), conclude that China as an economic power is insignificant and will remain so for some years to come. To help clarify the issue, this chapter reviews the growth record since 1978, identifies the major sources of economic growth, and assesses whether these contributing factors will continue to generate rapid growth in the near future.

THE GROWTH RECORD, 1978–1998

How fast has the Chinese economy been growing in the last two decades?

The question is relevant because the challenges of sustaining a 10 percent annual growth of GDP would be somewhat different from those of sustaining a 5 percent growth.[1] Table 5.1 compares China's economic growth in the 1980s and 1990s with those of selected

[1] For example, a 10 percent growth of capital inputs could almost guarantee a 5 percent GDP growth, but would be much less significant in sustaining a 10 percent GDP growth.

countries. The comparison shows that China's GDP growth rates were not only far above the averages for other low income countries, they also exceeded those of large developing countries like India and Indonesia, as well as the two neighboring newly industrialized economies, Taiwan and South Korea, not to mention such developed countries as Japan and the United States.

But how reliable are China's official statistics? Many economists question their accuracy. Table 5.2 compares the official growth rates with seven alternative estimates for various periods. In all cases, the alternative estimates are considerably lower than the official growth rates. The overstatement for the pre-1978 period is particularly noteworthy. For the post-1978 period, it is somewhat smaller but still substantial, ranging from 0.4 to 3.8 percentage points.

There are several reasons to believe that the official statistics overstate the GDP growth. First, the deflators used by the State Statistical Bureau (SSB) to convert nominal to real GDP growth understate the true inflation rate.[2] Second, the use of output growth rates as per

Table 5.1

GDP Growth: China and Selected Countries, 1980–1998 (in percentage)

	1980–1990	1990–1998
China	9.3	10.8
Other low-income countries	4.1	3.6
India	5.8	6.1
Indonesia	6.1	5.8
Taiwan	7.9	6.3
South Korea	9.4	6.2
Japan	4.0	1.3
United States	3.0	2.9

SOURCES: China: State Statistical Bureau (SSB), Statistical Survey (SA) 99, p. 14. *Taiwan: Industry of China*, August, 1999. Others: World Bank, 1999, pp. 250–251.

---

[2]For example, the factory price index for industrial products in 1995 was 338 percent of that in 1980, far above the implicit deflator for gross value added in industry, 222 percent over the same period. SY 98, p. 317; SA 99, pp. 11, 14.

formance indicators has led some enterprise managers and local government officials to exaggerate their reports.[3] Third, the SSB has underestimated the level of GDP, particularly those for the 1980s,[4] partly because of incomplete statistical coverage of some key sectors,[5] and partly because of the undervaluation of some goods and services.[6] Some downward biases in the 1990s, however, have been subsequently adjusted by the SSB.[7] More importantly, by the 1990s, most prices have been decontrolled so that the undervaluation of output has been corrected to some degree. The result is that the growth rates are exaggerated by the large understatements in the earlier years.

---

[3]See, for example, *Zhongguo tongji* (*China's Statistics*) No. 5, 1999, p. 29. At times the reported growth rates err on the high side for unknown reasons. For example, the average annual growth of consumption of all households in 1990–98 exceeds those of both the rural and urban households (SA 99, p. 27). Technically it would be impossible for the average index to fall below the lowest or exceed the highest index of the individual components.

[4]Estimates by Shuqing Guo, the World Bank, and Kiedel indicate that the true level of GDP in 1987 should be 16, 34, and 55 percent above the official figure, respectively. Guo and Han, 1991, p. 61; Szirmai and Ren, 1995, p. 3; World Bank, 1994, p. 25.

[5]For reasons of tax evasion or weaknesses of the statistical system, the output and income of many small businesses in the informal sector have been left out. These businesses include services provided by private traders, hawkers, craftsmen, packers, coolies, herbal medicine practitioners, domestic servants, handymen, moneylenders, and people with second jobs. Steven Cheung noted this long ago. See Cheung, 1989, p. 45. Another major item that has been excluded in the official statistics is rural consumption of noncommercial energy such as straws and stalks, wood, and biogas (SY 98, p. 261). The omission is nonnegligible. According to one estimate, rural consumption of noncommercial energy amounted to 22 percent of total reported energy consumption in 1992 (Yan, 1994, p. 186; SY 98, p. 251).

[6]During the early stage of economic transition, market prices and planned prices coexisted, and some goods and services were valued at planned prices set by the state at levels far below actual market prices or what market prices would have been. For example, in 1980, prices of farm products at rural free markets were 48 percent higher than those set by the state-owned enterprises (SOEs) (SY 93, p. 256). Other important items that have been undervalued include: urban housing, food, health care, education, urban facilities, transportation, energy, interest rates on loans to SOEs, and home consumption of farm products. There is, of course, overvaluation of some products, such as new products, substandard goods, and unsold inventories. But on balance, the official estimates are most probably on the low side.

[7]In 1993, the SSB revised the output of the service sector sharply upwards by 36 percent after a survey of that sector (SY 93, p. 32; SY 95, p. 32). The revision resulted in an 11 percent upward adjustment of the 1992 GDP. However, no significant adjustments have been made for the data for the 1980s.

Table 5.2

China's GDP Growth: Official and Alternative Estimates (percentage per year)

Source	Period	Alternative	Official
(1) Maddison (1990 prices)	1952–78	4.3	6.1
	1978–92	7.6	9.4
(2) Wu (1980 prices)	1952–78	4.9	6.1
	1978–91	8.6	9.0
(3) Li et al.	1952–78	5.6	6.1
	1978–90	8.4	9.0
(4) Chow (1980 prices)	1952–80	3.9	6.2
(5) World Bank	1978–95	8.2	9.9
	1978–86	8.8	9.7
	1986–95	7.9	10.0
(6) Ren (1985 prices)	1985-94	6.0	9.8
(7) Yeh (1990 prices)	1990-95	8.7	12.0

SOURCES: Official estimates are based on data in comparable prices from SSB 1989; SSB, SA 99, p. 14. The alternative estimates are taken from: (1) Maddison, 1995, p. 191. (2) Ren, 1997, p. 105; Wu, 1994, p. 64. (3) Li et al., 1995, p. 27. (4) Chow, 1994, p. 108. (5) World Bank, 1997a, pp. 3, 106; SSB, Statistical Yearbook (SY) 98, p. 105. (6) Ren, 1997, p. 108. (7) Charles Wolf et al., 2000.

Fourth, the distorted price structure in the initial years of reform also imparted an upward bias in the aggregate output index. This is because the GDP index is the weighted average of the real growth rates of the state and the nonstate sectors, the weights being their respective shares in GDP valued at prices of the initial year. Over time, the state sector has been growing more slowly than the nonstate sector. The initial weights, however, are biased against the state sector, because the prices of many of its products and services, such as energy, raw materials, transportation, and financial services, were still under state control at levels far below market prices, whereas most products of the nonstate sector were sold at market prices. An artificially smaller weight assigned to the slower-growing state sector has resulted in a faster GDP growth than if a larger weight were used. The bias is particularly serious for the growth rates for the 1980s, which are based on 1980 prices.

To say that the official growth rate is overstated is not to belittle China's impressive growth record. The purpose here is to place the recent growth trends in a more realistic perspective. Judging from the various estimates presented in Table 5.2, it seems clear that the true growth rate is considerably below the official 10 percent. Still, it is a remarkable achievement by any standards. The crucial issue is whether the growth rate is sustainable. The question is timely, because the official statistics indicate a persistent decline in GDP growth since 1992 as shown in Figure 5.1. Is the slowdown a temporary phenomenon, or is it the beginning of a long-term trend toward a level significantly below that of the last two decades?

SOURCES OF GDP GROWTH

To address that issue, we first examine how China's economy grew so fast in the past. Table 5.3 presents estimates of sources of growth

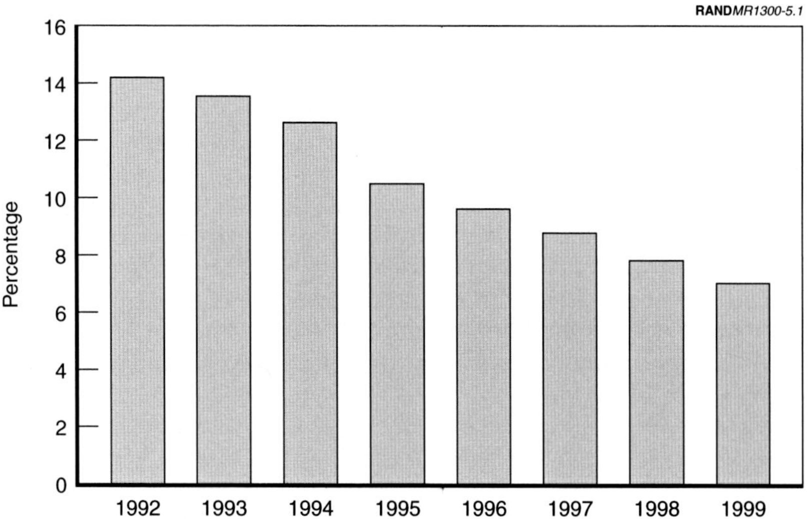

Figure 5.1—China's GDP Growth Rate

Table 5.3

Source of Economic Growth (Special Countries, 1960–2000) (in percentage)

	GDP Growth Rate	Contributions from		
		Capital	Labor	TFP
China	9.4	4.4	1.3	3.7
		(46.8)	(13.3)	(39.8)
Hong Kong	7.3	3.1	2.0	2.2
		(42.3)	(27.6)	(30.1)
Singapore	8.5	6.2	2.7	–0.4
		(73.1)	(31.6)	(–4.7)
South Korea	10.3	4.8	4.4	1.2
		(44.2)	(42.2)	(11.6)
Taiwan	9.1	3.7	3.6	1.8
		(40.5)	(39.8)	(19.8)
Japan	6.8	3.9	1.0	2.0
		(56.9)	(14.3)	(28.8)
U.S.	3.1	1.4	1.3	0.4
		(45.2)	(41.5)	(13.2)

SOURCES: China: GDP growth rate is based on Li's estimate for 1978–90 and the official growth rate for 1990–95 (Li, 1994, p. 91; SA 99, p. 14). The percentage shares of contribution of capital and productivity growth are from Li, 1998, p. 2. All others: Barro and Sala-I-Martin, 1995, pp. 380–381.

NOTES: Percentages for China are 1978–1995. Figures in parentheses refer to percentages of contribution to GDP growth. TFP is total factor productivity.

for China in 1978–95 and those of six other countries for 1960–90. The comparison brings out several interesting features in China's case. First, like all other economies, China's economic growth depended heavily on the growth of capital.[8] Second, unlike others, China's growth of total factor productivity (TFP) was much more significant, accounting for about 40 percent of GDP growth.[9] Third, by contrast, the contribution of labor growth was relatively small, though nonnegligible. To better understand the growth process, we

[8]It is not unusual for countries, including Japan and the U.S., to rely heavily on capital growth at the initial stage of development (Lau, 1996, p. 88).

[9]The figure is somewhat overstated, because GDP growth based on official statistics is exaggerated as noted above. Nonetheless, there are reasons to believe that significant improvements in productivity took place at the first phase of economic liberalization. See discussion below.

look further into the causes of growth of capital, labor, and productivity.

CAPITAL FORMATION

Capital growth depends mainly on investment. In the last two decades, China has consistently allocated a large share of GDP to investment. Many other developing countries too have been able to do the same, as shown in Table 5.4. However, China's case is distinctive in two respects: First, China sustains a high investment rate despite its low per-capita income. In terms of per-capita GDP in 1998, China ranks 129 in the world, way below all the other Asian countries listed in the table except India. Yet, its investment rate is higher than all others' (except Singapore's in 1980). Second, China's investment rate has been quite stable over time, in a period when its economic system underwent drastic changes, and when a severe and contagious financial crisis hit its neighboring countries. The average share of investment in GDP during 1978–1998 was 36.8 percent. The share was not very volatile, as indicated by the rather small coefficient of variation.[10]

Two sources of savings have been particularly important in sustaining a high and stable investment in China: a high household savings

Table 5.4

The Rate of Investment, Selected Countries, 1980 and 1998

	Rank: Per-Capita/GDP	1980 (%)	1998 (%)
China	129	35	39
Low-income countries	—	28	30
Singapore	5	46	37
Hong Kong	18	35	30
South Korea	55	32	35
Mexico	71	27	26
Malaysia	79	30	32
Thailand	91	29	35
India	163	20	23

SOURCE: World Bank, 1999, pp. 230–231, 254–255.

[10]The standard deviation is 2.72 percent, and the coefficient of variation, 0.07. For data, see SA 99, p. 21.

rate and a rising volume of foreign capital inflows. In the period 1978–95, domestic savings rose from 122 to 2,449 billion yuan (World Bank, 1995, p. 208; World Bank, 1997a, p. 121). The increase of household savings had been an important source of total savings. In 1978, it accounted for only 5 percent of total domestic savings (People's Bank, 1994, p. 76). By 1995, its share increased to 41 percent.[11] A number of factors contributed to the high household savings rate. At the micro level, Chinese households saved a substantial portion of their income for many reasons. By tradition or by necessity, the Chinese people are rather frugal. The sharp rise in per-capita income since 1978 (particularly transitory income) and subsidized urban housing greatly enhanced the households' capacity to save. At the same time, the households were highly motivated to save for contingencies when job security was no longer guaranteed, to set aside resources for retirement, health care expenses and children's education, and to accumulate money for large lump-sum expenditures such as weddings and purchases of houses and consumer durables, since consumer credit was not available. In particular, with the economy in transition, uncertainties abound, and it is quite natural for the households to save more for precautionary purposes.

At the macro level, several distinct trends also helped to sustain a high savings rate. One was the continued rise in the share of urban population, which, thus far, has a higher savings rate than the rural population.[12] Similarly, the share of employment in the nonstate sector has been increasing. These workers do not enjoy the free social benefits as those in the state sector and therefore tend to save a larger share of their income to hedge against unemployment and illness. Therefore, the distribution of income apparently has become more unequal between those in the coastal provinces and the interior provinces.

Table 5.5 shows the foreign capital inflows in 1985, 1990 and 1998. There has been a sharp increase since 1985, particularly in the case of direct investments. By 1990 direct investments constituted 77 per-

---

[11]Household savings are derived from household income given in Zhen, 1999, p. 569, and household consumption from SA 99, p. 22.

[12]See, for example, the average savings rates in 1995 and the marginal savings rates for 1985–1995. SY 96, pp. 69, 282, 288–289, 300, 353.

Table 5.5

Capital Inflow, 1985–1998
(Billions U.S.$)

	1985	1990	1998
Total	4.6	10.3	58.6
Loans	2.7	6.5	11.0
Direct Investments	1.7	3.5	45.4
Others	0.3	0.3	2.1

SOURCE: SA 99, p. 135.

cent of total capital inflows. This feature is important, because direct investments are less volatile than foreign loans in times of financial crisis. China had been able to attract large volumes of foreign capital for several reasons. The first is China's large potential market. Then, there is the case for moving one's manufacturing facilities from Hong Kong and Taiwan into China to take advantage of the relatively low labor and land costs. Also, the government had adopted various measures to attract foreign investment. Many such investments were made by overseas Chinese.

LABOR GROWTH

As Table 5.3 shows, the contribution of the growth of labor input to GDP growth was relatively modest, not only smaller than in the four newly industrialized economies, but also lower than the average for East Asian countries.[13] However, the estimate for China is probably on the low side for two reasons. First, there is probably a downward bias in the measurement of labor growth. For lack of information, labor input is measured in terms of the number of persons employed rather than man-hours worked. The presumption is strong that the actual man-hours worked per worker has increased, because workers in the nonstate sector generally put in more hours than those in the state sector, and employment in the nonstate sector has been growing faster than that in the state sector in the last two decades. Second, there is the likelihood that the labor share in GDP used in estimating sources of growth has been too low. According to one

[13]The average for East Asian countries for 1960–87 was 16 percent (World Bank, *World Economic Report, 1991*, Oxford University Press, New York, 1991, pp. 34, 45).

study, the labor share showed a distinct rising trend, increasing from 57.6 percent of GDP in 1984 to 60.6 percent in 1991 and 65.7 percent in 1995.[14] An adjustment of these biases would raise the growth rate of labor input.

In any event, the contribution of labor growth goes far beyond what the growth accounting figures suggest. This is because the indirect contribution of the large labor supply to GDP growth has been substantial. It has kept wages low and thereby maintained China's comparative advantage in international markets. Furthermore, the surplus labor that migrated to the coastal areas could displace the better-qualified workers in those areas so that the latter could move to more productive jobs. At the same time, the migrants could help to diffuse knowledge, promote factor mobility, and integrate markets, all of which would contribute to increasing income and employment in their home villages. Of course, the large proportion of unemployed created some problems. Overcrowding of coastal cities, wasted resources in subsidies, and social unrest are some of the consequences. More serious still is that concern over social stability might deter the leadership from pushing ahead with reforms. If that happens, the prospects of sustained economic growth would be jeopardized.

TFP GROWTH

Table 5.3 shows that TFP growth has been quite significant. For convenience of discussion, it will be useful to distinguish three sources of productivity gains: resource reallocation, improvements in the quality of inputs, and technological changes narrowly defined.[15] All have been important in the past, though to different degrees. One major source of increases in allocative efficiency is the structural shifts in resource use from low productivity to high productivity sectors. The most notable shift is that of labor from agriculture to industry and services. In the last two decades, employment in agriculture

---

[14]Zhen, 1999, p. 569. This means that the contribution of TFP growth shown in Table 5.3 might be too high.

[15]In technical terms, the allocative effect refers to the economy moving from a point below the production frontier toward the frontier, or along the frontier. The effects of quality improvements and technological advances would lead to a shift of the production frontier upwards. The three sources are, of course, not independent of each other.

dropped from 70 to 50 percent of total employment, while that in the nonagricultural sector rose correspondingly (SA 99, p. 34). Because the output per worker in agriculture was lower, the shift resulted in a dramatic increase in output per worker for the economy as a whole. Similarly, there had been a shift of investment in fixed capital from the state to the nonstate sector. In 1980, investment in the state sector accounted for 82 percent of total fixed investment. By 1997, it dropped to 52 percent (Zhen, 1999, pp. 899–900). In addition, the return to investment in nonstate enterprises was higher than that in state enterprises.[16]

A second important source of allocative efficiency has been the economies of scale resulting from the opening of the economy to internal and external markets. Economic liberalization since 1978 has torn down the barriers of the pre-1978 semi-closed village economy, and the expanding markets have allowed a higher degree of specialization and hence more efficient use of resources. Equally if not more important were the scale effects from opening to world markets. After China abandoned the closed-door policy and actively participated in world trade and in the globalization of industries, exports as a percentage of GDP rose from 4.6 percent to 19.1 percent in 1978–98 (SA 99, pp. 11, 130). The economy benefited not only from the usual advantages of international division of labor but also from foreign competition, the transfer of knowledge, and the inflow foreign capital—all of which contributed immensely to economic growth and reform.

A third type of allocative efficiency originates from the strong incentives and managerial skills to use resources efficiently at the enterprise level. A case in point is the dramatic increase in agricultural output per worker after China introduced agricultural reform.[17] When the commune system was replaced by the household responsibility system, the state in effect assigned to the farm households the rights to allocate their resources freely and to earn income there-

---

[16]For example, in 1997, among the industrial enterprises with independent accounts, total profits per unit of fixed asset in the SOEs were 8.1 percent, compared with 26.1 percent in the collectively owned enterprises (SY 98, pp. 425, 427).

[17]According to official statistics, output per worker increased at 3.92 percent per year during 1978–98, compared with 0.15 percent annual growth during 1952–78 (SY 98, pp. 57, 128; SA 99, pp. 14, 34).

from. These changes greatly motivated the peasants to increase output.[18] Similarly, the state left rural enterprises free to pursue higher economic gains. The result was a proliferation of small, independent enterprises that operated far more efficiently than the SOEs.

The significance of the productivity gains from reallocating resources is hard to quantify. But undoubtedly the gains were substantial. The World Bank (1996, Vol. I, p. 12) attributed 11 percent of GDP growth in 1985–94 to reallocation of employment, and 2 percent to ownership change. Sachs and Woo (1996, p. 78) estimated the contribution of reallocation of labor from agriculture at 13 percent of GDP growth in 1979–93. And, according to Lin (1992), the reintroduction of household farming accounted for nearly half of the growth of agricultural output in 1978–84. However, it is important to note that the improvements in allocative efficiency were one-time effects.

Apart from resource reallocation, there is the second major source of productivity growth: improvements in the quality of capital and labor. Because new technologies are generally embodied in new capital equipment, the younger the average age of the capital stock, the more new technologies have been introduced.[19] In the last two decades, large volumes of new equipment have been put in place.[20] Clearly, the quality of capital inputs has improved.

Improvement in the quality of the labor force is even more marked, as evidenced by the change in the educational level of the work force. Table 5.6 shows the percentage shares of the workforce with different levels of education in 1982 and 1997. The most notable change is the sharp reduction in the share of illiterate workers. At the same time, the shares of those with high school and college education increased discernibly. According to the World Bank (1997a, p. 106), education alone contributed 29 percent of GDP growth in 1978–95. In addition,

---

[18]Agricultural growth was virtually stagnant in the pre-1978 period. It rose abruptly to 7.8 percent annually during 1978–84 (SA 99, p. 14).

[19]For a formal model incorporating the concept of capital vintage, see Nelson, 1964.

[20]About one-third of the equipment in industry and transportation in the early 1980s was of the 1950s and 1960s vintage, one-half, the 1970s, and the rest was left over from the pre-1949 period (Sun, 1984, p. 177). At the end of 1995, equipment manufactured in the 1990s accounted for 34.5 percent, those in the 1980s, 55.6 percent, and less than 10 percent were from the 1970s (Li, 1998, p. 87).

Table 5.6

Composition of the Work Force by Educational Level, 1982 and 1997 (in percentage)

Workers	1982	1997
Total	100.0	100.0
College and above	0.9	3.5
Senior high school	10.5	12.1
Junior high school	26.0	37.9
Primary school	34.4	34.8
Illiterate or semi-illiterate	28.2	11.6

SOURCES: SY 86, pp. 114–115; SY 98, p. 171.

vocational training and learning by doing must have also improved the quality of workers.

Another source of TFP growth is technological change. Since 1978, the government has adopted a series of policies to promote technological advances by reorienting research and development (R&D) efforts toward developing industrial technologies, by encouraging the transfer of technology from the military to the civilian sector, and above all, by importing technology on a large scale. Expenditures on R&D increased from 4.6 to 52.6 billion yuan in the period 1978–1998 (SA 99, p. 145; SSB, 1989, p. 442). Considerable technological diffusion must have taken place, too, as suggested by the rise in the volume of transactions in technology markets, from 0.05 billion yuan in 1983 to 43 billion yuan in 1998 (State Science and Technology Commission, 1987, p. 42; SA 99, p. 145).

To sum up, in the last two decades, China has generated rapid economic growth primarily by sustained increases in capital formation and in productivity growth through reallocating resources, integrating with the world economy, and accumulating human capital.

PROSPECTS FOR GROWTH

Will China be able to repeat this high performance in the future? Interestingly, several economists unanimously say no. Table 5.7 presents the projections by the World Bank, Li, and Song, together with their estimates for 1978–95. Clearly, the consensus is that GDP growth will fall below the current level. The decline is probably less marked than the figures suggest, because, as noted above, the official statistics on which these estimates are based have overstated the growth rate. In any event, the rationales for these projections differ somewhat. Both the World Bank and Li believe that the investment rate will fall only slightly and will remain at a fairly high level, 30 percent or more for the next two decades. All expect labor growth to decline, rather sharply in World Bank's projections and moderately in others. The most marked difference is in their projected TFP growth. The World Bank expects a sharp drop. Li believes that it will remain more or less the same in the next decade but that its contribution will rise to as much as 60 percent of GDP growth by the year 2050. Song foresees a moderate decline in the next decade. To evaluate these projections, we explore the issue: What might happen to the three main sources of growth in the future?

In my judgment, the high investment rate will probably be maintained, but this is by no means certain. The conditions that increased the capacity and motivations to save are likely to persist for some time to come. Per-capita income will probably continue to grow, perhaps at a slower rate. The traditional basis of old-age support by the children of the family has weakened somewhat in recent years,

Table 5.7

GDP Projections, 1995–2050 (in percentage)

	GDP Growth	Investment Rate	Labor Growth	TFP Growth
World Bank				
1978–95	8.2	37	2.4	3.5
1995–20	6.6	35*	0.8	1.5**
2001–10	6.9	—	—	—
2011–20	5.5	—	—	—
Li				
1978–95	9.4	37	2.1	3.7
2001–10	8.1	33	1.0	3.4
2011–30	6.0	30	0.3	—
2030–50	4.5	—	–0.2	—
Song				
1978–98	8.2	—	2.2	3.7
1998–08	6.4	—	1.4	2.5

SOURCES: World Bank, 1997a, pp. 4, 21, 106, 113; 1997b, p. 34; Li, 1998, pp. 20, 23, 144, 359; Song, 1999, p. 18. See also notes to Table 5.3.

NOTES: *Figure is for the year 2005 and above. **Figure is for 2000–2020.

and this trend is likely to continue. Urban workers no longer have "iron rice bowls". Similarly the farmers themselves have to assume the risk of fluctuations in the prices of their products. At the same time, the state is privatizing some major social expenditures that the SOEs used to provide, such as pensions, unemployment insurance, medical expenses, education, and housing. Households must now prepare to bear partly or wholly these costs, until an effective social safety net is set up.

However, there are some negative forces in the making. First, as many observers anticipate, GDP growth in the next two decades may well decline. If and when that happens, the growth of per-capita income will slow. Second, China's population is rapidly aging. In 1990, China's population age 65 years and over constituted 5.6 percent of total population (Du Peng, 1994, p. 75). The proportion is projected to reach 6.8 percent in the year 2000 and 12.2 percent by 2025 (Lin and Zhai, 1996, p. 48). Unlike in other countries, the proportion of older people is rapidly increasing, and this increase occurs when China is still a developing country. An increasingly large proportion of aged population means more and more people living primarily on their own or others' savings.[21] Third, some economic reforms now in progress could affect people's savings behavior. For example, setting up an effective social safety net would lessen somewhat the need for precautionary savings. Eliminating subsidies to consumers, most notably housing subsidies to urban residents, would increase household expenditures.[22] Making consumer credit readily available to consumers might induce households to spend more on housing and consumer durables. Nonetheless, such negative effects should not be

[21] The potential drain of resources is indicated by the projected rise in the ratio of those working to the number of retirees from 6:1 in 1990 to 2:1 by the year 2020 (Lin and Zhai, 1996, p. 349). Offsetting this trend to some extent is the decreasing share of young dependents, as a result of declining fertility. But the cost of raising the young are likely to increase, too, as more and more households will be covering their own medical, educational, and housing expenses.

[22] At present, urban households' expenditures on housing accounted for only 4 percent of total consumption expenditures, a ridiculously low proportion (SA 99, p. 80). Government subsidies have been shown to be significant in determining urban residents' savings in Wang, 1995. Wang noted that, as the peasants' housing expenditures (which were not subsidized) in their total consumption expenditures increased from 9.8 percent in 1981 to 14.5 percent in 1987, their savings rate dropped from 23 percent in 1984 to 14 percent in 1987. The implication is that urban residents' savings rate will fall if their expenditures on housing increase.

overstated. While eliminating subsidies might reduce household savings, it creates an opportunity for the government to increase its savings, so that the total savings rate need not fall. A social security system is essentially an insurance plan funded by contributions of households and enterprises. These contributions are in effect forced savings that displace voluntary savings of individual households for the same purpose. What is different is that the burden and benefits are now distributed according to some social criteria. As for consumer credit, banks have recently begun to finance consumer spending in 1999, and it will take some time before consumers get used to the idea of spending one's future income.

The prospects for other sources of savings are even more uncertain. The problem with government savings in the last two decades is that the fiscal system has failed to generate sufficient revenues to cover the rapidly rising current expenditures. The share of government budget revenues in GDP dropped persistently, from 31.2 percent in 1978 to 10.7 percent in 1995 (SA 99, p. 58). Consequently the government savings rate declined from 32 percent in 1979 to 5 percent in 1995 (World Bank, 1996, Vol. II, pp. 53, 56; 1997a, pp. 139, 142). The fiscal squeeze is likely to persist since there will be enormous pressures to spend more on environmental protection, human capital formation, improving the infrastructure, funding institutional reforms, and defense spending. In anticipation of such demands, the government has made a great effort to reverse the downward trend in the share of government revenues in GDP. As a result, the share rose from 10.7 to 12.4 percent in 1995–98. The government planned to raise it further to 15 percent in two to three years and eventually to 20 percent.[23] It will not be easy because of strong resistance from various interest groups. But it is not infeasible, considering the potential of increasing tax revenues from the fast growing nonstate sector, revising personal income tax and property tax systems, and eliminating current tax loopholes. More importantly, government revenues and savings could rise sharply if economic reforms succeed in reducing subsidies to consumers and loss-making SOEs, shrinking the bloated government bureaucracy and diverting some extra-budget funds to the central government. Similarly, the outlook for busi-

[23]*Shijie ribao* (*Chinese Daily News*), May 21, 1999, p. C5.

ness and foreign savings is also clouded by the uncertain outcome of enterprise and fiscal reforms and China's open policy.

In light of these considerations, the stability of the savings rate cannot be taken for granted. Much depends on how institutional reforms might affect households, enterprises, and government incentives and capacity to save. In any event, economic growth in the future cannot rely solely on capital formation as in the pre-1978 days.

As Table 5.3 shows, the contribution of the growth of labor input to GDP growth in the last two decades was relatively small. According to many observers, it will be smaller still in the next two decades. The rationale underlying the projections is that the slowdown of population growth in the late 1980s and 1990s will change the age structure in the 2000s and beyond, so that the net increase of those entering the working force ages (15–64) will decline. This, in turn, will constrain labor supply and labor's contribution to economic growth.

The problem with this view is that it ignores a major component of labor supply: the massive hidden unemployed. Total labor supply comprises not only the new additions to the pool of labor available for employment (mainly those entering the working force and seeking employment), but also the existing stock of unemployed. To be sure, the net increase of those entering the working force will become smaller. But in China's case, the amount of existing unemployed is so overwhelmingly larger than the amount of new entrants that the declining amount of new additions really does not matter. The unemployed in China are composed of the urban registered unemployed, the urban hidden unemployed, and the rural hidden unemployed. The urban registered unemployed were reported at 5.7 million in 1997 (SY 98, p. 127). The hidden unemployed in urban and rural areas have been estimated at 30 million and 140 million, respectively (Zhen, 1999, pp. 513, 524). In the period 2000–2020, the average annual increase in the population of working age is estimated to be about 8 million, a minuscule number compared with the total existing unemployed of 170 million.[24]

---

[24]Li et al., 1995, p. 19. By the same token, the official unemployment rate is misleading and meaningless. It is misleading because it includes only the urban registered unemployed, which is only a fraction of the total number of unemployed. It is meaningless because the primary concern of the government is the effect of unemployment on

In my judgment, employment growth will probably slow, not so much because of a tightening of labor supply but because of a slowdown in the growth of demand for labor. The elasticity of nonagricultural employment with respect to output for 1980–85 was fairly high, 0.72, but it fell to 0.28 in the period 1995–98.[25] This rather sharp drop suggests that the high elasticity in the early 1980s might well have been the one-time effect of the upsurge in the labor-absorbing sectors, such as in rural industries and services during this period. The effect of a possible decline in GDP growth will be compounded by that of a low employment elasticity.

In recent years, the Chinese government has moved forward with releasing the excess labor in SOEs. The policy is a positive step in the right direction. But it unavoidably aggravated the unemployment problem. To mitigate the negative effects, various measures have been adopted, such as developing reemployment projects, controlling migration, and providing unemployment relief. All these measures are essentially short-term stopgaps. Perhaps an alternative strategy should be considered that focuses on the long-term demand for labor. At present, families, enterprises, and the state are supporting the 170 million hidden and openly unemployed. Perhaps through fiscal and financial measures, the state could divert some of the resources now being used to subsidize redundant workers to support the growth of more dynamic state and nonstate enterprises and let them absorb the surplus labor. The transfer of resources leaves the providers no worse off. The surplus labor would have jobs. The credit-starved enterprises would have the resources to grow.[26] A parallel and more direct approach would be to stimulate the growth of nonstate enterprises with resources now being used to subsidize loss-making SOEs. The workers from the bankrupt SOEs would be

---

social stability. But the official unemployment rate provides no warning to decision-makers. Even if the official unemployment rate is zero, a potential crisis still looms.

[25]For data used, see SA 99, pp. 11, 14, 34. GDP figures are official data in comparable prices.

[26]A project to increase employment by developing rural small towns is being funded by the World Bank, *South China Morning Post*, November 4, 1995, p. 8. However, the project appears to be putting the cart before the horse, since towns are developed mainly as a result of the growth of business activities and not the other way around. In any case, the idea of generating unemployment through growth promotion is basically sound. Another option is to develop the mid-size and small enterprises, which are more labor absorbing (see Chen, 1999).

absorbed by the growing nonstate enterprises. Because the employment elasticity of the nonstate enterprises is more than twice that of the state sector, the reallocation of funds could even generate new employment.[27]

If the savings rate in the next two decades will at best remain at the current level and if the growth of labor input will probably fall, the growth of total factor productivity will be the key to sustained economic growth. Will the trends in productivity growth continue into the near future? Much depends on the development potentials and challenges ahead and how effectively the leadership will be able to exploit these opportunities and meet the challenges. Consider first the potential of utilizing China's abundant surplus labor. Can productivity growth through reallocation of labor be sustained? Here the observers disagree. Sachs and Woo (1996, p. 81) believe that the labor allocation effect will remain significant in the medium run. Others expect a much more limited contribution in the future (World Bank, 1997a, p. 114; 1996, p. 11; Lardy, 1998, p. 10). To be sure, the growth of the two most important labor-absorbing sectors, rural industries and services, has been slowing in the 1990s. But the decline of rural enterprises was partly the result of the biased credit policy against nonstate enterprises. This trend could be reversed if the government would refrain from interfering with the market mechanism. Similarly, the slowdown in the growth of the service sector may be only temporary. International development experience indicates that the share of the service sector in GDP generally rises with per-capita income. By 1998, China's per-capita GDP rose to a level 89 percent above, that of India and over 50 percent above the average for low-income countries (World Bank, 1999, pp. 230–231). Yet, its share of the service sector in GDP was way below India's or the average for low-income countries.[28] If and when China's share of the service sector in GDP catches up with that of other countries, as is likely, structural shifts in employment will continue. To facilitate the transfer, the government has the important task of removing obstructions to factor mobility, such as the household registration system, restric-

[27]For data used to calculate the employment elasticities for 1978–95 (see SA 99, pp. 11, 14; SY 98, pp. 128, 138; Wang, 1998, p.1).

[28]China's share was 33 percent, lower than India's 45 percent, and the average for low-income countries, 38 percent (World Bank, 1999, pp. 252–253).

tions on the transfer of property rights, and regional barriers set up by local governments. But market forces should be left alone to initiate and direct the transfer.

What about the prospects for further benefits from market expansion? China has come a long way in developing markets. Nonetheless, much remains to be done. By and large, the development of factor markets has lagged behind product markets. Financial markets are still in a formative stage. Furthermore, the integration of nationwide markets has run into a number of problems. Bottlenecks are a major problem in some key sectors, such as water supply, energy, and transportation.[29] Another obstacle is the protectionist tendencies of local and central governments. Suboptimization by local governments has created vested interests that obstruct the expansion of markets. One striking example is the scattering over many provinces of numerous small automobile factories. Resistance to China's entry into the World Trade Organization from some industrial groups reflects the same protectionist sentiments. Supporting these tendencies are some party members who still hold on to the socialist dogma of self-sufficiency. There is thus uncertainty about whether and how far China would push ahead with further expansion of internal and external markets.

A set of integrated markets is a necessary but not sufficient condition for the economy to function efficiently. The competitive players, i.e., the enterprises, have to be present. Herein lies the most difficult challenge the current leadership faces: Large numbers of SOEs cannot survive in competitive markets and have been kept alive by fiscal subsidies and bank loans.[30] The unconditional support of loss-making SOEs violates one of the basic principles of the market economy: free entry and exit of firms. Indeed, one plausible explanation of why nonstate enterprises as a whole are more efficient than the SOEs is that the nonstate enterprises have to constantly face the Darwinian evolutionary struggle so that the inefficient ones die out,

---

[29]For example, coal production in Shanxi is limited not so much by the productive capacity of the mines as by the capacity of the railroads to ship the coal to users in coastal provinces.

[30]In 1978, 24 percent of industrial SOEs had a total loss of 4.4 billion yuan. By 1998, 41 percent incurred losses totaling 102.3 billion yuan (Ministry of Finance, 1992, p. 304; SA 99, p. 108).

leaving only the relatively efficient ones, whereas inefficient SOEs survive even if they persistently lose money. Whatever the cause of inefficiency, there is a pressing need to cope with inefficient SOEs, because, without reform, productivity growth will almost certainly fall. First, inefficiency in the state sector itself tends to lower overall productivity growth. More significantly, the growing losses of SOEs force banks to accumulate nonperforming loans, driving the latter toward insolvency. Then, the continued support of loss-making enterprises depletes the financial resources of banks and deprives nonstate enterprises of credit for more-productive uses.

There can be no doubt that China will continue to accumulate human capital through education and vocational training. The number of secondary school graduates has been increasing since 1985, and this trend will probably continue to rise as China implements the nine-year education program introduced in 1998. Because of the persistent shortage of skilled workers and educated manpower, the accumulation of human capital is likely to bring substantial productivity gains.

In the long run, technological change will be the key factor, because, unlike resource reallocation, it can be a continuous, on-going process rather than a one-time gain. But herein lies perhaps the weak link in China's economic growth. At present, China's R&D capability is rather poor, mainly because of the prolonged neglect of human capital formation under a regime that valued ideological piety above technical knowledge. In particular, the abrupt lapse in China's education program during the Cultural Revolution left a gap in the human capital structure. Around the year 2000, many senior rank scientists and engineers will retire, and there will not be enough qualified personnel to succeed them. The effects were not keenly felt in the 1980s and 1990s, partly because the market demand for all kinds of goods and services was so strong that innovation was hardly necessary. Also, China was able to borrow or transfer technology from abroad. According to one study, inventions accounted for only 10 percent of the total research achievements in the 1980s, whereas those based on imitation accounted for 50 percent, and those based on improvements of existing technologies, 40 percent (Ma, 1989, p. 294). But, as competition both at home and abroad intensified, the importance of innovation greatly increased. The current leadership reversed the pre-1978 policy and substantial progress in education and R&D has been made (see Zhen, 1999, pp. 418–419). Nonetheless, it is not clear if the renewed effort is sufficient to prepare China for the challenges ahead. One cause for concern is that the growth of both education expenditures and R&D expenditures has fallen behind GDP in the 1980s.[31] The shares of public expenditures and R&D in GDP in 1990 were far below the world average, and even lower than those in India, not to mention those of Japan and the United States (SY 98, pp. 942–943). More serious still is the lack of an effective incentive system to motivate innovations. Like the SOEs, China's R&D system traditionally never linked risks, effort, and rewards together. The system apparently changed little after 1978 despite reform efforts (Li et al., 1995, pp. 388–340). Again, the future of technological advances hinges to a large extent on institutional changes.

GDP GROWTH: ALTERNATIVE PROJECTIONS

To sum up, China's economic future is clouded with many uncertainties. Apart from the challenges and opportunities noted above, there are others. Not least are some political and social undercurrents that might erupt into open conflicts and undermine economic growth. Potential problems include intra-party disputes over key economic policies (e.g., the pace and direction of reforms); opposition of local governments, ministries, and departments to central government policies (e.g., joining the WTO); ethnic secession and rural unrest as a result of the widening gap in income distribution; protests of workers being laid off; and the general public's disgust with widespread corruption.[32] A second set of uncertainties relates to possible changes in the external environment. These include the changing economic conditions and trade policies in the United States, Europe, Japan, and other Asian-Pacific countries (the major markets for China's exports and sources of capital and technology imports); the pace and direction of technological breakthroughs; and also possible military conflicts directly or indirectly involving China.

---

[31]The share of education expenditures dropped from 3.8 percent of GDP in 1990 to 3.1 percent in 1997, and that of R&D expenditures, from 0.7 to 0.6 percent over the same period (SA 99, pp. 11, 142, 145).

[32]China's decision to join the WTO resolved the question of whether to join, but whether there will be opposition to implementation of the policy remains to be seen.

In view of the many uncertainties, it would seem more appropriate to have a series of projections under alternative scenarios than to have a single estimate with a rather wide margin of error. Table 5.8 shows what the GDP growth rates could be, given alternative parameters that reflect various possible scenarios. For example, in a stable growth scenario, where economic reforms proceed steadily and no major internal or external economic crisis occurs, savings rates are assumed to remain high, probably between 30–40 percent. Productivity growth is projected at 1–1.5 percent annually. GDP growth would be in the range of 4.8–6.4 percent. In a disrupted growth scenario, the savings rate would fall to 25 percent or below, and productivity, 0.5 percent or less. GDP would grow at an annual rate no higher than 3.8 percent.

CONCLUDING REMARKS

To recapitulate, China faces a problem of sustaining a current growth rate of 6–8 percent rather than the official 9–10 percent. Nonetheless, the challenge is by no means less arduous, mainly because the savings rate is coming close to the end of a plateau, and because accelerating productivity growth has become increasingly difficult. Our

Table 5.8

GDP Growth, 2000-2020: Alternative Projections (in percentage per year)

	Total	Total Factor Productivity Growth		
Savings Rate	0.5	1.0	1.5	2.0
25	3.8	4.3	4.8	5.3
30	4.3	4.8	5.3	5.8
35	4.9	5.4	5.9	6.4
40	5.4	5.9	6.4	6.9

NOTES: Growth of capital inputs is derived by dividing the savings rate by the capital-output ratio, 3.7, given in Li et al., 1995, p. 59. Thus, given the four alternative savings rates, the corresponding annual growth of capital inputs are: 6.8, 8.1, 9.5, and 10.8 percent, respectively. Assuming the output elasticity of capital to be 0.4, the contribution of capital inputs to GDP growth are: 2.7, 3.2, 3.8, and 4.3 percent, respectively. The annual growth of labor inputs is assumed to be 1 percent, and its output elasticity, 0.6. Its contribution is therefore 0.6 percent. GDP growth rates are derived as the sums of the contributions of capital inputs, labor inputs, and total factor productivity growth.

assessment is that the long-term growth rate is likely to be lower than the current one.[33] How much lower will depend largely on the pace, direction and effectiveness of economic reforms.

Indeed, in discussing possible constraints on the sources of economic growth, we keep running into institutional bottlenecks, some of which are legacies of the pre-1978 era while others are the byproducts of the transition. For example, decentralization of decisionmaking motivates households and enterprises to invest in pursuit of higher profits. Yet the state maintains centralized allocation of financial resources according to some credit plans that are biased against nonstate enterprises. This inconsistency has not only seriously weakened the financial system but also made it rather difficult for the more productive nonstate enterprises to accumulate capital. In the case of labor supply, the critical problem is not the dwindling of new labor supply due to demographic changes two decades ago, but the massive hidden unemployment, some of which is now surfacing. The fundamental solution calls for institutional changes, such as building a social safety net, developing labor markets, and financial reforms to ease the supply of credit to the productive state and nonstate enterprises to increase the demand for labor. In the case of productivity growth, the debt-laden SOEs have continued to drag down the overall growth rate, and there are still no signs of an end to

---

[33]In that respect our conclusion is similar to those of other observers. However, the reasons behind the conclusions are quite different. For example, the World Bank attributes the projected decline in GDP growth to three forces: The labor force will stop growing, capital accumulation will run into diminishing returns, and structural change will provide a smaller boost to growth because resources will be more efficiently allocated. In our opinion, each of these hypotheses is open to question. As noted above, the net increase in labor supply will certainly decline, but the total stock of available labor will remain so large that the effect of declining new additions will be negligible. In short, labor supply is not likely to be a constraint on GDP growth. The law of diminishing returns to investment applies only when other factors are held constant. Is it reasonable to assume that both labor supply and technological advance will stop growing altogether during the next two decades? And, even if productivity gains from resource reallocation drops, other sources of productivity growth could be the impetus to the growth of total factor productivity. One such source is human capital formation, which, according to the World Bank, 1997a, p. 106, constituted 33 percent of GDP growth in 1978–95. It would seem plausible that the educational level of the workforce and skill formation through training will continue to develop. In our judgment, there is still much gross inefficiency in the system. These inefficiencies also represent potentials to accelerate productivity growth if they can be removed. Unlike the World Bank, we do not rule out the possibility that productivity growth would fall only slightly.

subsidies. Moreover, one sees rampant corruption and fuzzy property rights that increase transaction costs and lower incentives to improve efficiency. To the extent that reform is indeed the key to sustained growth, one wonders if the primary policy focus should be placed on reform instead of on economic growth. Economic growth without reform is not sustainable, because the current system persistently drains resources into unproductive uses and that cannot go on indefinitely. If, however, the institutional framework of a market system were firmly established, economic growth would follow because it could then rely not just on factor accumulation alone but also on productivity gains, which in turn reinforces factor accumulation.

At this juncture, China's reforms still have a long way to go. This task will require huge financial costs, painful adjustments, and strong political will. Earlier reforms were relatively easy. The benefits from these reforms apparently have run their course. The next phase of high growth must come from new reforms that are more difficult because the economy has become more interdependent, because the vested interests are now more deeply entrenched, and because the new reforms are much more costly. But, painful as it may be, does China have any other viable option?

REFERENCES CITED

Barro, Robert J., and Xavier Sala-I-Martin. 1995. *Economic Growth*, MIT Press, Cambridge, Massachusetts.

Chen, Naixing. 1999. "The Focal Point of Economic Development and Re-employment," *Jingji wenti* (*Economic Problems*), No. 2, 1999, pp. 8–11.

Chen, Yuan, ed. 1994. *Zhongguo jiushihniandai de hobi zhengce* (*China's Monetary Policies in the 1990s*), China Economics Publishing House, Beijing.

Cheung, Steven N. S. 1989. *Quan wan zhi qiu* (*A Critical Stage*), Hong Kong Economic Daily, Hong Kong.

Chow, Gregory. 1994. *Understanding China's Economy*, World Scientific, Singapore.

Du Peng. 1994. *Zhongguo renkou laolinghua guozheng yanjiu* (*Studies in China's Population Aging Process*), People's University Press, Beijing.

Guo, Shuqing, and Wenxiu Han. 1991. *Zhongguo GNP de fengpei he shihyong* (*Allocation and Uses of China's GNP*), People's University Press, Beijing.

Han, Wenxiu. 1995. "An Analysis of China's Investment Rate Since Reform," *Jingji yanjiu* (*Economic Research*), No. 8, 1995, pp. 3-8.

Lardy, Nicholas. 1998. *China's Unfinished Economic Revolution,* Brookings Institution Press, Washington, D.C.

Lau, Lawrence J. 1996. "The Sources of Long-Term Economic Growth: Observations from the Experience of Developed and Developing Countries," in Ralph Landau, Timothy Taylor, and Gavin Wright, eds., *The Mosaic of Economic Growth,* Stanford University Press, Stanford.

Li, Jingwen. 1994. "A Comparison of Chinese and U.S/Productivity: Sino-American Economic and Trade Relations," *Journal of Asian Economics,* Vol. 5, No. 1, 1994, pp. 85–97.

———. 1998. *21sijih zhongguo jingji da qushih* (*General Trends in the Chinese Economy in the 21st Century*), Liaoning People's Press, Shengyang.

Li, Jingwen, Feihong, Gong, and Yisheng, Zheng. 1995. "Productivity and China's Economic Growth, 1953–1990," in Kai-yuan Tsui, Tien-tung Hsueh, and Thomas G. Rawski, eds., *Productivity, Efficiency and Reform in China's Economy,* Chinese University of Zhong Kong, Hong Kong, pp. 19–53.

Lin, Fude, and Shenwu Zhai, eds. 1996. *Zhoxiang 21 sijih de zhongguo renkou huanjing yu fazhan* (*China's Population, Environment and Development Towards the 21st Century*), Higher Education Publishing House, Beijing.

Lin, Y.F. 1992. "Rural Reform and Agricultural Growth in China," *American Economic Review,* March 1992, pp. 34–51.

Ma, Hong, ed. 1989. *2000 nian di zhongguo* (*China in the Year 2000*), China Social Sciences Publishing House, Beijing.

Maddison, Angus. 1995. *Monitoring the World Economy 1820–1992,* OECD, Paris.

Ministry of Finance. 1992. *Zhongguo caizheng tongji, 1950–1991* (*China Public Finance Statistics, 1950–1991*), Science Press, Beijing.

Nelson, Richard R. 1964. "Aggregate Production Function and Medium Range Growth Projections," *American Economic Review,* September 1964, pp. 575–606.

People's Bank of China. 1994. *Zhongguo jiushih niandai de hobi zhengce* (*China's Monetary Policy in the 1990s*), China Economic Publishing House, Beijing.

Qian Yingyi. 1988. "Urban and Rural Household Savings in China," *IMF Staff Papers,* December 1988.

Ren, Ruoen. 1997. *China's Economic Performance in an International Perspective,* OECD, Paris.

Restall, Hugo. 1999. "Is China Headed for a Crash?" *Wall Street Journal,* September 2, 1999, p. A14.

Sachs, Jeffrey D., and Wing Thye Woo. 1996. "Chinese Economic Growth: Explanations and the Tasks Ahead," in Joint Economic Committee, *China's Economic Future: Challenges to U.S. Policy,* U.S. Government Printing Office, Washington, D.C., pp. 70–85.

Segal, Gerald. 1999. "Does China Matter?" *Foreign Affairs,* Vol. 78, No. 5, pp. 24–36.

Song, Guoqing. 1999. "A Projection of China's Economic Growth in the Next Decade," *Guanli Shijie* (*Management World*), November 1, 1999, pp. 17–19.

State Science and Technology Commission. 1987. *Zhongguo kexue jixu zhengce zhinan* (*Guidelines for China's Science and Technology Policies*), Science and Technology Documents Publishing House, Beijing.

State Statistical Bureau. 1989. *Fengjin de sishinian 1949–1989* (*Four Decades of Striving and Advancing*), China Statistics Publishing House, Beijing.

———.1998. *Zhongguo tongji nianjian 1998* (*China Statistical Yearbook 1998*), China Statistics Publishing House, Beijing. Abbreviated as SY 98. Statistical yearbooks for other years are similarly cited.

———.1999. *Zhongguo tongji zheyiao 1999* (*A Statistical Survey of China 1999*), China Statistics Publishing House, Beijing. Abbreviated as SA 99.

Sun Shanqing, ed. 1984. *Lun jingji jieko duice (On Policies Concerning the Economic Structure*), China Social Sciences Publishing House, Beijing.

Szirmai, Adam, and Ruoen Ren. 1995. *China's Manufacturing Performance in Comparative Perspective, 1980–1992,* University of Groningen, Groningen.

Wang, Zhi. 1995. "The Ration System and the Consumption and Saving Behavior of China's Urban Residents," *Jingji yanjiu* (*Economic Research*), No. 8, 1995, pp. 57–68.

Wang, MengKui. 1998. "China's Ownership Structure at the Present Stage," *Guanli shijie* (*Management World*), No. 3, 1998, pp. 1–4.

Wolf, Charles, Jr., A. Bamezai, K. C. Yeh, B. Zycher. 2000. *Asian Economic Trends and Their Security Implications,* RAND, Santa Monica.

World Bank. 1992. *World Development Report 1992,* Oxford University Press, New York.

———. 1994. *China GNP Per Capita,* World Bank, Washington, D.C.

———. 1995. *World Tables 1995,* Johns Hopkins University Press, Baltimore.

———. 1996. *The Chinese Economy: Fighting Inflation, Deepening Reforms,* World Bank, Washington, D.C., Vol. I and II.

———. 1997a. *China 2020,* World Bank, Washington, D.C.

———. 1997b. *China Engaged,* World Bank, Washington, D.C.

———. 1999. *Entering the 21st Century,* Oxford University Press, New York.

Wu, Harry X. 1994. "Rural Enterprise Contributions to Growth and Structural Change," in C. Findley, A. Watson, and Harry X. Xu, eds., *Rural Enterprises in China*. St. Martin's Press, New York.

Yan, Changlo, ed. 1994. *Zhongguo nunyuan fazhan baokao* (*Report on China's Energy Development*), Economic Management Publishing House, Beijing.

Zhen Peiyian, ed. 1999. *Xin zhongguo jingji 50 nian 1949–99 (New China's Economy in the Last Fifty Years, 1949–1999),* China Planning Publishing House, Beijing.

Chapter Six

THE CHINESE ECONOMY IN PROSPECT

Angang Hu[1]

THE CATCH-UP MODEL OF CHINESE MODERNIZATION

From a historical perspective, modernization could generally be grouped into four types: innovators or forerunners, followers or latecomers, those who catch-up with and surpass, and those who stay behind, stumbling and not yet in the process of modernization, possibly stagnating. There are several large economies in the catch-up-with-and-surpass category. The first among these is the United States. The United States accelerated its modernization process during the period 1871–1913, rapidly catching up with and surpassing the United Kingdom. The second country is Japan, which started industrialization after the Meiji Reformation. Particularly after World War II (1950–1985), Japan's economy took off and didn't lose time in catching up with that of the United States. The third economy in this category is the group encompassing the East Asian "Four Dragons," which started their economic takeoff during the 1960s, and from 1965 to 1997 rapidly reduced the gap between themselves and developed nations, becoming newly industrialized countries and regions. The fourth county in this category is China, which entered the stage of economic takeoff in the 1980s.

[1]Editors' note: Despite our efforts to correct them, some discrepancies remain in the text between the author's references to numerical figures and those that appear in the tables. Generally, these discrepancies are minor but resolution of them can be obtained by contacting Professor Hu directly. He can be contacted at the Center for China Study at the Chinese Academy of Sciences, 18 Shangqing Road, Beijing, 100085, P. R. China. E-mail: anganghu@mail,rcees.ac.cn. Telephone and fax: 86-10-62919108.

Angus Maddison, an expert in economic history at the Organization for Economic Cooperation and Development (OECD), published *Chinese Economic Performance in the Long Run* (1998). In this book, Maddison used the PPP (purchasing power parity) method to calculate the GDP in China during 1820–1995 and the respective per-capita GDP, the shares of Chinese GDP of the world total, and the per-capita GDP in China as a percentage share of the world average. Based on his calculations, I summarize the characteristics of the historical process of the long-term economic development in China in the following text.

Economic Fall and Rise

To begin, economic development in China has undergone a process of falling first and then rising later on. The economic capacity of the country has also undergone a process of growing from strong to weak and then from weak to strong. In the 10th century, China was a leader on the economic indicator of per-capita income. China was also better off than European countries in the level of science and technology, the utilization of natural resources, and the management of a country with a huge territory. But in following century, European countries surpassed China in such areas as science and technology and real income per capita. During the period 1820–1952, the world economy experienced great development. The total world gross product increased eightfold. The per-capita income of European countries and Japan increased fourfold and threefold, respectively. But the share of China's GDP compared with that of the rest of the world decreased from one-third to one-twentieth, and China's per-capita income decreased to one-fourth of that of the rest of the world. In 1820, GDP in China accounted for 32.4 percent of the world total, ranking number one in the world. The share of Chinese GDP of the world total was reduced to 13.2 percent, 9.1 percent, and 5.2 percent, respectively, in 1890, 1919, and 1952. This is because the average annual growth rate of GDP in China (only about 0.22 percent) during 1820 to 1952 was much lower than the world average annual growth rate (1.62 percent) during the same period. As a result, the share of Chinese GDP in the world total declined substantially. The price of this backwardness was being laid open to outside aggression. Because of the "opium war" in 1840, 19 Western countries gained much. Japan invaded China three times. Twice Britain and France made colonial invasions into China. Russia forcibly occupied the Siberian regions of China, which were nearly 10 percent of China's total area.

China began the process of industrialization after the foundation of the People's Republic of China. During the period 1952–1978, China's economic growth significantly accelerated, and the total GDP increased by threefold. During this period, per-capita income and labor productivity in China increased by 38 percent and 6 percent, respectively. The share of industry in the national economy increased from 10 percent to 35 percent. Although the growth rate of China was very high, the speed of development was still slow compared with that of the rest of the prospering world at that time. By the end of 1978, China's GDP share of that of the world was reduced to 5.0 percent because of the even lower economic growth rate in China (4.4 percent) (according to data from the State Statistical Bureau (SSB) of China, 6.1 percent) compared with the world average growth rate (4.52 percent). Starting in 1979, China's growth share began a steady rise. By 1995, the share increased to nearly 11 percent (see Table 6.1) because the average economic growth rate in China during 1978–1995 increased to 7.49 percent (according to SSB data, 9.9 percent) and the world total GDP growth rate declined (to 2.7 percent). Thus, the share of Chinese GDP of the world's total increased distinctly.

Table 6.1

China's Geopolitical Standing, 1820–1995

	1820	1890	1913	1952	1978	1995
Share of world GDP (%)	32.4	13.2	9.1	5.2	5.0	10.9
Share of world population (%)	36.3	26.2	24.7	21.8	22.4	21.3
Per-capita GDP as % of world average	89.2	50.3	36.7	23.7	22.3	51.1
GDP ranking	1	2	3	3	4	2
Share of world exports (%)	N.A.	1.7	1.6	1.0	0.8	2.9
Per-capita exports as % of world average	N.A.	6.5	6.5	4.6	3.6	13.6

SOURCE: Angus Maddison, *Chinese Economic Performance in the Long Run*, Development Centre Studies, OECD, 1998, p. 56.

NOTE: N.A. is not available.

Per-Capita GDP

The relative difference between the per-capita GDP in China and the world average increased first, and later declined rapidly. In 1820, the per-capita GDP in China was about 89 percent of the world average. The share was reduced to 50 percent, 36.7 percent, and 23.7 percent, respectively, in 1890, 1919 and 1952. From 1820 to 1952, the growth rate of per-capita GDP in China was negative (–0.08 percent), and the world per-capita GDP average increased at a rate of positive 0.92 percent. Therefore, the relative difference between the per-capita GDP in China and the world average level clearly increased. In 1978, the per-capita GDP in China was about 22.3 percent of the world average, which was a little bit lower than that of 1952. From 1952 to 1978, the per-capita GDP growth rate was 2.34 percent (according to SSB data, 4.0 percent), which was a little bit lower than that of the world average (2.56 percent). During this period, not only was the gap between per-capita GDP in China and that of advanced countries not reduced, but also the gap between China's GDP and that of the world average was not reduced. Since 1979, the per-capita GDP in China increased rapidly: By 1995, China's per-capita GDP was 51.1 percent of the world average, which was 28.8 percentage points higher than that of 1978 (see Table 6.1). The per-capita GDP in China in 1995 was 11 percent of that of the United States, 13 percent of Japan, 20 percent of Taiwan, and 22 percent of South Korea. In 1995, the increase in the rate of per-capita GDP in China was 6.04 percent (according to SSB data, 7.5 percent), which was much higher than the world average (1.01 percent). Not only was the difference between China and the world average reduced substantially, but also the difference between China and developed countries was reduced to a large extent.

Economic Isolation

During the process of global modernization, which began in the 18th century, China was cut off from the outside world for a very long time. It wasn't until 1978 that China became a more open country and accelerated the process of integrating with the world economy. The role of a country in the world market can be measured by the share of the country's exports of the world total export volume. In 1890, the share for China was 1.7 percent, which was further reduced to 1.6 percent and 0.8 percent in 1913 and 1978, respectively (see

Table 6.1). A country's level of trade can be measured by the percentage share of per-capita exports of the country relative to that of the world average. In 1890, the percentage share for China was 6.5 percent, which continued to decline, to 4.6 percent and 3.6 percent in 1952 and 1978, respectively. All these data prove that, although China is a large country in terms of population, it is a small economy in terms of trade; it ranked 32nd in terms of world exports. Even though China began its industrialization in the 1950s, China has been typically self-supporting, economically cutting itself off from the outside world.

Since 1978, foreign trade in China has had the following four features. First, foreign trade volume has increased at an unprecedentedly high speed. From 1978 to 1997, the total foreign trade volume on average increased by 15.6 percent annually, which includes an average annual import trade volume increase of 14.5 percent and a total export volume average annual increase of 16.7 percent (all increases were higher than that of the world average). Second, the increase in the rate of trade surpassed the growth rate of the economy, and the shares of both total foreign trade and total export in GDP continued to grow rapidly. During the late 1970s, the total foreign trade accounted for only 13 percent of the GDP, which made China one of the countries that had the lowest trade dependency rate. By 1995, however, the rate had increased sharply to more than 30 percent of GDP. Third, the share of total export volume in China as a percentage of world total exports increased substantially. By 1995, the share had increased to 2.9 percent, which made China the tenth largest exporter in the world. However, compared with the total exports of the East Asian "Four Dragons," which exceed 10 percent of the world total exports, the share of Chinese trade was still very low. Fourth, China's per-capita export level has increased several dozen times. In 1952, China's per-capita export rate was only \$1.4; in 1978, \$10.7; and by 1997, \$122.8.[2]

Despite this upward trend, China's per-capita export level was still very low compared with the average per-capita export level of the world. In 1995, China's per-capita export level was only 13.6 percent of the world average (see Table 6.1). These percentages show that

---

[2]All dollar amounts are U.S. unless otherwise noted.

China's open policy propelled it into the world market amid international competition and helped China contribute more to world trade growth. However, in terms of China's export share of the world's total exports and its per-capita export level relative to that of the rest of the world, China is still at much lower level. Therefore, accelerating trade and investment liberalization and joining the WTO as soon as possible will help China to continue on its quest for economic openness and is in keeping with the basic interests of the country. The long-term benefits to the Chinese economy will far exceed the short-term costs of adjusting to an open policy. If China's per-capita export level increases to, or close to, one-half of the world average, then China's total exports will account for more than one-tenth of the world total.

Human Development Indicators

The relative difference in human development indicators between China and developed countries is decreasing. China's birth rate was as high as 37.0 percent in 1952, but in 1978 and 1995, it was reduced to 18.25 percent and 17.12 percent, respectively. Regarding life expectancy at birth, in 1952, it was only 38 years; in 1978 and 1995, life expectancy increased to 64 years and 70 years, respectively. In 1952, the average years of schooling for Chinese over 15 years of age was 1.7 years; in 1978 it increased to 5.33 years, and by 1995 it increased to 8.93 years (calculations by Maddison are higher than my estimates) (see Table 6.2). This 1995 rate was higher than India's (5.55 years). However, compared with the education levels in the 1950s of France (9.6 years), Germany (10.4 years), the United States (11.3 years), and the United Kingdom (10.8 years), it is still quite low (Maddison, 1998).

Production Factors and Economic Takeoff

The increase in all production factors in China and the respective market allocation have sped the growth of the Chinese economy. Considering the production factors that affect economic growth and comparing the period 1952–1978 with that of 1978–1995, the total population growth rate decreased, from 2.2 percent to 1.37 percent; the labor input rate increased slightly, from 2.57 percent to 2.62 per-

Table 6.2

Vital Statistics, Age Structure, Labor Input, and Education Levels, China, 1952–1995

Year	Crude Birth Rate Per 1,000	Life Expectancy at Birth (years)	Working Age Population (%)	Employed Population (%)	Years of Equivalent Primary Education Per Person Age 15 and Older
1952	37.00	38[a]	51.7	36.4	1.70
1978	18.25	64	53.6	41.9	5.33
1995	17.12	69	61.2	51.7	8.93

SOURCES: The first column is from SSB, *China Statistical Yearbook*, 1996, p. 69; the second column is from the World Bank, *World Development Report*, various issues; the third column is from *China Statistical Yearbook*, 1996, pp. 71–72; the fourth column is from Appendix D. The working age population in China refers to males aged 15–60 and females aged 15–55. Education levels are derived by extrapolation from population census estimates for 1964, 1982, and 1990; see *China Statistical Yearbook*, 1996, p. 71. Primary education is given a weight of 1, secondary 1.4, and higher 2—in line with international evidence on relative earnings associated with the different levels of education. The fifth column is based on data from Angus Maddison, *Chinese Economic Performance in the Long Run*, Development Centre Studies, OECD, 1998, p. 61.

[a]1950.

cent; the capital input rate also increased slightly; the nonresidential capital rate increased from 7.57 percent to 8.80 percent; the farmland rate decreased, from 0.47 percent to 0 percent; and the total factor productivity rate increased, from negative 0.78 percent to positive 2.23 percent. All these factors indicate that the reallocation of production factors and an increased role of market mechanisms since the economic reform have improved the total factor productivity. In the meantime, labor productivity has increased substantially. From 1952 to 1978, the labor productivity rate was 1.78 percent (according to SSB data, 3.5 percent) and, from 1978 to 1995, increased to 4.74 percent (according to SSB data, 7.1 percent) . However, capital productivity has continued to be negative. From 1952 to 1978, the average rate was negative 2.95 percent, and, from 1978 to 1995, the rate was negative 1.21 percent (see Table 6.3).

Comparing Chinese production factor rates with those of other countries shows that economic growth from 1978 to 1995 in China has been very similar to the growth in Japan and South Korea from 1952 to 1978. The population growth rate decreased substantially, 1.37 percent in China, 1.11 percent in Japan, and 2.26 percent in

Table 6.3

Basic Growth Accounts, China, Japan, South Korea and the United States, 1952–1995 (annual average compound growth rates)

	China		Japan		United States		South Korea	
	1952–78	1978–95	1952–78	1978–95	1952–78	1978–95	1952–78	1978–95
Population	2.02	1.37	1.11	0.52	1.34	0.99	2.26	1.14
GDP	4.40	7.49	7.85	3.21	3.49	2.47	7.84	7.84
Per-capita GDP	2.34	6.04	6.66	2.68	2.12	1.47	5.46	6.62
Labor input	2.57	2.62	1.12	0.45	1.12	1.19	3.40	2.48
Quality adjusted labor input	4.85	4.19	1.72	1.00	1.77	1.78	5.02	4.36
Nonresidential capital	7.57	8.86	9.57	6.37	3.39	2.98	8.49	11.46
Farmland	0.47	0.00	–0.12	–0.60	0.13	0.09	0.46	–0.52
Labor productivity	1.78	4.47	6.65	2.75	2.26	1.26	4.31	5.23
Capital productivity	–2.95	–1.26	–1.58	–2.97	0.09	–0.49	–0.55	–3.25
Capital stock per person working	4.87	6.08	8.03	5.27	1.74	1.47	5.50	8.76
Total factor productivity	–0.78	2.23	3.74	0.66	1.26	0.38	1.84[a]	1.46[a]
Export volume	6.42	13.50	13.17	6.49	5.19	6.63	26.09	10.65

SOURCES: Japan and United States from Maddison (1995a), pp. 253–254, updated. Korean GDP 1952–83 from Pilat (1994), 1983–95 from OECD, *National Accounts 1983–1995*, Paris, 1997, Korean capital stock derived by cumulating real investment series from Mizoguchi and Umemura (1988), p. 288, Korea national accounts and OECD, *op. cit*, with rough assumptions about the breakdown of prewar investment and the level of wartime investment. War damage assumed to be 40 per cent of pre-1953 investment. Employment, hours, education levels and population from Pilat (1994) and Maddison (1995a) updated. Labor input from Appendix D. Labor quality is improved by increases in the education level of the working population (see Table 3.8). It is assumed that the impact of more education on the quality of labor was half of the rate of growth of education. Nonresidential gross fixed capital stock was all assets of the same age being scrapped when their expected life was reached. Farm land for Japan, Korea, and the United States refers to cultivated area, derived from FAO, *Production Yearbooks*, for China it gives irrigated land a double weight (as in Table 3.14). In calculating total factor productivity for China, labor input was given a weight of 0.6, capital 0.3 and 0.1. For the growth accounts of Japan and the United States, labor inputs were given a weight of .67, capital .03. The results for Korea are shown with both sets of weighs. Angus Maddison, *Chinese Economic Performance in the Long Run*, Development Centre Studies, OECD, 1998, pp. 66.

[a]Rates shown are with the same factor weights as for Japan and the United States, the corresponding rates would be 2.16 and 1.80 with Chinese factor weights.

South Korea. The labor input rate was relatively high. The non-residential capital rate was also high, 8.8 percent in China, 9.57 percent in Japan, and 8.49 percent in South Korea. There was either no increase or a decrease in the growth of farmland, 0.00 percent in China, –0.12 percent in Japan, and 0.46 percent in South Korea. The total factor productivity rate improved remarkably, 2.23 percent in China, 3.74 percent in Japan, and 1.84 percent in South Korea. The export rate was very high, 13.5 percent in China, 13.17 percent in Japan and 26.09 percent in South Korea. The labor productivity rate was also high, while the capital productivity rate decreased, and per-capita capital stock increased by a large amount (see Table 6.3).

In Sum

The above data show that two centuries ago, China was economically strong, with relatively high per-capita income. However, during the process of global industrialization, China has fallen far behind: By the middle of the 20th century, it had become one of the poorest countries. From the early 1950s to the late 1970s, despite starting the process of industrialization and having an economic development rate increasing relatively quickly, China's economic growth rate was lower than the world average rate. Therefore, China's per-capita GDP, relative to the average world level, declined slightly. However, since 1978, reform and openness policies have improved China's economic growth rate substantially, while the world average economic growth rate declined during the same period. Thus, China is catching up to the average economic development in the rest of the world. The process of increased economic development has encompassed many other aspects in China, including economic aggregate and per-capita GDP, as well as social development indicators. As in the past, when the United States economically caught up with the United Kingdom, when Japan caught up with the United States, and when the "Four Dragons" caught up with developed nations, China, with one-fifth of the world's population, will also catch up. As of the present, China still has a way to go, but it's role in the development of humanity and its contribution to world trade will be ever increasing.

THE LONG-TERM TREND OF ECONOMIC GROWTH IN CHINA

Forecasts for the Chinese economy show that the trend of high speed economic growth will be maintained. The following are the general forecasts and estimates for the long-term trends of Chinese economic development.

In 1995, the Center for China Study in the Chinese Academy of Sciences forecasted that the annual average economic growth rate would be 9.3–10.2 percent for 1995–2000,[3] 8.0–8.7 percent for 2000–2010, and 7.0–7.8 percent for 2010–2020 (see Table 6.4). For their base scenario, the authors estimated that the per-capita GDP in China would be $2,100 in 1994. For 1994–2015, they estimated that the average annual growth rate would be 7.6 percent. It was estimated that Chinese GDP would surpass that of the United States

Table 6.4

Annual Growth Rate of GDP in China

Period	Years	Average	Range (%)
1952–1980[a]	28	6.3	
1980–1990[b]	10	8.9	
1990–1995[b]	5	11.9	
1995–2000[c]	5	9.3	9.3–10.2
2000–2010[c]	10	8.0	8.0–7.8
2010–2020[c]	10	7.0	7.0–7.8
2020–2030[c]	10	6.3	6.3–7.0

[a]World Bank, *World Tables 1992*, Johns Hopkins University Press, Baltimore and London, 1992.

[b]SSB, *China Statistical Yearbook*, 1996.

[c]Based on research from the Group for National Condition Analysis of Chinese Academy of Sciences, *Opportunities and Challenges: Economic Development Goals and Strategies for China Going to the 21st Century*, Science Press, Beijing, 1995.

---

[3]Center for China Study, Chinese Academy of Sciences, *Opportunities and Challenges: Study on the Economic Development Strategic Objectives and Essential Development Strategy for China Entering 21st Century*, Beijing Science Publication House, Beijing, 1995.

around the year 2015. In their best-case scenario, they estimated that per-capita GDP in China would be $2,510 in 1994, based on the World Bank (1996) estimate. For 1994–2015, under their best-case scenario, the average annual growth rate was estimated to be 8.1 percent and the total GDP in China was estimated to exceed that of the United States around the year 2010. However, under this scenario, the per-capita GDP of China would only be one-fourth of that of the United States. (See Tables 6.5 and 6.6).

In 1996, RAND conducted a study on the long-term economic development trends in China for the period 1994–2015. The authors overestimated the U.S. dollar denominated initial per-capita GDP in China (based on the PPP method)—$4,200 in 1994, which is equivalent to 16.3 percent of the U.S. per-capita GDP for the same period. While they underestimated the future average annual growth rate of. According to their best scenario estimate, the average annual growth rate for China is only 4.9 percent. Based on the above assumption, they estimated that by 2006 China's GDP will surpass the U.S. GDP, and by 2010 and 2015 the GDP in China will be equivalent to 110 percent and 127 percent, respectively, of that of the United States. They also estimated that, by 2000, the per-capita GDP in China would be 18.8 percent of that of the United States, and that, by 2010 and 2015, the per-capita GDP in China will continue to increase to 25.6 percent and 28.9 percent, respectively, of that of the United States.

In 1997, the World Bank published *China 2020: Development Challenges in the New Century*. In this report, it is assumed that in the coming 10 years, the domestic saving rate in China would decrease gradually from 40 percent to 35 percent. In addition, the total factor productivity growth rate would decrease slightly to an annual rate of 1.5 percent. Based on these assumptions, the average annual growth rate for China's GDP would be 8.6 percent in the period 1995–2000. And then the growth rate would slow down gradually from the present 9–10 percent to 5 percent by 2020. The authors from the World Bank state that three forces will drive down GDP growth. The first is population, which they predict will fall and that, by 2020, the labor force population will stop increasing. The second is capital accumulation, which they predict will be affected by the economic law of decreasing returns to scale. The third is a decrease in the contribution of structural reform to economic growth, because of improve-

Table 6.5

GDP of United States, Japan, China and India

County	1985	1990	1994	2000	2006	2010	2015	1994–2015 Average Growth Rate (%)
GDP (billions of PPP 1994 $)								
United States			6,704	7,791	8,852	9,657	10,673	3.0
Japan			2,593	3,114	3,642	4,277	4,509	4.1
China-1			4,950	6,602	8,808	10,665	13,569	4.9
China-2			2,989	5,096	8,087	11,002	15,431	8.1
China-3			2,695	4,160	6,600	9,000	12,600	7.6
India			1,193	1,675	2,324	2,698	3,693	3.8
Level of U.S.'s GDP %								
United States			100.0	100.0	100.0	100.0	100.0	
Japan	35.5	39.4	38.7	40.0	41.1	44.3	42.2	
China-1			73.9	84.7	99.5	110.4	127.1	
China-2	35.0	41.9	44.6	65.4	91.4	113.9	144.6	
China-3			40.2	5.34	74.6	93.2	118.1	
India	15.3	18.4	17.8	21.5	26.3	27.9	34.6	

NOTES: China-1 is RAND's prediction (1995); China-2 is a higher prediction based on PPP 1994 dollars of per-capita GDP estimated by the World Bank (1996); China-3 is a low prediction based on PPP 1994 dollars of per-capita GDP estimated by the author. The data for 1985 and 1990 come from the World Bank (1992). Other data are from RAND's forecasts (1995).

Table 6.6

Per-Capita GDP of the United States, Japan, China, and India

County	1985	1990	1994	2000	2006	2010	2015	1994–2015 Average Growth Rate (%)
Per-Capita GDP (billions of PPP 1994 $)								
United States			25,700	28,200	30,300	30,673	33,200	1.23
Japan			20,700	24,400	28,300	31,153	34,300	2.43
China-1			4,200	5,300	6,700	7,844	9,600	4.02
China-2			2,510	3,920	5,983	7,966	11,280	7.42
China-3			2,100	3,200	4,800	6,300	8,632	6.96
India			1,300	1,700	2,100	2,446	2,900	3.89
Level of U.S. per-capita GDP (%)								
United States			100.0	100.0	100.0	100.0	100.0	
Japan	71.6	79.4	80.5	86.5	93.4	101.6	103.3	22.8
China-1			16.3	18.8	22.1	25.6	28.9	12.6
China-2	7.6	9.1	9.7	13.9	19.7	26.0	34.0	24.3
China-3			8.2	11.3	15.8	20.5	26.0	17.8
India			51.	6.0	6.9	8.0	8.7	3.6

NOTES: China-1 is RAND's prediction (1995); China-2 is the World Bank forecast for 1994–2015; China-3 is the author's projection (1995). The data for 1985 and 1990 come from World Bank (1992). Other date are from RAND's forecasts (1995).

ment in resource distribution efficiency, including a reduction in returns from reallocation of agricultural surplus laborers. The authors of this report estimate that the gap in technology between China and other developed countries has decreased, causing a reduction in technology progress. They also conclude that, by 2020, China's total GDP will far exceed that of the United States. According to World Bank estimates, the per-capita GDP in 1995 was $2,900 and that, by 2020, China's per-capita GDP would be close to that of Portugal, which will be equivalent to half of the U.S. per-capita GDP. Also, the report estimates that by 2020 China may be the world's second largest exporter and importer. Therefore, the residential purchasing power in China would surpass that of all of Europe. And in financial markets, as a capital supplier and user, the authors predict that China could compete with most industrialized countries.[4]

In 1997, the Asian Development Bank published *Emerging Asia: Change and Challenge,* which uses three alternative scenarios to estimate economic development trends in China. Under the optimistic scenario, China will continue economic reform and maintain a relatively high rate in productivity forces and capital formation. Under this scenario, during 1995–2025, China's annual per-capita GDP growth rate would be 6.6 percent. Under the pessimistic scenario, China will not complete necessary reforms, causing industrial bottlenecks to constrain economic development. Under this scenario, China's annual per-capita GDP growth rate would be 4.4 percent. The base scenario assumes that China maintains its political conditions of 1995. Under this assumption, the annual per-capita GDP growth rate would be 6.05 percent, which is much higher than the average level of East Asian countries (2.8 percent) and slightly higher than that of South East Asian countries (4.5 percent). Under the base scenario, the difference in per-capita GDP between China and the United States will rapidly decrease. The percentage share of per-capita GDP in China relative to that of the United States will improve, from 3.2 percent in 1965 to 10.8 percent in 1995 and to 38.2 percent in 2025.[5]

---

[4]World Bank, *China 2020: Development Challenges in the New Century,* 1997.

[5]Asia Development Bank, *Emerging Asia: Change and Challenge, The Asia Development,* 1997.

In 1998, Angus Maddison published his estimates on the future of China, which he considered to be conservative estimates. The basic assumptions for his estimates were as follows: First, labor input will grow relatively slowly, the share of labor force in the total population will decrease slightly, and the labor participation of women will decrease somewhat. Second, the growth rate for education level will slow down. Third, the growth rate of per-capita capital stock will not exceed 5 percent. Fourth, the growth rate of total factor productivity will also slow down. Based on the above assumptions, he estimated that the growth rate for China's GDP will decrease from 7.5 percent during 1978–1995 to 5.5 percent during 1995–2010, and the growth rate for per-capita GDP will also decrease from 6.04 percent to 4.5 percent for the two respective periods. Even under these assumptions, according to the PPP method, by 2015 China will exceed the United States in total GDP and will account for 17 percent of the world total GDP, which will improve by close to 6 percentage points compared with the percentage in 1995 (Maddison, 1998). Since the total population in China is huge, by 2015 China's per-capita GDP will be close to the world average level, which is equivalent to one-fifth of that of the United States. China will still be a middle-income country. However, because of the large economic aggregate, China will play an important role in the world economy.

Based on the estimates above of Chinese economic development, and without social unrest, a split of the country, or major mistakes in important economic decisions, it is foreseeable that China will surpass the United States in total GDP during the period 2010–2020. Thus, as a newly industrialized country and after 20 years of reform and opening, China has greatly reduced its relative gaps in economic aggregate and per-capita GDP between itself and the United States. If China can maintain this trend of development, in the coming 20 years it will catch up with the United States in terms of total GDP, and the total trade volume will be slightly lower than that of the United States. Therefore, China will be in a position to make positive contributions to world development and peace.

THE EFFECT OF THE ASIAN FINANCIAL CRISIS ON CHINA

Because of globalization's rapid progress and the interdependent trade relationship among nations, direct investment and finance have deepened. As a result of the progress of the technological revolution in information and telecommunications, crises in one country can affect the macroeconomic situations of other countries in the same region—for example, economic depression in one country can reduce the export demand of other countries and depreciation of one currency can increase the competitiveness of other countries in the world market.[6] The Asian financial crisis has affected the world economy in terms of economic growth, international trade, financial transactions, debt/credit relationships, and global price fluctuations, while the negative effects of the Asian financial crisis on China are mounting.

Delayed Economic Recovery

The economic growth rate of East Asia and the world economy has decreased sharply and will likely not recover until 2000. According to the World Bank (1998), the world economic growth rate was 2.3 percent during 1991–1997, 3.2 percent in 1997, and 1.8 percent in 1998, which was 2.4 percentage points lower than the previous year. It was estimated that the world economic growth rate would be 1.9 percent in 1999. The economic growth rate in East Asia and the Pacific region was 1.9 percent during 1991–1997, 7.1 percent in 1997, negative 1.8 percent in 1998, and will likely recover gradually (see Table 6.7). Among the 13 countries and regions in East Asia and the Pacific region, in 1997 and 1998, seven experienced negative growth, from –0.4 percent to –15.0 percent. In 1998, China enjoyed the highest economic growth rate, 7.8 percent, which is substantially lower than previous record highs (see Table 6.8).

The major reasons behind the sharp reduction in the world economic growth rate in 1998 can be summarized as follows: (1) the contribution of Japan and East Asian "crisis" countries to the world economy was –0.4 percent and –0.3 percent, respectively, which together reduced the world economic growth rate by 0.7 percentage points; (2) the United States, China, and Latin American countries contributed positively to world economic growth; however, the contribution of all was 0.1 percentage points lower than in the past,

[6]World Bank, *Global Economic Prospects and the Developing Countries*, 1998.

Table 6.7

World Output Growth, 1981–2007

				Forecasts				
				Global Economic Prospects (1998–99)				Global Economic Prospects (1997)
	1981–90	1991–97	1997	1998	1999	2000	2001–07	2001–06
World total	3.1	2.3	3.2	1.8	1.9	2.7	3.2	3.4
High-income countries	3.1	2.1	2.8	1.7	1.6	2.3	2.6	2.8
OECD countries	3.0	2.0	2.7	1.9	1.6	2.2	2.5	2.7
Non-OECD countries	6.6	6.4	5.3	–1.8	2.0	3.9	5.2	5.7
Developing countries	3.0	3.1	4.8	2.0	2.7	4.3	5.2	5.5
East Asia and Pacific	7.7	9.9	7.1	1.3	4.8	5.9	6.6	7.5
Europe and Central Asia	2.6	–4.4	2.6	0.5	0.1	3.4	5.0	5.2
Latin America and the Caribbean	1.9	3.4	5.1	2.5	0.6	3.3	4.4	4.4
Middle East and North Africa	1.0	2.9	3.1	2.0	2.8	3.1	3.7	3.7
South Asia	5.7	5.7	5.0	4.6	4.9	5.6	5.5	5.9
Sub-Saharan Africa	1.9	2.2	3.5	2.4	3.2	3.8	4.1	4.2

SOURCE: World Bank data and baseline projections, November 1998. World Bank, *Global Economic Prospects and the Developing Countries*, 1998, pp. 6.

NOTE: GDP is measured by market prices and expressed in 1987 prices and exchange rates. Growth rates over historic intervals are computed using least squares method.

Table 6.8

Output Growth in East Asia and the Pacific Region

	GDP Growth, %			
Country	1997	1998	1999	2000
Japan	0.9	–2.5	0 to 1	1.5
China	8.8	7.8	5 to 6	5 to 6
Hong Kong	5.2	–5.0	–1 to 1	2.5
South Korea	5.5	–5.8	–0.5 to 0.5	2 to 4
Taiwan	6.8	4.5	4.7	5.5
Indonesia	4.7	–15.0	–3	0
Malaysia	7.8	–6.0	–1 to 1	2 to 3
Philippines	5.2	0.5	2.3	3 to 4
Singapore	7.8	1.3	–1 to 0	3 to 4
Thailand	–0.4	–0.8	–1 to 0	4
Vietnam	8.8	5.2	4.6	5.5
Australia	3.8	4.4	2.4	2.9
New Zealand	2.3	–0.4	1.8	2 to 3

SOURCE: The Economist Group, January 1999.

Table 6.9

Contributions to World GDP Growth, 1997–99

				Change[a]	
	1997	1998	1999	1997–98	1998–99
World GDP growth (%)	3.2	1.8	1.9	–1.4	0.1
Contributions to world growth (percentage points)					
OECD Europe	0.7	0.8	0.7	0.1	–0.1
United States	1.0	0.9	0.5	–0.1	–0.4
Japan	0.1	–0.4	0.0	–0.5	0.4
East Asia crisis countries	0.1	–0.3	0.0	–0.4	0.3
China	0.3	0.2	0.3	0.0	0.0
Latin America and the Caribbean	0.2	0.1	0.0	–0.1	–0.1
Republics of the former Soviet Union	0.0	–0.1	0.1	–0.1	0.0
Other developing regions[b]	0.3	0.3	0.3	0.0	0.0

SOURCE: World Bank estimates. World Bank, *Global Economic Prospects and the Developing Countries,* 1998, p. 15.

NOTE: Contributions may not sum to world growth because of the omission of certain countries.

[a]Percentage may not equal differences in level columns because of rounding.

[b]Aggregate of Middle East and North Africa, Sub-Saharan Africa, South Asia, and Central and Eastern Europe regions.

which reduced the world economic growth rate by 0.3 percentage points. It is estimated that in 1999, the United States and the Latin American countries will reduce their contributions to world economic growth by 0.4 percentage points and 0.1 percentage points, respectively. In addition, in 1999 Japan and crisis-stricken East Asian countries will begin to recover and their contribution to the world economy will be neutral (that is zero), while the contribution of China will increase by 0.1 percentage points to 0.3 percent (see Table 6.9).

Effects of Competition and Depreciation

Vicious competition and sharp depreciation have exerted a great influence on the Chinese economy. The East Asian countries' reliance on exports is remarkably higher than the world export market. Thus, competition among nations in this region is much tougher than the competition in other regions (World Bank, 1998). From June 1997 to August 28, 1998, the currencies in Indonesia, South Korea, Malaysia, the Philippines, Thailand, and Russia have depreciated by 76 percent, 34 percent, 40 percent, 40 percent, 43 percent, and 52 percent, respectively (see Table 6.10). While the surrounding countries' currencies have experienced sharp depreciation, the Chinese currency, Renminbi yuan, on the contrary, has appreciated, which definitely affects the competitiveness of Chinese exports. However, at the same time, because of currency depreciation, asset prices denominated in U.S. dollars have declined in surrounding countries, increasing their competitiveness in attracting foreign direct investment away from China. For instance, by August 1998, the U.S. foreign direct investment in Asian countries reached $8 billion, which was more than twice the amount of the same month in the previous year.

Reduced Exports

The effects of the Asian financial crisis have been transmitted through trade. The Asian financial crisis has directly contributed to the increase in export trade and has indirectly affected the trade of the crisis-stricken countries' trade partners. According to a WTO estimate, the world trade growth rate in 1998 was only 5.3 percent,

Table 6.10

Changes in Financial Variables for Selected Emerging Markets

	Exchange Rate (US$/local currency) % Change from: [a]			Equity Markets % Change from:			Short-Term Interest Rates Level	% Change from:	
Country	Last Month[b]	Dec. 1997	June 1997	Last Month[b]	Dec. 1997	June 1997	Real[c] (Aug. 28)	Last Month[b] (basis points)	June 1997 (basis points)
Indonesia	32	–47	–76	–30	–16	–53	–8.9	236	4130
South Korea	–8	20	–34	–10	–18	–59	2.8	–267	61
Malaysia	–1	–8	–40	–25	–49	–72	3.1	–99	214
Philippines	–5	–11	–40	–26	–36	–57	6.4	61	554
Thailand	–4	11	–42	–18	–41	–58	3.2	–488	–380
Argentina	0	0	0	–38	–47	–55	8.4	93	155
Brazil	–1	–5	–8	–37	–34	–46	17.0	–126	–122
Mexico	–11	–19	–21	–26	–40	–29	17.9	483	505
Venezuela	–3	–13	–16	–42	–70	–72	—	—	—
Czech Republic	–7	4	–1	–23	–23	–22	2.6	–29	–779
Hungary	–5	–10	–17	–37	–35	–24	2.1	–70	–429
Poland	–9	–7	–13	–29	–20	–22	6.6	–121	–314
Russian Federation	–48	–50	–52	–44	–79	–79	115.5	386	7906
South Africa	–6	–25	–30	–28	–20	–33	16.3	57	484

SOURCES: World Bank, *Global Economic Prospects and the Developing Countries*, 1998, p. 12.

NOTE: [—] indicates that data are not available.

[a] [–] denotes depreciation.

[b] Last month refers to July 31, 1998, except for interest rate where the changes are monthly averages.

[c] Nominal three-month interest rate (one-month for Brazil) on August 28, 1998, deflated by the inflation rate in July.

which was much lower than the estimate for 1997—9.5 percent. Based on World Bank estimates (1998), the world export growth rate has declined from 10.1 percent in 1997 to 5.3 percent in 1998, while the import rate has declined from 8.8 percent in 1997 to 5.8 percent in 1998. The financial crisis caused stagnation in domestic demand in East Asian countries and greatly reduced import and export volume. The rate of foreign trade volume in East Asian crisis countries declined from 3.0 percent in 1997 to –17.0 percent in 1998. The trade volume rate in Japan declined from 1.7 percent in 1997 to –7.5 percent in 1998. To cope with the crisis, these East Asian countries took measures to control demand. Enterprises reduced spending because of huge debts, while banks could not issue import credit because of the chaos caused by the crisis. Huge nonperforming debts also impeded the expansion of domestic demand. Exports from the United State, Europe, Japan, and China to East Asian regions have all reduced to varying degrees. The export growth rate has declined from 15.4 percent in 1997 to 2.3 percent in 1998 in the United States, from 9.6 percent to 6.3 percent in 15 European Union (EU) countries, and from 11.8 percent to –1.5 percent in Japan (World Bank, 1998) (see Table 6.11). In 1997, the export growth rate in China was 20.5 percent which contribution rate of net export to GDP growth rate was about one-fifth.

At the beginning of 1998, without an accurate estimate of the effects of the Asian financial crisis, the Chinese government set the goal of increasing trade by 10 percent. For 1998, the export growth rate continued to decline to 0.5 percent, (with an all-time low in October of –17.2 percent). The sharp decline in exports to East Asian regions was the major reason. During January to November of 1998, the export growth rate to Asia was –9.6 percent (Xinhua News Agency, Beijing, December 10, 1998). According to World Bank estimates, the world export growth rate would be 5.3 percent in 1999 and 6.3 percent in 2000, while the import growth rate would be 5.8 percent in 1999 and 6.4 percent in 2000. Under this world trade environment, China's exports would experience negative growth in 1999. During the second half of 1998, China's domestic demand returned to the trend of expansion and likely continued to expand in 1999. However, because of the decline in export demand, China's real GDP growth rate will de-

Table 6.11

World Merchandise Trade Growth, 1991–2007 (in percentage)

Indicator and Region	1991–97	1997[a]	1998	1999	2000	1998–2007
World trade growth[b]	6.8	9.5	5.3	5.7	6.2	6.1
World output growth	2.3	3.2	1.8	1.9	2.7	2.9
Import growth						
High-income countries	6.2	8.8	5.8	6.4	5.9	6.1
OECD countries	5.4	9.4	7.2	6.6	5.6	6.0
United States	8.3	14.7	11.8	8.7	5.2	6.3
EU-15	4.3	7.9	7.3	6.5	5.9	6.2
Japan	6.3	1.7	–7.5	–0.8	4.0	3.6
Non-OECD countries	11.5	5.4	–2.7	5.4	8.1	6.5
Developing countries	9.2	8.8	2.8	4.4	6.2	6.2
Sub-Saharan Africa	3.5	5.8	4.7	5.9	5.9	5.3
East Asia and Pacific	13.5	3.5	–5.2	5.7	8.2	7.3
South Asia	12.1	7.9	6.1	7.6	8.3	8.4
Europe and Central Asia	5.8	9.1	5.7	5.1	5.2	5.2
Latin America and the Caribbean	14.1	16.1	7.8	0.9	5.2	5.4
Middle East and North Africa	1.3	10.8	4.0	4.9	4.7	5.5
Export growth						
High-income countries	6.4	10.1	5.3	5.3	6.3	5.9
OECD countries	5.9	10.7	4.7	5.0	6.1	5.6
United States	7.5	15.4	2.3	3.0	6.6	5.1
EU-15	5.7	9.6	6.3	6.0	6.2	5.8
Japan	2.8	11.8	–1.5	1.2	4.1	4.7
Non-OECD countries	10.3	7.1	8.9	6.7	7.3	7.5
Developing countries	8.7	9.8	6.4	6.3	7.0	6.9
Sub-Saharan Africa	2.6	7.7	3.7	4.5	4.7	5.1
East Asia and Pacific	15.2	12.7	9.4	8.5	9.0	8.5
South Asia	11.1	8.7	5.6	7.3	9.0	9.9
Europe and Central Asia	5.3	6.2	3.4	5.1	5.5	5.5
Latin America and the Caribbean	9.7	11.1	7.1	6.3	6.7	6.7
Middle East and North Africa	4.2	8.3	3.6	3.2	4.8	4.3
Memorandum items[c]						
East Asia crisis country imports	12.0	3.0	–17.0	4.9	9.8	5.8
East Asia crisis country exports	12.6	7.9	15.3	8.1	8.2	8.3

SOURCE: World Bank data and baseline projections, November 1998.

NOTE: Growth rates over intervals are compound averages. EU-15 is Austria, Belgium, Denmark, Finland, France, Germany, Greece, Ireland, Italy, Luxembourg, the Netherlands, Portugal, Spain, Sweden, and the United Kingdom.

[a]Estimate.

[b]Growth rate of the sum of merchandise exports and import volumes.

[c]Indonesia, South Korea, Malaysia, Philippines, and Thailand.

crease by about 1 percentage point. Consequently, the profitability of export enterprises will be influenced, which will indirectly affect employment.

Foreign Direct Investment

The Asian financial crisis also influence the world and Chinese economies via foreign direct investment (FDI). According to a report from the United Nations Trade and Development Conference, in 1997 the Asian financial crisis caused international direct investments to be diverted from Asian countries to Europe and the United States. Total capital flow to developing countries was $140 billion, while private capital flow declined by 7.1 percent and capital flow to Asian emerging market economies declined by about 14 percent. It is estimated that this trend will continue for some time. In addition, foreign direct investment from Southeast Asia, East Asia, and Hong Kong—which accounts for a large share of the total foreign direct investment in China—will decline to a large extent.

Global Deflation

The Asian financial crisis not only reduced the world economic growth rate, but also caused the prices for nonenergy and energy products to fall sharply. According to World Bank statistics, the growth rate for nonenergy products' price index declined from 2.2 percent in 1997 to –15.7 percent in 1998, from 2.6 percent to –16.5 percent for agriculture products, –10.5 percent to –24.1 percent for metal and mineral products, 1.2 percent to –15.4 percent for fertilizer, and –6.9 percent to –28.5 percent for energy products (World Bank, 1998) (see Table 6.12). The price of crude oil on the world market declined from $20 per barrel in 1997 to below $10, which was a record low for the last 12 years. East Asian nations are the major importers of crude oil and agricultural and mineral products. The slump in demand due to severe economic depression in this region was the major cause for the sharp decline of agricultural and mineral product prices. Since the outbreak of the crisis in 1997, the price index of the British journal *Economists* shows an agricultural and mineral product decline of 30 percent. More deeply felt are the productivity surpluses in many industries worldwide and serious banking

Table 6.12

Annual Percentage Change in Energy and Nonenergy Commodity Prices, 1981–2007

	1981–90	1991–96	1996	1997	1998	1999	1998–2007
Nonenergy commodities	–2.3	2.4	–5.8	2.2	–15.7	–2.2	–0.2
Agriculture	–3.2	3.9	4.4	2.6	–16.5	–3.7	–0.4
Food	–3.3	3.6	5.7	–6.1	–9.9	–1.1	0.4
Grains	–2.9	5.8	16.8	–20.3	–9.6	2.4	1.3
Beverages	–5.8	4.0	–16.3	35.2	–17.5	–11.7	–3.3
Raw materials	–0.5	4.4	–6.0	–10.5	–24.1	2.0	1.2
Metals and minerals	0.5	–1.9	–12.3	1.2	–15.4	2.6	0.5
Fertilizers	–2.5	3.1	15.6	–0.1	2.8	–2.0	–0.3
Energy	–4.7	–1.9	18.9	–6.7	28.5	9.5	0.3
Memorandum item G-5 manufactures unit value	3.3	3.2	4.4	–5.1	–3.8	1.3	1.8

SOURCE: World Bank, *Global Economic Prospects and the Developing Countries*, The World Bank, Development Prospects Group, November 1998, p. 24.

problems, which are probably at the roots of the Asian financial crisis (International Pioneer Forum, January 30, 1999). Global deflation has the mechanism of transnational transmission and as the external environment has made the persistent deflation since 1997 even worse. Domestic deflation has seriously affected the coal, oil, steel, nonferrous metal, and agricultural industries, in addition to impeding export growth of primary products.

In Sum

My estimates show that the ratio of China's exports to GDP and that of FDI to GDP increased drastically during the early 1990s, together with the continuing increase of economic growth, but that these indicators decreased substantially after 1994 in addition to a significant decline in economic growth (see Table 6.13). Because of globalization, the Asian financial crisis and economic crises in other regions exert deepening effects on the Chinese economy as external shocks. We cannot prepare for the worst if we neglect these contingent or obvious factors in establishing macroeconomic policies.

Table 6.13

The Growth Rate of GDP and the Share of Exports and FDI to GDP (in percentage)

Year	GDP Growth Rate	Ratio of Exports to GDP	Ratio of FDI to GDP	Ratio of Foreign Funds to Investment	Share of Foreign Enterprises to Total Gross Industrial Products
1990	3.8	16.1	0.9	6.3	4.38
1991	9.2	17.7	1.1	8.7	6.01
1992	14.2	17.6	2.3	5.8	7.61
1993	13.5	15.3	4.6	7.3	11.06
1994	12.6	22.3	6.2	9.9	14.84
1995	10.5	21.3	5.4	11.2	16.57
1996	9.6	18.5	5.1	11.8	16.64
1997	8.8	20.4	5.0	10.3	17.02
1998	7.8	19.2	4.7	9.1	19.91

SOURCE: Calculated on the basis of the *China Statistical Yearbook*, 1999.

THE SHORT-TERM PROSPECTS FOR CHINESE ECONOMIC GROWTH

The recent decrease in the economic growth rate in China was mainly because of a common economic cyclical effect, not a result of external shocks. However, external shocks could reinforce cyclical effects. Since the "South China Inspection" of Deng Xiaoping in 1992, China has experienced an overheated economy and high inflation. The GDP growth rate was 14.2 percent in 1992 and 13.5 percent in 1993, and the inflation rate was 13.2 percent in 1993 and 21.7 percent in 1994. In 1993, the Chinese government began implementing appropriately stabilizing macroeconomic policies that have effectively controlled the high inflation. The inflation rate was reduced from 21.4 percent in 1994 to 6.1 percent in 1996, and in 1996 the GDP growth rate was 9.7 percent (for the first time realizing a "soft-landing"). In 1997, when the Asian financial crisis broke out, the Chinese government continued its appropriate macroeconomic policy of austerity. As of March 1998, the Chinese government was still emphasizing adherence to this principle in its work report. However, due to the negative effects of the Asian financial crisis and the role of long-term accumulated conflicts, domestic economic development has been facing serious challenges since 1997.

Economic Recession

To begin, China's economic growth rate is continuing to fall below the potential output level, indicating recession. In economics terms, the output gap is the difference between the real output growth rate and the natural economic growth rate. The "natural economic growth rate," also referred to as the "potential economic growth rate," is the real economic growth rate when inflation equals a constant (that is, when inflation is neither accelerating nor decelerating). Recession is defined as the trend of enlarging the output gap. From historical statistics we can see that, during the 1980s, China's economic growth potential or trend rate was 9.5 percent, and, for the first half of the 1990s, the trend growth rate increased to 10.9 percent. However, for the second half of the 1990s, the growth rate started to fall, to 8–9 percent. The growth rate was 8.8 percent in 1997 and decreased to 7.8 percent in 1998. For the first quarter of 1999, the economic growth rate declined to 7.1 percent, compared with 9.6 percent for the rate at the same time of the previous year.

Since 1978 and for almost 20 years, China has experienced an unprecedentedly high speed of economic growth and entered a new stage for both stable economic growth and structural adjustment. This new stage has two implications: (1) the growth rate will decline compared to that of the previous 20 years and will show obvious features of structural adjustment—i.e., from aggregate-expansion-oriented growth to structural-adjustment-oriented growth; and from supply-pushed growth to demand-pulled growth. (2) Compared with the growth rate of other countries during the same period, China's growth rate will still remain high. China's domestic saving rate will also remain at a relatively high level, and FDI will slow down. But nevertheless, China will still rank second among all nations in attracting FDI. Fixed-asset investment will continue to be the engine for development, and the distinct advantages of being a large economy will help in expanding domestic demand. Therefore, although China's GDP growth rate in 1999 and 2000 will not achieve the double digit growth rate seen during the "Eighth Five-Year Plan" (1991–1995), China will not experience the very low or even negative growth rates of its neighbors. There were many forecasts for the 1999 GDP growth rate, such as the estimate of 8–8.5 percent by the State Statistical Bureau, the estimate of 8.6 percent of the China Academy of Social Science, and the estimate of 5–6 percent by the British

Economist Group. My personal forecast was 7–8 percent. If exports achieve positive growth, the GDP growth rate could reach 8 percent or higher. If exports fall into negative growth, the GDP growth rate would be 7 percent or lower. Or if there was no change in total exports, the GDP growth rate would be around 7.5 percent. The 1999 economic growth target of the Chinese government was about 7 percent, which was no longer an instructive order or planned indicator but a forecasting indicator or an economic indicator with natural guidance (see Table 6.14).

In 1998, investment's contribution to GDP growth was much higher than consumption's contribution. Of the 8.8 percent GDP growth in 1997, investment growth was 2.2 percent, consumption increase was 4.9 percent, net export growth was 1.7 percent, and their respective contribution rates for GDP growth were 25.2 percent, 55.5 percent, and 19.1 percent. Of the 7.8 percent economic growth rate of 1998, investment growth was about 4.7 percent, and consumption growth was about 3.2 percent. The respective contribution rates of investment and consumption to GDP growth were 63 percent and 32 percent, and the contribution of net export was 5 percent. In 1998, investment was still a driving force for economic growth and its reinforcing effects for economic growth were evident. In 1998, the total fixed asset investment rate was 14.1 percent, of which the rate for state-owned entities was 19.6 percent, which likely further increased

Table 6.14

Chinese Economic Growth

	1979–97	1997	1998	1999	2000
SSB	9.8	8.8	7.8	8 to 8.5[a]	
Economist[b]				5 to 6	5 to 6
BNP[c]			7.5	7.2	8.0
CASS[a]			7.7 to 8.1	8.6	
Government target			8	7	
Hu	9.5			7 to 8	
World Bank			7.3 to 7.5	5.0	4.4 to 5.0

SOURCES:

[a]Lin Quoguang, ed., *China in 1999: Analysis and Forecast*, Social Sciences Literature Publisher, Beijing, December 1998.

[b]Economist Group, January 1999.

[c]BNP Prime Peregrine, *China Outlook 1999*, January 6, 1999.

in that and the following year. Presently, insufficiencies in domestic demand are mainly a result of insufficient consumption. Since 1994, various consumption growth rates were sharply reduced. Based on current price calculations, by 1998, the total consumption growth rate declined from 32.8 percent to 6.5 percent. For the same period, the rural consumption growth rate was reduced from 33 percent to 6.5 percent; the urban consumption growth rate was reduced from 37.4 percent to 10.5 percent, and government consumption growth declined from 33 percent to 8.7 percent. The fall of the consumption growth rate has become the major constraint to GDP growth. According to calculations of the Industrial Economic Research Center of the Chinese Academy of Social Sciences, in 1998–1999, a 1 percent increase in consumption would lead to an increase of 0.5 percent in economic growth, while an increase of 1 percent in gross fixed-capital formation could lead to an increase of only 0.17 percent in GDP, and a 1 percent increase in exports could lead to only a 0.06 percent increase in economic growth (see Table 6.15). Therefore, it is clear that expansion to meet consumption needs is both the objective of economic growth and the major driving force behind economic growth. For the future, instead of allowing investment to drive growth, China should coax economic growth through increased investment and by stimulating consumption. When consumption accounts for close to 60 percent of China's GDP, long-term economic development policies should focus on expanding urban and rural residents' consumption demand, particularly on stimulating the consumption of the more than 900 million rural Chinese residents.

Economic Surpluses

Economic growth is also being affected by excessive surpluses in production capacity, causing the supply of consumer products to be greater than demand. Since economic reform policies have been adopted, China's industrial production capacity has increased unprecedentedly. Based on constant-price calculations, industrial value added increased 7.6 times from 1978 to 1997. In 1978, industrial sectors' total net assets were over 200 billion yuan, and by 1997 they were over 4 trillion yuan. The International Pioneer Forum observed that for developing countries, China ranks first in production capacity surplus—for almost all major products supply is much greater

Table 6.15

Demand Analysis of China's Economic Growth (the explained variable is Ln (GDP))

Explaining Variable	Variable Number	T-Test Value
The constant item	1.2662	9.3327
Consumption	0.5039	10.1044
Government consumption	0.2045	3.6600
Growth of fixed capital	0.1739	4.7766
Growth of stock	0.0580	4.8787
Growth of exports	0.0597	2.8166

SOURCES: The Research Institute of Industrial Economy of Chinese Academy of Social Sciences, *The Report on China's Industrial Development,* 1999; *Chinese Industry: After the Shortage Economy,* Economic Management Publishing House, 1999.

NOTES: $R2 = 0.99$; $DW = 1.40$; $F = 22533$. Sample period is 1978–1997.

than demand. This production capacity surplus is the latest threat to the health of the Chinese economy and trade. In the early 1990s, a trend of textile and household electrical appliance oversupply emerged in China. In the mid 1990s, a general consumption and manufacturing industry oversupply emerged in China. For most enterprises in China, the average rate of productivity utilization is below 70 percent.

According to analyses by the Commercial Statistics Information Administration Office of the State Bureau of Domestic Trade on more than 600 major commercial product markets, at the beginning of 1998, about 25 percent of the surveyed product markets were in surplus, and, in May 1998, the share of surplus markets increased to 27.4 percent. By the beginning of 1999, the share of surplus markets increased to two-thirds. For example, the supply of textile and articles of everyday use is 100 percent higher than demand (see Table 6.16). Also, the supplies of household electronics and chemical products were 90 percent higher than demand. In addition, the share of surpluses for agricultural and animal byproducts and agricultural means of production increased substantially. The remaining one-third of markets are in supply/demand equilibrium, and only one market category (grain and cooking oil) is in shortage (*Economic Information Daily,* Xinhua News Agency, January 26, 1999). The conditions needed for most industries to show a profit have van-

Table 6.16

The Relationship Between Supply and Demand for Main Commerce Goods

Survey Date	Number of Goods	Balance (%)	Supply over Demand (%)
January 1998	601	75	25
May 1998	606	72.6	27.4
January 1999	605	33.3	66.7

NOTE: These data are based on a survey conducted by the Ministry of Commercial, China Economic Time, February 2. 1999.

ished. Traditional industrial enterprises have entered a period of low, or even negative, profits (The Industrial Economic Research Center of the Chinese Academy of Social Sciences, 1999). Manufacturing capacity surpluses were a result of excessive investment in these sectors, duplicative construction, and vicious competition. Many projects are domed to lose money from the very first day of investment. This trend shows that the Chinese economy has changed from a sellers' market to a buyers' market—structural competition has become more obvious. The current economic structure can neither meet the needs of domestic market demand, nor cope with the challenge of international competition.

What should especially be pointed out is that, except for the retail and restaurant industries, most of the service sectors remain an economic phenomenon. State-owned entities still have a highly monopolistic hold on most service sectors, particularly the banking and insurance industry, the telecommunications service industry, higher education, health care services, the television and motion picture sector, science, and the research and technology service sector. The rates of value added for these industries are very high and have great potential for development (see Table 6.17), but unfortunately they are controlled by state-owned economic entities. The average Chinese resident's consumption is depressed, but the ability of these industries to absorb excess employment is low.

Consumer and Retail Price Indexes

Deflation has become more and more obvious, severely hurting the initiative of average workers and further constricting economic growth. From an economics perspective, the output gap directly af-

Table 6.17

Growth Rate of the Value-Added from "Tertiary" Industries (in percentage)

Sector	1991	1992	1993	1994	1995	1996
Transport and storage	8.6	7.9	5.9	7.1	5.0	3.8
Post and telecommunications	35.5	30.3	53.3	20.1	39.0	34.0
Wholesale and retail trade and catering services	4.5	13.1	6.6	7.7	5.9	5.4
Banking and insurance	2.3	8.0	10.9	9.4	8.5	7.5
Real estate	12.0	34.7	10.8	12.0	12.4	4.0
Social services	26.8	19.3	18.9	8.3	5.8	5.0
Health care, sports, and social welfare	14.9	9.4	11.8	8.2	6.4	10.3
Education, culture, arts, radio, film, and television	07.8	8.0	14.9	15.0	8.0	13.9
Scientific research and polytechnic services	12.0	15.3	6.9	17.9	10.5	14.0
Government agencies, parties, and social organizations	14.5	8.6	7.7	8.3	6.0	6.2
Other	14.8	19.5	17.9	10.6	8.6	9.5

SOURCE: SSB, *China Statistical Yearbook*, 1998, p. 61.

fects the direction of inflation. When real output is higher than potential output (that is, the output gap is positive), inflation increases tend to accelerate. If the gap is negative (that is, the real output is lower than the potential output), inflation decreases tend to accelerate. Not only did various consumption indexes decline generally, but price indexes in various regions also declined (see Table 6.18).

Since October 1997, the rate of retail price indexes has maintained negative growth. By 1998, the rate was –2.6 percent, and the rate for residential consumption price indexes was –0.8 percent, which includes the rate of the food consumption price index (–3.2 percent) and the rates of the transportation and means of communication price indexes (–4.2 percent). The purchasing price index of farm products was –4.5 percent in 1997 and –8.0 percent in 1998, and the ex-factory price index of industrial products was –0.3 percent in 1997 and –4.1 percent in 1998 (Xinhua News Agency, February 26, 1999). Since economic reform, China has been constantly challenged by high inflation, and for the first time finds itself threatened by deflation. High inflation jeopardizes the interests of the average consumer, while deflation tends to hurt producers directly. From the

Table 6.18

Consume and Retail Price Indexes of Commodities by Region (1998)

Region	Consumer Price Index	Retail Price Index of Commodity
Total	99.2	97.4
Beijing	102.4	98.3
Tianjin	99.5	96.6
Hebei	98.4	97.7
Shanxi	98.6	97.0
Inner Mongolia	99.3	98.1
Liaoning	99.3	97.6
Jilin	99.2	97.9
Heilongjiang	100.4	98.4
Shanghai	100.0	95.1
Jiangsu	99.4	98.2
Zhejiang	99.7	98.4
Anhui	100.0	98.1
Fujian	99.7	98.5
Jiangxi	101.0	98.8
Shandong	99.4	97.1
Henan	97.5	96.6
Hubei	98.4	97.1
Hunan	100.2	97.9
Guangdong	98.2	97.0
Guangxi	97.0	96.3
Hainan	97.3	96.5
Chongqing	96.4	94.5
Sichuan	99.6	97.7
Guizhou	100.1	98.9
Yunnan	101.7	99.2
Shanxi	98.4	96.2
Gansu	99.0	98.1
Qinghai	100.7	99.6
Ningxia	100.0	97.5
Xinjiang	100.2	99.7

SOURCE: *A Survey of China's Statistics,* 1999, p. 298.

NOTE: Statistics for 1997 = 100.

perspective of the average consumer, a fall in prices is a good thing, and consumers expect to benefit from it. But persistently falling prices for products and services will force enterprises to cut back on spending, reduce supply, decrease wages, and increase unemployment, forming a vicious cycle. The greater the production capability surplus, the greater are the price falls, and the slower the wage increases or the more the worker layoffs. In turn, residential consumption demand will be restrained.

It is important to note that we lack the experience and measures to control deflation. Usually, a government can effectively control inflation and an overheated economy through tight fiscal and monetary policies. However, such policies are very difficult to use for controlling deflation or stopping recession. Deflation can bring about a crisis of confidence, causing people to have negative expectations about the future. Of course, in the situation of excessive supply and falling prices, one of the major measures to control deflation is to close inefficient, out-of-date, and polluting enterprises. For instance, in 1998 the key state-owned coal enterprises accumulated a loss of 3.7 billion RMB yuan—about 81 percent of these enterprises were operating at a loss. It was estimated that 2.4 million coal industry workers were laid off, and about 25,800 small coal mining enterprises of all kinds were closed. In 1998, coal output was almost 300 million tons less than that of 1996 (Xinhua News Agency, January 22, 1999). Also, in 1998, 5.12 million cotton spindles became obsolete, and 660,000 workers were laid off in this industry. It was estimated that in 1999 4.38 million spindles would become obsolete and that 1.1 million workers would be laid off. In addition, due to production capability surpluses in the metallurgical, forest, defense, and oil industries (about 40 percent), huge amounts of workers would be laid off and production would be further cut back.

Unemployment Rates

Sharp unemployment increases have reached record highs since the establishment of the People's Republic of China, further debilitating the economy. On the one hand, the urban registered unemployed increased from 4.2 million in 1993 to 6.2 million in 1998, an increase of 47.6 percent. On the other hand, the number of laid off workers increased from 3 million in 1993 to 18–19 million in 1998, including laid off (xiagang) workers from state-owned enterprises (12 million). The number of those unemployed because of layoffs also increased, from 1.2–1.8 million in 1993 to 8.6–9.6 million in 1998, including laid-off workers from state-owned enterprises (about 7.1 million). Adding to these numbers were unemployed rural workers who moved to urban areas; therefore, the real number of urban unemployed was 5.4–6 million in 1993, 13–15 million in 1997, and 15.4–16.0 million in 1998. The real unemployment rate was about 7.9–8.3 percent, which was the unemployment peak since the establishment of the People's Republic of China (see Table 6.19).

In the 1990s, the employment rate in agriculture sectors declined by 10 percent, while the employment rate for secondary industries and service industries increased by 20 percent and 55 percent, respectively. These two types of industries became the major channel for employment increases during the decade. Meanwhile, urban employment increased by 21.6 percent, including employment in urban collectively owned enterprises (a decrease of nearly 20 percent) and employment in state-owned enterprises (which increased early in the decade and then later declined). However, during the 1990s employment in other enterprises (private enterprises, small and/or self-owned businesses, and foreign-invested enterprises) increased by 130 percent and have become the main channel for urban employment growth.

High unemployment is not only a prominent issue on the national social agenda, but also a prominent problem in economic development and social stability in all regions of China. Liaoning province has the largest real urban unemployment (960,000), followed by Heilongjiang (810,000), Henan (728,000), Hunan (769,000), Hubei (671,000), Shandong (668,000), and Sichuan (646,000). Chongqing City has the largest real unemployment (266,000) among the four municipalities (see Table 6.20).

The real unemployment rate in China's midwest region is generally higher than that of the coastal region. The real urban unemployment rate in Qinghai ranks first nationwide (11.5 percent), followed by Shannxi (11.4 percent), Guizhou (10.5 percent), Jilin (9.3 percent), Hunan (9.0 percent), Shanghai (4.9 percent), Guangdong (4.8 percent), and Fujian (4.0 percent). However, the real urban unemployment in Tianjin and Beijing is only 2.8 percent and 1.4 percent, respectively. The difference between the highest and lowest real urban unemployment rate is close to 10 percentage points (see Table 6.20). Not only do the great differences in per-capita GDP and economic growth rates show the economic development disparity throughout China, but so do these great differences in real unemployment rates in various regions. Geographically, although many areas of China experienced high unemployment rates, it was mainly the midwest that maintained high unemployment levels.

Reform of State-Owned Enterprises

The lack of reform of state-owned enterprises also contributed to economic stagnation. In 1993, state-owned enterprises totaled losses as high as 48.3 billion yuan, while total profits were 82.9 million yuan, and total net profits were 36.5 million yuan. In 1997, state-owned enterprises totaled losses of 83.1 million yuan, but total profits were only 42.8 billion yuan, while net losses were 40.3 billion yuan. According to the State Statistical Bureau, in 1997 the total losses for 58,000 enterprises reached 100 billion yuan, which was 2.7 percent higher than for the same period of the previous year. Among these losses, the losses of large and medium-sized enterprises increased by 30.4 percent (Economic Daily, January 29, 1999). When we take into consideration the trend of gradually declining profits, the total losses in 1998 were expected to be about 70 billion yuan.

The investment rate of return on state-owned enterprises has declined sharply. In 1990, the capital rate of return for state owned enterprises was 3.2 percent, and by 1997 the rate declined to 0.9 percent. The sharp decline in state-owned enterprises' capital rate of return is the major reason for the fall of state owned enterprises' investment rate of return. From a productivity index for various economic entities, based on the 1990 constant price, the productivity growth rate for state-owned manufacturers increased by 59 percent from 1991 to 1997, but the productivity rate for other forms of economic entities increased by 114 percent for the same period. For comparison, in 1985 the productivity ratio of other forms of businesses to state-owned enterprises was 1.5 to 1; in 1991 the ratio was 2.1 to 1, and in 1997 the ratio was 2.8 to 1. Therefore, generally state-owned enterprises could not compete with other types of enterprises.

State-Owned Commercial Banks

Another factor affecting economic growth was the high rate of nonperforming loans among state-owned commercial banks. Although China still regulates foreign exchange on capital accounts and has forbidden the entrance of hot money, the Chinese financial system is very risky because of lagging financial reform. The nonperforming

Table 6.19

Various Estimates of Unemployment in Urban Areas

Year	Registered Unemployment (tens of thousands of people)	Investigated Unemployment (tens of thousands of people)	Laid-Off Workers (tens of thousands of people)		Unemployment Due to Layoffs (tens of thousands of people)		Real Unemployment (tens of thousands of people)	Rural Labor Unemployment (tens of thousands of people)	Real Unemployment Rate (%)
			Total	SOEs	Total	SOEs			
1993	420		300[a]	200	120–180[e]		450–600[e]		3.3–3.7
1994	476		360[a]	24	144–216[e]		620–692[e]		3.6–4.1
1995	520	790	564[a]	376	226–338[e]		800–913	55	4.4–5.0
1996	557	815	892[b]	574[b]	356–535[e]		970–1148	60	5.1–6.0
1997	570	980	1435[c]	929[c]	670–770[f]	465[c]	1,310–1,510[f]	69	6.8–7.8
1998	600	1145	1,720–1,820[d]	1218[d]	860–960[f]	610[d]	1,540–1,640[f]	80	7.9–8.5

SOURCES: The scope of unemployment (the investigated number) in urban areas is limited to that within the districts of the cities without street areas, and resident committees: *China Labor Statistical Yearbook*, 1997, p. 3; *China Labor Statistical Yearbook*, 1998, p. 3. The data for 1998 are the author's estimates. The registered unemployment is the registered population from local employment agencies. This population has nonagricultural registered permanent residence, working ability, and a desire for employment: *China Statistical Yearbook*, 1998, p. 127.

[a]Refer to Yiyong Yang, "What Is the Number of the Unemployment in China?" *Economic Highlights*, March 10, 1998.

[b]Refer to *China Labor Statistical Yearbook*, 1997, p. 213.

[c]Refer to *China Labor Statistical Yearbook*, 1998, p. 230.

[d]According to data provided by the Ministry of Labor and Social Security, there were 6.09 million laid-off workers from SOEs who have become reemployed, obtaining a reemployment rate of 50 percent: News Agencies, Beijing, January 22, 1999. According to this reference, the real estimated number of laid-off workers from SOEs was about 12.18 million. According to the share of laid-off workers of the total number of unemployed, which is below 65 percent, the author estimated that the total number of laid-off workers of various enterprises was about 17.20–18.20 million.

Table 6.19—continued

[e]The author's estimate based on a reemployment rate of 40–60 percent: See Angang Hu et al., *Employment and Development,* Group for China Study, Chinese Academy of Sciences, Liaoning People's Publishing House, Beijing, 1998, Table 3.5.

[f]The author's most recent estimate: Unemployment of agricultural labor is estimated on the basis of an unemployment rate of 1.5 percent. The real unemployment of various labor forces is based on the following: (1) the registered unemployment rate; (2) unemployment from laid-off workers; and (3) unemployment from the agricultural labor force.

Table 6.20

The Number of Unemployed and the Real Unemployment Rate, 1997

Area	Registered Unemployment (tens of thousands of people)[a]	Unemployment Due to Layoffs (tens of thousands of people)[b]	Real Unemployment (tens of thousands of people)[c]	Registered Unemployment rate (%)[a]	Real Unemployment Rate (%)[c]
Beijing	3.3	3.2	6.5	0.7	1.4
Tianjin	4.3	4.9	9.2	1.3	2.8
Hebei	16.2	21.2	37.4	2.0	4.6
Shanxi	12.6	19.5	32.1	2.4	6.1
Inner Mongolia	17.7	16.9	36.6	3.8	7.9
Liaoning	46.0	50.0	96.0	3.9	7.6
Jilin	13.6	46.6	60.2	2.1	9.3
Heilongjiang	25.5	55.5	81.0	2.6	8.3
Shanghai	14.9	11.9	26.8	2.7	4.9
Jiangsu	25.1	35.5	60.6	2.5	6.0
Zhejiang	21.2	12.2	33.4	3.4	5.4
Anhui	21.6	13.2	34.8	3.2	5.2
Fujian	10.4	6.8	17.2	2.4	4.0
Jiangxi	16.3	26.5	42.8	3.0	7.9
Shandong	38.9	27.9	66.8	3.4	5.8
Henan	24.0	53.8	77.8	2.3	7.5
Hubei	33.9	33.2	67.1	3.5	6.9
Hunan	30.9	46.0	76.9	3.6	9.0
Guangdong	31.9	24.6	56.5	2.7	4.8
Guangxi	18.2	10.1	28.3	4.2	6.5
Hainan	5.5	4.0	9.5	4.3	7.4
Chongqing	10.9	15.7	26.6	2.9	7.1
Sichuan	32.3	32.3	64.6	3.9	7.8
Guizhou	19.6	12.2	31.8	6.8	10.5
Yunnan	10.4	6.3	16.7	2.8	4.5
	NA	NA	NA	NA	NA
Shanxi	32.0	25.1	57.1	6.4	11.4
Gansu	15.7	7.6	23.1	5.2	7.7
Qinghai	5.9	3.3	9.2	7.4	11.5
Ningxia	4.2	2.1	6.3	4.8	7.2
Xinjiang	13.8	6.3	20.1	3.7	5.4

[a]Refer to *China Labor Statistical Yearbook*, 1998, p. 93.

[b]Based on the only available statistics for unemployment rates of laid-off workers from SOEs: *China Labor Statistical Yearbook*, 1998, p. 435.

[c]Based on the author's estimates. This estimate is conservative because of the lack of data for unemployment of laid-off workers from collectively owned and similar enterprises, as well as the lack of data regarding rural labors who were laid off but then reemployed in urban areas.

loans of state-owned commercial banks can be divided into three groups—overdue loans (for example, one state-owned bank has overdue loans amounting to about 10 percent of its assets), ideal loans (for example, about 3–4 percent of assets), and bad debts that need to be written off (for example, about 1–2 percent).[7] According to government statistics, the share of nonperforming loans of state-owned banks is over 20 percent, which includes nearly 5–6 percent of bad debts. In addition, medium and small financial institutions have incurred serious losses, and some financial institutions are facing bankruptcy. Serious losses combined with the inability of some borrowers to repay mature loans have brought some financial institutions to the brink of bankruptcy. The closure of Guangdong International Trust and Investment Corporation (ITIC) has had very negative effects on the international financial market, increasing costs for the banking system to raise overseas funds and causing difficulties in entering the international financial market at all. This bank's closure could possibly lead to a new financial crisis (Zhou Xiaochuan, Xinhua News Agency, February 8, 1999). Chinese society as a whole lacks proper debt-credit relationships in general, showing an inability to pay back debts on time and abide by contracts. In addition, there are great sums of "hidden foreign liabilities," that is, foreign debt beyond government supervision.

STIMULATING DOMESTIC DEMAND IS KEY

Because China is facing serious challenges from home and abroad, it is appropriate

for it to emphasize economic policies to stimulate domestic demand while continuing the process of opening its economy to the outside world. It should further develop domestic

markets and specialization, as well as promoting fair competition and economies of scale.

Maintaining a prosperous economy under the unfavorable circumstances of Asian financial crises should be a priority. Prosperity will

---

[7] Zhou Xiaochuan, *The Issues Regarding the Non-Performing Loans in the Banking System in China,* August 19, 1998.

come from proactive policies to increase domestic consumption and investments to stimulate the economic growth, creating employment opportunities and increasing fiscal revenues.

Compared with many other Asian countries, China has many advantages in promoting policies that stimulate domestic demand and promote economic growth:

1. The unique advantage of being a large country with a huge population.
2. Development disparities between urban and rural areas as well as among different regions.
3. As a newcomer in the industrialized world, China has the advantage of the "backwardness effect."
4. From the viewpoint of developmental stages, China is in an economic rising period of its total domestic demand and per-capita consumption. According to forecasts of World Bank experts, the service sector will significantly change in the next 25 years, when China gradually will enter the mid-income country category.
5. Stable and sustainable high savings rates and domestic investment rates.
6. Physical and technological strength, resulting from high-speed economic development over the past 20 years, will help China build on capabilities that reduce the effects of external shocks.
7. Government restructuring will help promote administrative abilities that can deal with outside strikes.

Stimulating domestic demand will not only increase government and public demand but, more importantly, will expand social and private demand. The government should take the lead—its key role being to guarantee that the economy has a sustainable, fast, healthy, and balanced development. Therefore, government policies should help expand residential consumption, especially the spending of low and mid-income residents, and increase social investments, especially private and foreign investments. Stimulating domestic demands does not exclude exploring possible foreign demand and export markets. These ventures can be met by streamlining production in export enterprises, facilitating and promoting technological innovations, strengthening internal management, reducing export costs, and generally increasing the ability to compete internationally. Meanwhile, multi-export-market strategies should be adopted so that more emerging markets can be developed. The basic policy for China's participation in the global economy is to develop both domestic and international resources and markets, which are not mutually exclusive—the two types of resources and markets are linked and promote each other.

MACROECONOMIC POLICY SUGGESTIONS

Fiscal and Monetary Policy

China should follow a policy package that includes an appropriately expansionary fiscal policy and a "disinflationary" monetary policy. The core of fiscal policy is to stimulate economic growth, while currency value embodies the core of monetary policy. The policy package should include the following elements:

- Fiscal policy should be the dominant economic policy, while monetary policy maintains a relatively supporting role.
- An appropriate expansionary fiscal policy does not mean reducing tax but increasing tax sources through tax system restructuring. China's tax revenue accounts for a very low level of GDP while the various fees levied on businesses and farmers are very high. Therefore, fiscal policy should adjust the tax burden and attempt structural optimization by reducing the real tax and fee burdens of investors. In doing so, greater investment flows to enterprises would be encouraged, expanding effective demand and creating employment opportunities.
- Fiscal expenditure structures should be adjusted so that public spending is more efficient. SOE loss subsidies and other price subsidies should be discontinued, and fiscal money should not be channeled to spending on competitive products (such as technological innovations). Instead it should go to efforts that help minimize social costs resulting from reform and crisis (such as a social safety net) and to meet basic public service needs for all citizens.

- The main target of current monetary policy is curbing deflation. It should be noted that there are differences between deflation and "disflation." Deflation denotes a continuous downward trend of prices and disflation means the fall of inflation. Since the cost of deflation is higher than that of low inflation, it is necessary to further expand the money supply to achieve disinflation. To support an expansionary fiscal policy, monetary policies should increase credits for infrastructure, housing, education, public transportation and communications needs, export and import credit, and credit for medium and small size and private businesses as well as for foreign enterprises.
- Monetary policy operations should be forward looking, flexible, and quickly response to external conditions.

Policies for Industrial Development

China's new industrial policies' main objective is to create a sound economic environment. However, the role of government is not to choose a plan for industrial development and then raise subsidies for this plan, but rather to encourage open markets and competition, to stimulate private investment and technology innovation, and to eliminate restrictions on free enterprise, including introducing competition in the public-sector monopolistic service industry.

Government should expand infrastructure construction to attract investment from home and abroad. It should encourage competition, by setting up transparent bidding procedures that are open not only to domestic enterprises, but also foreign ones. It should especially break up the highly monopolistic telecommunications industry. In addition, the Chinese government should focus on

- promoting technological innovation
- facilitating the development of high-tech and new communications, microelectronic, information, medical, and environmental protection industries
- raising the ability of the country as a whole and enterprises in general to compete
- helping medium and small enterprises to develop

- developing a non-SOE economy by creating a strong, competitive, stable, and effective private sector
- opening up the monopolistic service industries—special efforts in breaking down the markets run solely by SOEs.
- promoting emerging and new economic participants and industries.

Trade and Investment Liberalization Policies

From an economic view, China's open trade policy is fundamentally a liberalization of trade and investment. But China must go further to transform from a semi-open, semi-protected country to a totally open economy. To complete this economic transformation, China must take the following steps:

- Further reduce the nominal import custom tax rate and cancel trade protection and various tariff barriers. Sharply reduce the custom tax rates for capital products, technology equipment, automobile and telecommunications equipment, raw materials, and the resources in which China does not have a competitive advantage (such as oil, chemicals, food, and timber). In addition, streamline or cancel the irregular policies of exempting and reducing custom taxes.
- Make further efforts to attract foreign capital, especially from multinational corporations. Permit and even encourage foreign capital to enter competitive merchandise and service markets. Open domestic and foreign trade markets; the banking and insurance market (not including the capital market); the communications service sector, including e-mail, electronic information, data transfer, and fax services; the tourism service sector; higher education and vocational education; the cultural sector; the sports sector; publishing; transportation; port construction; air, sea, and inland water transport sectors; channel transportation; highway transportation; and the construction industry including public construction projects.
- Treat foreign enterprises civilly. On the one hand, cancel the "super-civil" tax treatment for foreign enterprises. On the other

hand, cancel discriminatory policies regarding loans, financing, and investment.

- Stabilize foreign exchange rates, gradually transiting to a free conversion exchange rate system, making the link between foreign and domestic markets complete. Transition to international market prices.
- Participate in the WTO as soon as possible. The WTO should be seen as the international "economic Olympics." The world needs China and China needs the world even more. The long-term advantages of a liberal trade system and more-transparent market competition to China's economy will far surpass the short-term cost adjustments of open trade.

Employment Policies

Economic growth is the key to expanding employment. The Chinese government should commit to expanding the scale of employment and reducing the unemployment rate. Also local governments should make reducing real unemployment the main objective of economic development. Sustainable high-speed economic growth is part of the process of continuously creating employment opportunities. Great efforts should be made to develop labor-intensive industries by adopting the strategy "save capital, use more labor," selectively developing capital-intensive, resource-intensive and technology-intensive industries. Also, the development of labor-intensive small-sized enterprises, private enterprises, and high-tech enterprises should be encouraged. In addition, various "irregular" flexible shifts (such as part time and split shift) should be encouraged. The central and local governments should also set up an unemployment insurance system and career development and employment facilitation services to encourage the free flow of labor throughout the economy. By reallocating labor resources and changing employment structures, economic and employment growth will be promoted.

Policies for Expanding the Consumption Demand of Urban Populations

The government should increase the income of the urban poor. The following concrete measures should be taken:

- Raise basic living expenses by 30 percent.
- Elevate unemployment insurance for the registered unemployed by 30 percent.
- Increase the urban population's living security expenditure by 30 percent.
- Boost the wage level and the standard pension for public servants.

The above measures can directly benefit 8.4 million of the low-income population. At the same time, the government should levy a 20 percent tax on the interest from savings. This would accrue about ¥ 20–30 billion for the central government in the first year. In addition, abolishing various informal and random taxes and fees in rural areas can also directly help increase the real income of the rural population.

Policies for Expanding Housing and Education Expenditures

The goal for education should be raising enrollment in higher education by 41.7 percent (or about 450,000 students) of the rate in 1998. In the short run, this policy would delay the population studying in universities from entering the employment sector and promote expenditures on higher education as well as promoting the development of the education sector. In the long run, this policy would improve the quality and the productivity of the labor force. In a similar vein, accelerating housing reform can stimulate consumption expenditures on housing and property. Therefore, the government should promote reform of housing privatization, housing-related credit, and development of the secondary estate market.

REFERENCES

A Survey of China's Statistics, 1999.

Asia Development Bank, *Emerging Asia: Change and Challenge, The Asia Development,* 1997.

BNP Prime Peregrine, *China Outlook 1999,* January 6, 1999.

Center for China Study, Chinese Academy of Sciences, *Opportunities and Challenges: Study on the Economic Development Strategic Objectives and Essential Development Strategy for China Entering 21st Century,* Beijing Science Publication House, Beijing, 1995.

China Labor Statistical Yearbook, 1997.

China Labor Statistical Yearbook, 1998.

China Statistical Yearbook, 1996.

China Statistical Yearbook, 1999.

SSB, *China Statistical Yearbook*, 1996.

SSB, *China Statistical Yearbook*, 1998.

Economic Daily, January 29, 1999.

Economic Information Daily, Xinhua News Agency, January 26, 1999.

The Economist Group, January 1999.

Economist Group, January 1999.

FAO, *Production Yearbooks.*

Group for National Condition Analysis of Chinese Academy of Sciences, *Opportunities and Challenges: Economic Development Goals and Strategies for China Going to the 21st Century,* Science Press, Beijing, 1995.

Hu, Angang, et al., *Employment and Development,* Group for China Study, Chinese Academy of Sciences, Liaoning People's Publishing House, 1998, Table 3.5.

The Industrial Economic Research Center of Chinese Academy of Social Sciences, 1999.

International Pioneer Forum, January 30, 1999.

Maddison (1995a), pp. 253–254, updated.

Maddison, Angus, *Chinese Economic Performance in the Long Run*, Development Centre Studies, OECD, 1998.

Ministry of Commercial, China Economic Time, February 2. 1999.

Mizoguchi and Umemura (1988).

News Agencies, Beijing, January 22, 1999.

OECD, *National Accounts 1983–1995*, Paris, 1997.

Pilat (1994).

Quoguang, Lin, ed., *China in 1999: Analysis and Forecast*, Social Sciences Literature Publisher, Beijing, December 1998.

RAND's forecasts (1995).

RAND's prediction (1995) (in table 6.5).

The Research Institute of Industrial Economy of Chinese Academy of Social Sciences, *The Report on China's Industrial Development*, 1999; *Chinese Industry: After the Shortage Economy*, Economic Management Publishing House, 1999.

United Nations Trade and Development Conference, report, 1997

World Bank (1996).

World Bank data and baseline projections, November 1998.

World Bank forecast for 1994–2015.

World Bank, *China 2020: Development Challenges in the New Century*, 1997.

World Bank, *Global Economic Prospects and the Developing Countries*, 1998.

World Bank, *Global Economic Prospects and the Developing Countries,* The World Bank, Development Prospects Group, November 1998.

World Bank, *World Development Report,* various issues.

World Bank, *World Tables 1992,* Johns Hopkins University Press, Baltimore and London, 1992.

Xiaochuan, Zhou, *The Issues Regarding the Non-Performing Loans in the Banking System in China,* August 19, 1998.

Xiaochuan, Zhou, Xinhua News Agency, February 8, 1999.

Xinhua News Agency, Beijing, December 10, 1998.

Xinhua News Agency, January 22, 1999.

Yang, Yiyong, "What Is the Number of the Unemployment in China on Earth?" *Economic Highlights,* March 10, 1998.

Chapter Seven

THE ROLE OF FOREIGN-INVESTED ENTERPRISES IN THE CHINESE ECONOMY: AN INSTITUTIONAL FOUNDATION APPROACH

Yasheng Huang

THE ROLE OF FOREIGN-INVESTED ENTERPRISES IN THE CHINESE ECONOMY

In 1999, the Chinese government reported a foreign direct investment (FDI) inflow in the amount of $40.4 billion.[1] This was a sharp drop from $45.6 billion in 1998, and government officials and economic analysts have begun to voice concerns about the economic effects of FDI contraction for China. Indeed, one of the alleged benefits associated with the impending Chinese membership in the World Trade Organization is to stem the contractionary FDI trend.

During the reform era and especially since 1992, foreign-invested enterprises (FIEs) have become an important component in the Chinese economy, often to an extent that outside analysts fail to appreciate fully. Just a few numbers may be helpful to illustrate this point. In 1995, manufacturing FIEs accounted for about 47 percent of Chinese manufacturing exports and 24 percent of manufacturing sales. In a number of industries, FIEs have established a dominant business position. In the electronics and telecommunications industry, for example, FIEs accounted for 95 percent of the Chinese exports and 61 percent of the sales. On average, foreign firms controlled 55 percent of equity of the manufacturing FIEs in China. If we

---

[1] All dollar amounts are in U.S. dollars unless otherwise stated.

use 50 percent as the cutoff point to measure the allocation of control rights of a firm, by 1995, multinational corporations (MNCs) already established effective managerial control over FIEs in China, and the Chinese firms in joint ventures were minority shareholders.[2] FIEs have become industrial leaders in a number of areas in the Chinese economy. Table 7.1 lists a number of such sectors and firms. The information is based on a study by the State Planning Commission (SPC). The FIEs' encroaching market share is still a sensitive issue in China. The SPC presents the statistics in Table 7.1 in a sharply critical manner. In addition, the same report notes that in light industries, electronics, and the chemical industry, FIEs' shares in sales have already exceeded 30 percent.

The growing financing and economic roles of FIEs in the Chinese economy can be described as an "FIE phenomenon." This chapter explains this phenomenon in two ways. One shows that much of the presently accepted explanation does not hold up to close scrutiny and that there is need for a more rigorous interpretation of this issue. The other lays out an analytical framework that stresses the importance of China's institutions and policies in understanding the FIE phenomenon. I call this framework an institutional foundation ap-

Table 7.1

Estimates for the Share of Foreign-Invested Enterprises of the Total Domestic Sales and of the Number of Firms (percentages)

	Shares of Domestic Sales	Shares of Firms
Industries		
Baby Food	20	
Cosmetics	30	18.8
Glassware	30	3/5[a]
Firms		
Xerox	42	
Motorola	70	

[a]Three out of the five largest firms are FIEs.
SOURCE: State Planning Commission (1994).

[2]These figures are based on Office of Third Industrial Census (1997).

[3]Much of the argument presented here is laid out in Huang (2000).

proach with the basic premise that the important financing and economic roles of FIEs in the Chinese economy have institutional roots.[3] My approach has two main differences from conventional explanations. One is that the institutional foundation approach aims to uncover the alliance motivations of and the characteristics of Chinese shareholder firms, as opposed to the motivations and characteristics of foreign investing firms. I argue that Chinese motivations and their operating constraints are a critical part of the story underlying the FIE phenomenon. The other difference is that the institutional foundation approach constructs a micro story explaining growth and performance of FIEs. The typical approach relies on macro factors, such as economic fundamentals and the evolution of FDI regulations, as explanations.

There is also a microeconomic approach, which postulates that the most significant benefit associated with FDI is the technology that FDI capital is supposed to bring to a country. Indeed technology acquisition constituted the strongest motivation for China to open its doors to foreign trade and investment in the early 1980s. In an 1980 interview with journalists, Deng Xiaoping gave the rationale for establishing the four Special Economic Zones (SEZs) as follows:

> Technology, science and even advanced production management, which is also a kind of science, will be useful in any society or country. We intend to acquire technology, science and management skills to serve our socialist production.[4]

Technology acquisition is nothing short of an intellectual mantra justifying FDI, but surprisingly there is little evidence that FDI inflows into China embody much hard or soft technology. FDI is more abundant in industries that are relatively low-tech, and foreign controls of Chinese firms are found to be quite significant even in those industries in which Chinese firms and entrepreneurs should possess competitive advantages. For example, foreign control of operations in China's traditional handicraft industries is substantial despite the fact that these are industries the Chinese have practiced for thousands of years.

---

[4]See Ziaoping (1993 <1984>).

These analytical and empirical anomalies call for a more rigorous examination of FDI inflows into China than hitherto has been provided. The institutional foundation approach does that, and it argues that much of the explanation lies with gaining a better and detailed understanding of Chinese financial and economic institutions. This chapter begins by describing what is meant by the "FIE phenomenon" in China during the reform era and especially in the 1990s. The second section sketches a number of conventional explanations and describes their problems. The third section presents the institutional foundation approach and discusses some empirical evidence. This section concludes with a discussion of policy issues related to rising intra-firm trade associated with China's large FDI inflows.

THE FIE PHENOMENON

Foreign investment is most commonly defined as "direct" when the investment gives rise to "foreign control" of domestic assets. Thus according to the International Monetary Fund (IMF), FDI "is made to acquire a lasting interest in an enterprise operating in an economy, other than that of the investor, the investor's purpose being to have an effective voice in the management of the enterprise." In the United States, the Department of Commerce defines FDI as a foreign investor's stake exceeding 10 percent. A 10 percent threshold is quite common among countries in the Organization for Economic Cooperation and Development (OECD). Under this definition, if a foreign firm acquires more than a 10 percent stake in a U.S. concern on the New York Stock Exchange, this capital inflow is credited to the FDI account of the balance of payment statistics, not to the portfolio account. This brings up an important difference between the U.S. and China. A large share of FDI inflows into China finances foreign equity stakes in joint ventures—i.e., ownership alliances between foreign and domestic firms. There are usually only two investors in a joint venture, and unlike the diffused shareholding of publicly traded corporations, foreigners need to acquire a greater equity stake to establish "an effective voice in the management of the enterprise" in China.

The other purpose according to the IMF is to preclude "fake" FIEs from enjoying many of the policy benefits granted to FIEs, but to establish "an effective voice in the management of the enterprise" also requires a higher foreign equity stake in China since most Chinese joint venture partners are state-owned enterprises (SOEs), whose shares, like closed corporations, are not traded.

FDI inflows are the most widely cited and watched measure of FDI. As the name suggests, FDI inflows connote the quantity of FDI received by the host country during a given period of time. This is to be distinguished from FDI stocks, which refer to the accumulation of FDI inflows at a given point in time. Table 7.2 reports FDI inflows as measured by the number of approved applications and the dollar values of approved and actual inward FDI inflows.

FDI/Capital Formation Ratio

As shown in Table 7.2, the absolute size of FDI inflows into China has been huge. In the 1990s, China accounted for about half of the total FDI going to developing countries. In 1996, the FDI inflow, on the

Table 7.2

Measures of FDI Inflows: Number of Projects, and Values of Approved and Actual FDI, 1979–1997

	Number of approved FDI applications	Approved FDI inflows ($ billions)	Actual FDI Inflows ($ billions)
1979–1982	922	6.01	1.17
1983	470	1.73	0.64
1984	1,856	2.65	1.26
1985	3,073	5.93	1.66
1986	1,498	2.83	1.87
1987	2,233	3.71	2.31
1988	5,945	5.30	3.19
1989	5,779	5.60	3.39
1990	7,273	6.60	3.49
1991	12,978	11.98	4.37
1992	48,764	58.12	11.01
1993	83,437	111.44	27.52
1994	47,549	82.68	33.77
1995	37,011	91.28	37.52
1996	24,556	73.28	41.73
1997	21,001	51.00	45.26

SOURCE: State Statistical Bureau, 1998, p. 138.

paid-in basis, amounted to $41.7 billion. This compares to about $80 billion that went to the United States in the same year. The third largest destination of FDI capital is the United Kingdom, which received $30 billion. This type of comparison led to the claim in the press that China was the second largest recipient of FDI capital in the world.

A more relevant measure is the relative size of FDI. Countries vary in their economic and market size, and the size of FDI flows ought to be gauged relative to the size of the host economy. The absolute size of FDI flows for the United States in 1996 is twice as large as the Chinese FDI, but the U.S. economy is roughly seven times as large (on the basis of official foreign exchange conversion). In that sense, the United States is less "dependent" on FDI than China is even though the absolute size of FDI flows is much greater.

A more useful measure is what is sometimes known as the "FDI/capital formation ratio." The ratio is given by FDI divided by the total fixed asset investments made by foreign and domestic entities in a given year. This is a more empirically and conceptually useful measure. Empirically, the ratio tells us something about the relative importance of FDI to a country's economy. Conceptually, the FDI/capital formation ratio is driven by the willingness on the part of foreign investors to invest in a country relative to the willingness on the part of domestic investors to do the same. If the FDI/capital formation ratio rises or falls within a short period of time (as it did in China in the 1990s), this would raise an interesting research question as to why foreign and domestic investors should view the same market growth opportunities differently.

Frequently business and academic analysts invoke China's growing market size as an explanation for the explosive FDI growth in the 1990s. But this reasoning does not really settle the issue. When a firm invests in fixed assets (machinery, equipment, and other productive facilities), it puts down money today in the expectation of greater *future* profit payoffs. The key word here is future because investment is an inter-temporal activity and amounts to a decision to forgo current consumption in exchange of greater consumption possibilities in the future. Because there is no guarantee that the firm will make more money by investing in fixed assets as compared to investing the same money in safer bank deposits, a firm's investment decision is guided by its belief of what the future holds in store. It will put down more money if it believes that the market prospects in the future are promising. It will put down less if it believes otherwise. If the growing Chinese market size attracts lots of FDI (as measured by the increasing share of FDI of capital formation), one has to prepare to argue that for some reason domestic firms are not in the same position to take advantage of the future market opportunities. A rising FDI/capital formation ratio obviously suggests that domestic firms are not investing as much as foreign firms. Is it because domestic firms perceive the future market opportunities differently from foreign firms? Or is it because foreign firms are in a better position to reap the rewards of the market growth than domestic firms? For example, foreign firms may be able to offer a product lineup that is more income elastic than what domestic firms can offer. Nokia and Ericsson may offer mobile phone units to affluent Chinese consumers that Chinese telecommunication equipment makers are unable to match. Or foreign firms may possess entrepreneurial talents to spot future market opportunities that have eluded domestic firms. Another possibility is that domestic firms are bogged down by poor performance, burdened by mounting financial and social liabilities, and beset with incentive problems and managerial incompetence. No matter what explains the asymmetric investment behavior on the part of foreign and domestic firms, a simple macro explanation focusing on market size (or on labor costs) is inadequate. Strictly speaking, an account of FDI growth is not about FDI growth *per se* but is about why foreign firms have invested more than domestic firms. To address why foreign investors are more willing than domestic investors to invest (or vice versa), the FDI/capital formation ratio comes in handy.

Between 1993 and 1997, on average, in China FDI flows accounted for about 15 percent of total capital formation. This ratio is one of the highest among all developing countries. Only Singapore, Chad, and Hungary have a substantially higher ratio. As pointed out before, even though the United States attracted a greater amount of FDI, the relative importance of FDI in the case of the United States is far smaller than it is in the case of China. FDI only accounts for some 6 percent of total investments; China's FDI dependency is almost three times as large. It is worth noting that China is commonly viewed as a closed and controlled economy. According to the economic freedom ranking devised by the Heritage Foundation in the United States, China is classified as a "mostly unfree economy." Yet its FDI dependency is higher—and in some cases substantially higher—than such completely open economies as those of the United States (with an FDI/capital formation ratio of 6.38 percent), the United Kingdom (12.4 percent), Hong Kong (10.24 percent), Taiwan (2.78 percent), Thailand (3.76 percent), and Malaysia (14.12 percent).

Commanding Positions of Foreign-Invested Enterprises (FIEs) in the Chinese Economy

A few statistics in Table 7.3 are quite startling. As of 1995, FIEs controlled almost half of China's manufacturing exports (47.11 percent). In a number of industries, such as electronics and telecommunications, garments, leather products, printing and record pressing, cultural products, and plastics, FIEs have acquired a dominant position. They account for over 60 percent of Chinese exports. Their sales are not insignificant either. In four industries, their sales exceeded 50 percent of industry sales, and altogether FIEs accounted for 24 percent of the sales.

Often, China's overall success in increasing export production is attributed to the strong export orientation of FIEs. That FIEs account for over 47 percent of Chinese export is often taken as evidence that FDI has contributed to China's export success. The real story is far more complex, depending on two developments in China's export front. One is export/GDP shares; the other is FIEs' shares of Chinese exports. Between 1991 and 1997, FIEs' share of Chinese exports has risen from about 15 percent to 40 percent, while export/GDP share rose by only 5 percent. This is *prima facie* evidence that FIEs have both created exports and diverted exports at the same time. During the course of the 1990s, as more FDI flowed in, foreign firms have taken over those Chinese firms engaged in export production. Thus the high share of FIEs in Chinese exports needs to be interpreted carefully. Export orientation is only a part of the story; export diversion from Chinese-owned firms is another—and frequently neglected—story.

The significant position of FIEs in the Chinese economy raises a natural question about who controls FIEs. Corporate control is a complicated concept, but the simplest measure is an investor's share of equity ownership of a firm. The higher the share, the more control an investor is said to have of a corporation since equity ownership is usually proportional to the amount of decisionmaking power. Since many FIEs in China are joint ventures, decisionmaking is shared between Chinese and foreign investors, and allocation of decision-making power is determined on the basis of respective shares of equity ownership.

Foreign firms have established majority controls over FIEs in most industries. Only in seven out of 28 manufacturing industries are foreign firms found with an average minority equity position—i.e., an equity stake less than 0.50. State-owned monopolies or oligopolies are typically found in those industries where foreign firms only command a minority stake. The tobacco industry is probably the best illustration. But it should be noted that even in this heavily monopolistic industry, foreign firms already enjoy a sizable minority stake, at 46.88 percent. As I will show in this chapter, while foreign firms have been able to make inroads into industries explicitly reserved for the most powerful government corporations, nonstate firms have been completely excluded. Another characteristic is that foreign majority equity controls seem unrelated to some of the well-known features of these industries. Foreign majority controls span both labor-intensive industries, such as garments and leather products, and capital-intensive industries, such as chemicals, machinery, and instrument manufacturing.

Performance of FIEs

In China, no less than in other countries, foreigners' growing presence in industries steeped in national and political symbolism can be an emotionally wrenching experience. It is no longer considered normal business competition, proclaimed one worried Chinese official from the auto industry; it is nothing short of geopolitical war. Of the four so-called pillar industries designated by the Chinese government, FIEs have a significant presence in two of them. In electronics and telecommunications, FIEs' equity stake has already exceeded that of domestic firms, at 53 percent in 1997. FIEs accounted for 47 percent of the assets and 63 percent of pretax profits. In the

Table 7.3

Sectoral Characteristics of FIEs in the Chinese Manufacturing Industries, 1995 (percentages)

Manufacturing Industries (2-digit Chinese SIC)	Industry Distribution of Foreign Actual Capital	Ratio of FIE Exports to Exports of All Firms	Ratio of FIE Sales to Sales of All Firms	Ratio of FIE Exports to FIE Sales	Foreign Equity Shares of FIEs
Food processing	1.47	57.46	21.15	24.47	57.50
Food manufacturing	4.56	38.65	30.48	16.57	63.96
Beverage manufacturing	4.42	37.84	26.20	4.46	56.43
Tobacco processing	0.08	2.51	0.56	17.27	46.88
Textile industry	8.89	28.58	17.88	48.59	52.02
Garments and other fiber products	6.00	60.51	50.81	71.74	63.30
Leather and related products	3.55	73.21	54.14	73.58	63.94
Timber processing and related products	1.44	57.70	27.27	31.54	54.19
Furniture manufacturing	0.78	75.09	30.67	45.77	53.87
Papermaking and paper products	3.13	53.41	17.01	20.80	61.77
Printing and record pressing	1.58	79.39	18.26	19.79	51.68
Cultural, educational, and sports activities	1.90	69.02	50.71	81.29	73.56
Petroleum processing and products	0.18	8.50	1.41	21.84	48.14
Chemical materials and products	5.82	31.62	12.62	22.67	57.46
Medical and pharmaceutical products	1.98	21.89	18.28	16.89	46.22
Chemical fibers	1.42	41.48	12.65	26.27	48.92
Rubber products	1.79	53.29	24.98	39.73	59.09
Plastic products	5.06	77.17	33.05	42.59	54.43
Nonmetal mineral products	7.72	38.93	11.40	21.41	51.46
Smelting and pressing of ferrous metals	1.73	6.30	6.23	9.34	42.73
Smelting and pressing of nonferrous metals	1.18	24.40	12.51	17.97	40.44

Table 7.3 —continued

Manufacturing Industries (2-digit Chinese SIC)	Industry Distribution of Foreign Actual Capital	Ratio of FIE Exports to Exports of All Firms	Ratio of FIE Sales to Sales of All Firms	Ratio of FIE Exports to FIE Sales	Foreign Equity Shares of FIEs
Metal products	5.53	61.14	26.64	47.21	59.52
Ordinary machinery manufacturing	3.98	30.58	14.50	21.92	52.63
Special purpose equipment	1.94	35.47	8.95	27.68	51.01
Transportation equipment	5.86	30.42	25.21	7.58	46.54
Electric equipment and machinery	6.61	58.31	21.80	34.28	57.69
Electronic and telecommunications	9.62	94.45	60.80	59.11	61.02
Instruments	1.79	71.81	38.83	51.21	65.79
All manufacturing (total or average values)	100.00	47.11	24.11	32.98	55.08

auto industry, where state-owned enterprises (SOEs) are more entrenched than those in electronics and telecommunications, and the government has attempted to tailor and limit foreigners' equity participation, by 1997, foreign firms accumulated a significant stake in this industry, at 21 percent, as compared with 63 percent held by the government and only 3 percent held by Chinese private firms. Foreign shares of the seven largest auto firms came to 16 percent; the rest is exclusively held by the state.[5]

FIEs are also much more profitable than domestic firms are. In 1996, China's balance of payment account recorded a profit expenditure figure of $11.6 billion, a sharp increase from past years. Profit expenditure represents profit distribution to foreign investors. The profit figures look even more impressive if one looks beyond FIEs themselves and compares their performance with China's main form of corporate organizations—SOEs. The story about the sharply differing fortunes of FIEs and SOEs can be told from a number of perspectives. The simplest is the rise of FIEs as a significant force in China's economy from a de novo presence only 18 years ago. As of 1996, there were 43,542 industrial FIEs and 240,447 FIEs in the entire economy. Industrial FIEs accounted for 16 percent of the industrial value-added and 17 percent of assets.[6]

Probably, the thing that distinguishes FIEs most from SOEs is their financial performance. In 1996, 43,542 industrial FIEs reported a posttax profit of Renminbi (RMB) 40.79 billion, while some 86,982 SOEs managed to churn out a paltry 500 million more, at RMB 41.26 billion. Other financial measures tell exactly the same tale. In all likelihood, these amounts understate FIEs' success and SOEs' woes. FIEs are suspected of using transfer pricing to hide profits (discussed later); SOEs, on the other hand, exaggerate their profit and sale figures to make their income statements look attractive to banks and have very conservative write-off policies on their accumulated inventories and conservative provisions against their large accounts receivable.

---

[5]These data are reported in State Bureau of Machinery Industry (1998).

[6]All these figures and those reported below cover only enterprises that are independent accounting units.

THE FAILURE OF CONVENTIONAL WISDOM

Despite the growing importance of FIEs in the Chinese economy, most of the academic literature has not attempted to explain the FIE phenomenon as defined here—i.e., the factors that account for the growth of FDI over time and the increasing importance of FIEs in the Chinese economy. Academic writing on FDI in China have focused on relatively targeted subjects.[7] For example, economists have focused on the economic effects of FDI in China, such as export performance and economic growth via effects on productivity and competitiveness of markets. Economic writings thus approach FDI from a developmental perspective and focus on an issue that all developmental economists care about—economic growth. Exactly how FDI gets to be so important is usually left out in this discussion; instead the financing and economic roles of FIEs are taken as a starting point of analysis, and the interest is to explore their implications. Political scientists have approached the study of FDI from a totally different perspective. Their principal focus is on the effect of increasing FDI on the ability of the state to maintain control over its own economic and political agenda. This approach is rooted in the "bargaining" literature on FDI. Again why there is a high demand for FDI in the Chinese economy and why FIEs have grown so quickly are left out in this account.

What is important to note is that the Chinese patterns of FDI described above are not easily clarified by conventional explanations. In this section, I discuss the explanations based on conventional wisdom into macroeconomic and microeconomic explanations and discuss them in turn.

Macroeconomic Explanations

Macroeconomists often invoke the so-called "savings-investment" gap theory to explain FDI flows.[8] The reasoning is straightforward. An internal imbalance in a developing economy—a resource gap

[7]See Kamath (1990) and Pomfret (1991) in economics and Pearson (1991) in political science. In addition, Shirk (1994) tangentially addresses the issue of state control, although the subject matter is not limited to FDI.

[8]The discussion in this section is based on Meier (1995, especially pp. 247–263).

between its savings and its investment requirements—leads to an external imbalance on the country's balance of payment: Shortage of foreign exchange. This shortage must be financed by a combination of drawing down the foreign exchange reserves and an inflow of foreign exchange in a variety of forms. FDI is one such inflow.

The saving-investment gap, however, is conspicuously incongruous with China's large FDI absorption. In the 1990s, China had one of the highest savings rates in the world, at 41.76 percent between 1994 and 1997. The puzzle is that China's reliance on FDI deepened at the very time when the capital shortage was being alleviated. By all indications, China should be awash in capital. China's savings rate rose from an initially high level throughout the reform era. Between 1986 and 1992, the savings rate hovered around 36 percent, but between 1994 and 1997, the savings rate rose to 42 percent, second only to Singapore (51 percent).[9] The acceleration of the savings rate coincided closely with an explosive growth of FDI. Between 1979 and 1997, the gross cumulative FDI flows were $220 billion on the paid-in basis. Much of this FDI was invested since 1992. Between 1992 and 1997, the total FDI inflow was a whopping $196.8 billion. Thus China imported more capital when it saved more and imported less capital when it saved less! China's balance of payment statistics bear out this suspicion. In the 1990s, China ran a current account deficit only in 1993, and simple economic logic would predict that in other current account surplus years China is a net capital exporter, not an importer. This is precisely what happened. On average between 1994 and 1997, China exported capital to the rest of the world to the tune of almost 3 percent of its GDP. The large FDI inflows, on top of large current account surpluses throughout much of the 1990s, led to a huge accumulation of foreign exchange reserves, to the tune of $140.9 billion six months into 1998.

The simultaneous large FDI inflows and the large capital outflows at a very low rate of return are rather strange from the point of view of the capital shortage argument for FDI. The Chinese are striving to give up the ownership of their economy only to use the capital surpluses to invest in low-yielding government bonds in America. In a

---

[9]The savings rate is defined as the difference between GDP and final consumption divided by GDP. The data are reported in State Statistical Bureau (1998).

country of poor peasants, China borrows heavily from the rest of the world so that it can finance government spending in industrialized countries, an outcome a former Chinese central banker calls "scandalous."[10] By all indications, the Chinese are poor arbitrageurs. The country pays on average 8 percent on its foreign debt but only gets 5 percent returns on its investments abroad. One is hard pressed to think of an economic justification for this outcome but if there is, fund shortage is not one of them. Given China's status as a capital exporter, any convincing explanation for China's high FDI dependency needs to move beyond the capital shortage argument.

Another version of the macroeconomic story postulates that FDI is driven by China's market size. The idea is simple and straightforward: MNCs are attracted to China's economic fundamentals—fast income growth, a large population, a cheap and disciplined labor force, etc. This explanation, which focuses on the economic fundamentals, is correct, by definition and default. It is not hard to imagine that FDI inflows would have to be modest if these economic fundamentals were not sufficiently attractive to investing firms. However, it is important to recall that the rapid growth of the roles of foreign companies in China is relatively recent. The real surge in FDI inflows took place after 1992; the cumulative FDI inflows between 1992 and 1997 accounted for some 89 percent of FDI stock between 1979 and 1997. During the 1980s, FDI grew steadily, but not at a spectacular rate, even though Chinese economic growth was already quite impressive during this period. Thus, if we accept the notion that economic fundamentals drive FDI inflows, this gap in timing needs to be explained.

The economic fundamentals explanation poses other puzzles. The good economic fundamentals themselves do not automatically drive up FDI inflows. For one thing, foreign firms may prefer exporting to investing in foreign sites, and overseas investments thus occur only when there are impediments to exporting. In addition, FDI policies of host countries can be promotional or restrictive, and these policies have a big effect on the levels of FDI. This is abundantly clear when one examines the history of FDI in East Asian newly industrialized economies (NIEs)—countries that grew extremely fast in the 1970s

[10]Quoted in Smith (1998).

and 1980s but without much foreign equity participation. Amsden (1989) points out that the number of multinationals in Korea is smaller than in any other late industrializing countries. Policy barriers against FDI were an important reason. In a 1980 survey, 23 percent of the foreign executives in Korea listed "cumbersome bureaucratic procedures" as the number one impediment Stallings (1990). Japan, the world's second largest economy, has a level of FDI inflows lower than the level of Greece Graham (1994). Thus, the economic fundamentals explanation provides a *necessary* but not a sufficient account of FDI growth—i.e., those countries with high levels of FDI must have good economic fundamentals but there can be countries with good economic fundamentals but with low levels of FDI. This distinction between necessary and sufficient conditions for FDI growth often gets blurred in the business press.

To a large extent, the economic fundamentals explanation asks the wrong question in the first place. Even if good economic fundamentals drive up FDI inflows, the core issue is not the growth of FDI inflows *per se*. The core issue is the growth of FDI inflows relative to the growth of domestic investments. If the foreign share in fixed asset investment is expanding, it must mean that domestic investment is not rising as fast. To be sure, good economic fundamentals induce more investment, but why have there been more *foreign* investments? Do foreign firms have a better edge in responding to the growth opportunities than domestic firms? Do foreign firms, for some reason, see the market opportunities that elude domestic firms? Or do foreign firms have an optimistic bias, while domestic firms have a pessimistic bias? This is an especially important issue because more and more of FDI inflows are now financing asset purchases from domestic firms, rather than newly generated investments. Strictly speaking, an account of FDI growth is not about FDI growth *per se* but is about why foreign firms have invested more than domestic firms (as the increasing share of FDI of domestic capital formation indicates). Thus our story has to start with explaining why, over time, foreign firms have gained advantages relative to domestic firms and the factors causing the advantages of foreign firms to rise over time.

Cheap labor, in and of itself, does not drive up FDI. It is important to stress that FDI is an *ownership* arrangement—i.e., each investor puts up the capital to establish an equity stake in a firm. As an ownership arrangement, FDI is one of many cross-border alliances between a foreign and a Chinese firm. Low labor costs motivate MNCs to locate their production in China, but low labor costs per se do not mean that MNCs have to resort to an FDI arrangement. Except for those situations in which contractual complications naturally arise, such as asset-specificity and the associated opportunism, contract production results in the same cost-saving benefits as does FDI. For example, a Hong Kong firm can contract out a firm in China to produce goods and services according to the exact specifications it lays out, and the Hong Kong firm will reap the same labor-saving benefits as investing in China. The question is not whether or not producing in China is cheaper or more expensive than in Hong Kong; the question is, why do so many firms from Hong Kong resort to FDI rather than contractual production to realize labor-cost savings benefits.

One form of market transactions is export processing. Under export processing, a Chinese firm still relies on a foreign firm for the latter's overseas marketing capabilities, but it remains a separate *ownership* entity from the foreign firm. The foreign firm has no equity stakes in the Chinese firm, and the relationship between the Chinese and foreign firms is fundamentally contractual. But their relationship is not completely arms-length either, since a lot of coordination is involved between them. For example, the foreign firm supplies designs, specifications, and components to the Chinese firm, and the Chinese firm produces the goods in accordance and receives a payment for the goods delivered to the satisfaction of the foreign firm.

The history of export-oriented FDI in China is one of replacing market transaction mechanisms, such as export processing, with nonmarket transactions through intra-affiliate cross-border sales. National figures on FIE exports and contractual exports are only available since 1996, but more systematic data are available for Fujian and Guangdong provinces—which have received the lion's share of FDI. In Fujian province, in 1988, the FIE exports to export processing ratio was 3.64; it rose sharply to 22.45 in 1990 and then to 45.47 in 1992. In Guangdong province, FIE exports rose less dramatically but still far faster than export processing. At the national level, in 1996, FIE exports were about twice the size of contractual exports.

Another measure is to compare the amount of capital that finances FDI with the amount of the capital that finances contractual production. In the Chinese statistical classification, investment data are broken down by direct investments (FDI) and other investments. Other investments are essentially contractual capital flows, such as leasing, compensation trade, and export processing. In 1983, contractual capital flows were about 45 percent of the FDI inflows, but they took a sharp decline in 1984 and experienced further declines since 1988. Between 1992 and 1996, contractual capital flows virtually disappeared, but since 1996, they have risen in magnitude. The declining contractual capital flows relative to ownership capital flows coincided closely with the rounds of FDI liberalization in the 1980s and 1990s. In 1984, fourteen coastal cities were given expanded power to approve FDI projects; in 1988, the government pushed for further economic openings. Between 1992 and 1996, the Chinese government initiated another round of extensive and far-reaching liberalization of FDI controls. Thus, when a domestic firm and a foreign firm are given a choice between an ownership and a contractual arrangement, they prefer to enter into an ownership arrangement. This preference for an ownership arrangement over a contractual one needs to be explained.

Microeconomic Explanations

Microeconomic explanations for FDI are also problematic. Microeconomic explanations start with the notion that FDI transfers know-how from home firms to host firms and to the extent that transferring such know-how is costly, via a contractual arrangement home firms then extend common ownership over facilities overseas to facilitate such a transfer.

The know-how explanation is problematic. First, if know-how refers to knowledge to operate advanced equipment and machinery, there is simply no evidence that FDI has brought much "hardware" know-how to China. No doubt, some FDI projects bring advanced technology to China, but many do not. The industries in China with the largest share of FDI are often those with a low capital content and low "knowledge worker ratios" (i.e., engineers to blue collar worker ratios). In the 1990s, FDI originating from Hong Kong and Taiwan accounted for between 50 to 70 percent of Chinese total FDI inflows, and much of this kind of FDI contains a low content of hardware know-how. Many Hong Kong and Taiwanese simply capitalized their standard and mature equipment and machinery as equity stakes in FIEs in China.

Contrast this pattern with China's technology imports through trade. Technology imports refer to importation of technology licensing, patents, and turnkey projects. In contrast to FDI, technology imports transfer technology to the host country via arms-length market transactions rather than through an ownership arrangement. Research by United Nations Centre on Transnational Corporations (1992) shows that typically the level of technology transfer associated with FDI is of more recent vintage and is more sophisticated as compared with the kind of technology transferred via arms-length market transactions. China, however, exhibits precisely the opposite patterns. This is shown by the country origins of technology trade vis-à-vis country origins of FDI. The majority of China's technology trade is with OECD countries, whereas the majority of China's FDI originates from non-OECD economies.

In the standard account of FDI, FDI materializes only when the know-how needed to operate the capital assets cannot be disembodied from the capital itself. Given the high degree of maturity and standardization of the capitalized equipment, it is a mystery why Chinese firms could not simply import these items. It would be a win-win situation for both sides. The equipment and machinery of Hong Kong and Taiwanese firms have been rendered increasingly uneconomical because of rising labor costs since the late 1970s, and the opening of China would have provided an opportunity for these two economies to transition very quickly to service economies.[11] Not only is there thin evidence of "hardware technology transfer," some researchers have reported on "negative technology transfer" associated with FDI—i.e., Chinese firms possessed more advanced hard-

---

[11]Despite the image of Hong Kong as one of the most important financial centers in the world, manufacturing and its ancillary operations were still an important part of Hong Kong's economy until quite recently. In 1993, manufacturing employment accounted for 22.6 percent of total employment. Thus, at a per-capita income greater than that of the Great Britain and at a rental price several times as that of Manhattan, Hong Kong still retained a substantial tie to labor-intensive manufacturing activities. I argue in my book (Huang, 2000) that this is strongly related to the fact that investing in China was made cheaper to Hong Kong manufacturing firms because of the institutional configuration of the Chinese economy. This allowed Hong Kong firms to retain their labor-intensive manufacturing operations in the territory longer than would have been economically feasible.

ware than the investing firms from Hong Kong and Taiwan.[12] Thus, overseas Chinese firms invest in China not to transfer technology but to exploit the strong research and development capabilities of mainland Chinese firms.

There is in fact a negative correlation between FIEs' equity shares and asset intensity. The fixed asset turnover ratio is the ratio of sales to net fixed assets. It measures the sales generated per unit of net fixed assets deployed and measures capital intensity of an industry, with a high ratio denoting low capital intensity and a low ratio denoting high capital intensity. Table 7.4 shows the equity ratios of FIEs and the fixed asset turnover ratios of eight industries—four of these FIEs have the highest equity shares and four of them have the lowest equity shares. The average asset intensity levels of the high FIE equity group is actually higher than that for the low group, 3.17 compared to 2.09. Tobacco processing and petroleum processing are heavily

Table 7.4

FIEs' Equity Shares and Asset Intensity of Eight Industrial Sectors, 1996

Industries	FIEs' equity shares	Fixed asset turnover ratio
Top four industries		
Electronics and telecommunications	0.55	3.21
Leather products	0.52	3.87
Garments	0.49	3.64
Food manufacturing	0.47	1.94
Average	0.51	3.17
Bottom four industries		
Tobacco processing	0.02	2.69
Petroleum processing	0.03	1.36
Smelting and pressing of ferrous metals	0.10	2.03
Special purpose equipment	0.10	2.03
Average	0.05	2.09

SOURCE: Based on the data in State Statistical Bureau (1997).

NOTES: Industries selected for this table refer to those in manufacturing only; FDI is restricted in mining and public utilities. FIEs' equity shares are calculated as the ratio of FIEs' equity in a sector to the value of equity of that sector. Fixed asset turnover ratios equal sales divided by net fixed assets.

---

[12]See Young and Lan (1997).

capital-intensive activities, and yet FIEs have almost no presence.[13] This suggests that FIEs are more dominant in industries of low capital intensity. The same pattern holds when one looks at the data for all industries. The simple bivariate correlation between fixed asset turnover ratio and FIEs' industrial equity shares for 1996 was not only positive but large, at 0.70.

The second type of evidence is more direct. It comes from survey and interview research conducted by scholars. Two researchers, Stephen Young and Ping Lan, have conducted the most systematic study on this topic so far. Their data come from a postal survey of 361 FIEs in Dalian city and interviews with managers from 36 of these FIEs. Their findings suggest that, on average, the level of technology as embodied in the FDI was two years ahead of China's existing level even though the "technology gap" between investing countries and China was commonly perceived to be 20 years. The "technology package" was in most cases incomplete, meaning that the package included only one or two of the three components that constitute a complete technology transfer—product, process, and organizational technology. Less than 25 percent of technology transfer projects incorporated all three components. One interesting finding of their research is that foreign firms apparently invested in China to source Chinese technology, in that a significant number of Chinese firms were more technologically advanced than their foreign investors.[14]

Technology is an intrinsically difficult concept to measure and quantify. FDI researchers correctly point out that what FDI brings to China is not hardware but software—referring broadly to foreign managerial and organizational skills and expertise. It is again important not to take such a claim at its face value, and it is important to examine the empirical evidence indicating such a function of FDI inflows into China. Organizational know-how transfer is harder to document because of its intangible nature, but again anecdotal and piecemeal evidence suggests that it is implausible to argue that the organizational know-how is present in all FDI projects (numbering

---

[13]It is likely that the government's restrictions on FIEs explain this outcome.

[14]See Young and Lan (1997).

over 80,000 in 1993 and more recently declining to about 20,000).[15] For one thing, FDI is not the only mechanism to import organizational know-how; for relatively simple and standard organizational know-how, again a contractual arrangement is entirely feasible. A Chinese firm can hire a foreign manager—for example by hiring a retired foreign manager at a cost that would be a fraction of the present value of the future cash flows on the sold equity. For years, Korean firms did exactly that to build up their organizational and managerial expertise when the economy was shifting from light and labor-intensive industries to capital and technology-intensive industries in the 1970s.

As any business owner would know, ceding equity is an expensive way to access managerial expertise and usually one only gives up equity in absence of alternative sources of financing. In venture capital projects, for example, debt financing is usually unavailable because banks value a stable source of cash flow, while technology entrepreneurial start-ups entail high risks (defined as high variance of their cash flows) and therefore they have to rely on equity capital from venture capitalists who are seeking to reap the huge upside if the project succeeds. In other situations, stock options are given to managers when these managers possess hard-to-measure and intangible attributes or when owners use stock options as a monitoring device. None of these conditions readily applies to Chinese firms in labor-intensive and mature industries actively seeking FDI, and, even if some of these conditions apply, there is no reason why foreign suppliers of capital should disproportionately be sought out at the expense of domestic capital suppliers in many situations.

The anomaly does not stop there. According to the Office of Third Industrial Census (1997), in 1995, there were 49,559 industrial FIEs at or above the level township and yet there were only 31,992 foreign employees. Assuming at minimum one foreign employee needs to be present to transfer intangible skills and know-how, this is a strange result indeed. There were 17,567 FIEs without any foreign employees.

---

[15]It is interesting that, in interviews, SOE managers typically invoke importing organizational know-how as a motivation to seek out foreign joint venture partners. Often in the same conversations, they also describe their own reluctance to spend money on training and human resource development.

AN INSTITUTIONAL FOUNDATION APPROACH

The fundamental premise in this chapter is that the growing roles of FIEs in the Chinese economy are driven not only by foreigners' supply of equity capital but also by the Chinese *demand* for foreign equity capital. The demand side of the story relates to the perceived benefits associated with foreign equity capital and to the Chinese motivations to form alliances with foreign firms. The central idea of this chapter is that desire for capital and technology do not constitute the full universe of Chinese alliance motivations and that Chinese alliance motivations are partially a function of Chinese economic institutions and policies. Thus, I term this the institutional and policy factors approach. Four such institutional factors are examined below: state ownership, economic decentralization, financial market inefficiency, and policy benefits.

State Ownership

An important feature of SOEs' behavior in China and in other reforming socialist economies is that SOEs have an insatiable investment appetite. Despite the impressive results of its economic reforms, China remains a partially reformed Centrally-Planned Economy (CPE). In 1994, state-owned enterprises employed 67 percent of all urban employees and accounted for 57 percent of the total gross fixed capital formation. In comparison, as of the late 1970s, the state sector accounted for 32 percent and 23 percent, respectively, of the gross fixed capital formation in Taiwan and Korea.[16] The investment demand of state-owned enterprises is viewed as inefficient and excessive in reforming or partially reformed CPEs. Excess investment demand implies two kinds of behavior unique to SOEs in CPEs. *Ex ante*— excess investment demand means there are weak self-enforcing constraints on investment demand; *ex post*—demand for investments constantly exceeds the potential supply of investible resources, such as capital, intermediate goods, or, as the case may be, foreign exchange. Excess investment demand arises because there is a fundamental asymmetry in the incidence of costs and benefits associated with undertaking investment activities

[16]Wade, 1990, p. 177.

in a CPE. Benefits—enhanced reputation and higher financial rewards—accrue to the investors, while investment costs are borne by society at large. This is a situation analogous to "negative externalities" in market economies, and the consequences are similar: The costs of the affected activities are lower than socially optimal; therefore incentives to undertake these activities are stronger than when the external costs are taken into account. As Kornai[17] comments:

> Expansion drive is a fact of life for the bureaucracy. And because this system has only bureaucrats and no real owners, there is an almost total lack of internal, self-imposed restraint that might resist this drive.

A second and closely related characteristic of SOEs has to do with the budgetary environment in which they operate. SOEs are said to face "soft budget constraints," which refer to a bureaucratic readiness to provide financial assistance and, ultimately, to prevent bankruptcy.[18] Soft budget constraints, in essence, imply zero risks for the investment activities undertaken by a SOE. They are the second reason why restraints on investment demand are not self-enforcing on SOEs.[19] The lack of a credible threat of bankruptcy shapes alliance motivations and behavior profoundly. For one thing, it is entirely possible that forming joint ventures is an extension of the excess investment demand on the part of SOEs. But there are more subtle connections. Launching joint ventures can be a costly proposition, especially for cash-constrained SOEs. There are two common funding approaches. One is that SOEs contribute their best-performing fixed assets and workforce to new ventures to finance their equity stakes when they have low cash reserves. The other approach is that SOEs borrow heavily to finance their equity injections into new ven-

---

[17]Kornai, 1992, p. 163.

[18]For further illustrations, see Kornai, 1980, #228.

[19]One may object by pointing to a similar phenomenon in market economies—savings and loan institutions in the U.S. economy. But this observation is a mere restatement of the same point. Savings and loan institutions are federally insured and hence face a similar budgetary environment as a normal CPE firm. The recklessness of their behavior then critically depends on the degree of government supervision; if government supervision becomes lax, as it did in the 1980s, behavior tends to be reckless. For a more substantial treatment of this topic, see Huang (2000).

tures. This is evidenced by the fact that in sectors with a high foreign equity stake, SOEs tend to be highly leveraged, as measured by debt to equity and debt to asset ratios.[20] The simple bivariate correlation between SOEs' debt levels and FIEs' sectoral equity stake is very high. For the debt to asset ratio, it was 0.74 and for debt to equity ratio, it was 0.72. The four sectors with highest foreign equity stakes are electronics and telecommunications equipment (55 percent), leather and related products (52 percent), garments and fiber products (49 percent), and food manufacturing (47 percent). The SOEs' debt to asset ratios in these four sectors are, respectively, 0.76, 0.86, 0.71, and 0.77. The average debt to asset ratio for all the industrial sectors is 0.68.[21]

There are both balance sheet and income statement implications from these asset contribution methods. By forming joint ventures, SOEs essentially convert their fixed assets into long-term financial holdings on their balance sheets. In a number of cases, because SOEs took on so much debt to finance their equity stakes in FIEs, they put themselves in a technical bankruptcy under Chinese law, when shareholder equity is negative and when sudden collapse of operating revenue creates a default situation. In less dramatic situations, because the shareholder SOEs are left with the least productive assets and workforce, their profits tend to plummet after joint ventures are created. Those SOEs that contribute cash became highly leveraged and heavily burdened with interest payments. Here a critical driver of SOE alliance behavior is the *ex ante* expectation of bailouts by the state, and thus SOE managers tend to discount the costs and even the real bankruptcy prospects as a result of the aforementioned manners of financing joint ventures. Because loan obligations are soft or fiscal subsidy is readily available to SOEs in distress, SOE management may not feel constrained by the excessive burdens of asset conversion and expansions.[22]

---

[20]It is important to note that this is one of a few possible interpretations. Another possibility is that FIEs tend to gain advantages in sectors in which SOEs are failing. Thus high debt levels are not *ex post* but *ex ante*.

[21]All the data here refer to 1996.

[22]Their *ex ante* expectations can turn out to be false *ex post*, and this is highly likely when conflicts between Chinese shareholders and foreign shareholders escalate, with the Chinese shareholders insisting on dividend distribution while foreign shareholders insist on profit retention.

SOEs are also motivated positively to launch projects. A World Bank study finds an "engineering" motive particularly strong among Chinese SOEs (Byrd, 1987). An engineering motive can refer to a desire to produce an excellent product or to adopt the newest technology. The benefits are both psychological and tangible. A system of ranking enterprises and varying bonus, wage, and credit treatments according to their technological sophistication accentuate enormously the appetite for new technology.

The effect of a strong engineering motive on FDI can be illustrated by either the demand or supply sides of the story. On the demand side, it accentuates the demand for the type of capital closely bundled with technology. On the supply side, the high demand of Chinese SOEs for technology increases the owner-specific advantages possessed by MNCs. Many foreign investors readily confirm the constant demand for technology transfer from their Chinese partners and often such a demand is economically wasteful. The Chinese capacity to integrate technology is often poor, and as one Chinese economist pointed out, on average, the Chinese spend $1 on technological absorption for every $10 of technology import, an opposite ratio from Korean and Japanese firms in the 1960s and 1970s.[23] A senior Otis Elevator Company executive reflected on this issue in a Harvard Business School case study (1997, p. 8):

> We found the Chinese employees were always very eager to learn and improve their operations, but we still faced many difficulties in transferring technology. There were few engineers at the plants and a serious shortage of trained staff. When we transferred our drawings, CTOEC [China Tianjin Otis Elevator Company] often did not know what to do with them. This didn't, however, stop them from pressuring us to transfer our latest technology.

A third connection between state ownership and demand for FDI has to do with the sharp differences in terms of operational autonomy granted to SOEs vis-à-vis that granted to FIEs. Although many foreign executives complain about governmental restrictions placed on their operations, FIEs enjoy far greater autonomy than SOEs. SOE managers are appointed by the government (specifically by the

---

[23]See Wu (1996).

Organization Department of the Chinese Communist Party). Appointment decisions can often be a politicized process. In addition, SOEs are often subject to detailed and discretionary bureaucratic interference and to predatory taxes and fees. Herein lies a strong incentive to convert SOEs into FIEs on the part of the SOE managers—to arbitrage the significant differences in the legal, regulatory, and organizational autonomy between these two corporate forms. This motive gives rise to one of the most widely observed asset stripping actions undertaken by Chinese SOE managers—i.e., to deliberately undervalue the contributed assets and to evade the asset appraisal procedures stipulated by Chinese law. The reason is straightforward: Chinese SOE managers are motivated to increase the probability of creating joint ventures with foreign firms by giving up control.[24]

The arms-length relationship between government and FIEs is evidenced in a number of ways. First, the political control is much weaker in FIEs as compared with SOEs, not only by default but also by a rather explicit regulatory design. None of the FIE laws makes any explicit references to the Communist Party and mandates the establishment of party organizations within FIEs. To some extent, this is in contravention of the Charter of the Chinese Communist Party, which requires a party organization where there are more than three Communist Party members. A brief reference to the role of the party within FIEs is found in a manual prepared under the auspices of the Ministry of Foreign Economic Relations and Trade, which describes the role of the party as monitoring illicit conduct and educating FIE workers on ideology. No managerial role is prescribed.[25] In contrast, the 1986 Factory Director Regulations governing SOEs assigned broad and specific powers to the Communist Party, such as those ensuring the "socialist character of management," compliance with laws, fair distribution of interests among state, enterprise and workers, etc.[26] These functions would directly affect managers' production and wage/bonus setting policies. The reference to the Communist Party in the 1988 SOE Law was briefer, stipulating a

[24]According to one study, about 90 percent of joint ventures were formed without going through an asset appraisal process. See Qian (1996).

[25]See Li (1995, pp. 178–179).

[26]1986 Factory Director Regulations, Article 16, 1993 [1986] #1812.

monitoring and supervisory role to ensure compliance with party and state policies and regulations (Article 8). Interestingly, almost exactly identical wording referring to the Communist Party also appears in the 1991 Collectively Owned Enterprise (COE) Law (Article 10), although there is no similar provision in the 1990 Township and Village Enterprise (TVE) Law.[27]

The 1979 Equity Joint Venture Law established FIEs as independent legal persons separate from that of their shareholders and with a corporate structure broadly similar to that found in market economies. FIEs were to be shareholding corporations with limited liability and with a board of directors representing the interests of their shareholders. The ownership interests were transferable. Thus, from the onset of the open-door policy, FIEs acquired a corporate form that SOEs did not achieve until the 1993 Company Law, which gave legislative recognition to the legal independence of SOEs. Under the company law, SOEs acquired the set of organizational and corporate attributes that FIEs acquired 14 years earlier.

As an independent legal entity, FIEs were endowed with a set of *de jure* decision rights that exceeded those of SOEs, at least in the 1980s if not today. The division of these decision rights between government and enterprises has a large effect on the degree of operational autonomy available to firms. Probably the most important control right is the right to appoint managers. The 1979 Equity Joint Venture Law and an assortment of laws on other forms of FIEs vest this power with a board of directors. For SOEs, until the Company Law of 1993, which also established a board of directors for SOEs, this power resided with the supervisory line bureaus or ministries.

The differences in the *de jure* treatments of FIEs and SOEs do have a tangible effect on the actual operations of firms. In the 1980s and 1990s, several rounds of SOE reforms aimed at assigning significant fiduciary responsibilities to SOE managers. The 1988 SOE Law gave broad powers to SOE managers, including asset disposal. However, a number of surveys suggest that SOE managers are sharply constrained, even in the areas of operations in which they have been given explicit autonomy. A World Bank survey of 156 SOEs in 1994

---

[27]See [1991 Collectively Owned Enterprise Law, 1993 [1991] #1814] and [1990 Township and Village Enterprise Law, 1993 [1990] #1813].

shows that more than 60 percent of the SOEs surveyed indicated that they did not have autonomy in decisionmaking over trade, disposal of assets, and mergers and acquisitions. The Communist Party wields considerable power over personnel issues. A State Council study, cited in the aforementioned World Bank study, indicates that most SOEs did not have full investment authority, personnel decision rights, and the right to set wages. The conclusion from the study was that most of the 14 rights specified by the 1988 SOE Law remained with the line bureaus.[28]

Survey data indicate that FIEs are more independent from the government. In a 1995 survey, American firms in China ranked "bureaucratic interference" as the number three problem after inflation and rising accounts receivable,[29] even though only a few years earlier, it routinely took years to negotiate an investment deal with the Chinese government. In the early 1990s, Shanghai pioneered in setting up a "one-stop agency" to approve FDI applications, a practice copied by many regions. However, there is no similar agency for dealing with domestic investment applications. In 1995, ten government departments organized a comprehensive survey on managerial evaluations of their operational autonomy. Unlike the previous studies I cited, this survey included SOEs, collective firms, FIEs, and private enterprises, making a direct comparison possible.[30] The survey reveals, in a convincing fashion, that non-SOE managers enjoyed a far higher degree of operational autonomy, at least in their subjective evaluations. When asked what were the difficulties of improving enterprise management, the top three impediments cited by the SOE managers were, in descending order, (1) wrong managerial selection system, (2) incomplete delegation of authority over labor and personnel issues, and (3) too many surplus workers. All these factors were fundamentally driven by the structure of government-business relationships.

In contrast, the top three impediments cited by FIE managers all focused on internal operations of firms. They were (1) poor quality of

[28]World Bank (1997).

[29]Cited in Huang (1998). Survey Team of Chinese Managers 1996. [Almanac of China's Economy]. Beijing, pp. 943–960.

[30]The survey is reported in previous citation (1996).

managers, (2) lacking advanced managerial techniques, and (3) poor asset management.[31] Considering that many FIEs are affiliates of SOEs, this ranking is remarkable, in that it was almost exactly identical to the one given by private enterprise managers, indicating that FIEs have come to enjoy a similar level of operational autonomy as private enterprises.[32] In the same survey, 67.3 percent of SOE manager-respondents picked "evaluation by supervisory authorities" as their top concern, while only 39.7 percent of FIE manager-respondents did so. Of SOE manager-respondents, 15.4 percent gave "coordinating relationship with government agencies" when asked to pick activities to which they devote most of their time and effort. Only 7.9 percent of FIE manager-respondents did so.

Economic Decentralization

Arguably, one of the most prominent characteristics of contemporary China is the decentralized management of its economy. Compared with those of other developing and reforming centrally planned economies, Chinese regional officials not only control an enormous amount of economic resources but also make many decisions and policies quite autonomously from the central government. A proxy (although imperfect) indicator is the share of tax revenue collected by regional governments. In the early 1990s, regional governments collected about 66 percent of consolidated tax revenues and accounted for 67.4 percent of the total expenditure. In 1995, after the 1994 fiscal recentralization, the regional share was 47.8 percent on the revenue side but was still 70.7 percent on the expenditure side.[33]

The first and foremost manifestation of economic decentralization is that a vast majority of SOEs are under the direct control of regional governments. "Control" here means broadly *de facto* ownership

---

[31]The survey does not give the size breakdowns of the enterprises. The survey noted that 87.7 percent of the surveyed enterprises were large and medium sized. However it is not known whether the SOEs were larger than the FIEs. Size matters because government controls large enterprises more tightly than smaller enterprises.

[32]The top three impediments cited by private enterprise managers were (1) lacking advanced managerial techniques, (2) poor asset management, and (3) low quality of managers.

[33]This is calculated from SSB (1997), p. 235.

rights—the rights to make crucial decisions, to receive residual cash flows, and to dispose of assets. In 1995, there were 87,905 industrial SOEs, of which 83,167 were owned by regional governments. The locally owned SOEs accounted for 65 percent of total SOE assets and 64 percent of sales.[34] The ownership functions of regional governments are complemented by the broad regulatory power in their hands. Despite central policy prohibitions, it is widely known that local governments set up trade barriers against interregional trade as well as to curtail capital exports. This means that often it is difficult for a firm located in Province A to invest in Province B because of capital restraints.

The combination of ownership and regulatory functions in the hands of regional governments has a strong effect on interregional investment patterns. Consider the contrast between Shanghai Automotive Industrial Corporation (SAIC) and First Automotive Work (FAW) in Changchun, Jilin province. In 1997, SAIC had 36 billion yuan in assets, about four times of that of FAW (9.4 billion yuan). Yet each one of its 38 subsidiaries and affiliates are located in Shanghai. FAW, despite its smaller size, made active acquisitions outside Jilin province. Its subsidiaries and affiliates are located in Beijing, Xinjiang, Shandong, Qinghuai, etc. The fundamental difference between SAIC and FAW is that SAIC is controlled by the Shanghai municipal government, whereas FAW is controlled by the Ministry of Machinery Industry in Beijing, and thus it is not tied to the Jilin province.

The local ownership arrangement means that foreign capital plays a unique role that would be absent under an alternative ownership arrangement. Because there are no similar constraints on the mobility of foreign capital, foreign firms are free to fund firms wherever there is a capital shortage. Given the immobility of domestic capital, interregional capital competition then becomes indistinguishable from competition for foreign capital at the international level. This dynamic plausibly explains why China can have high FDI inflows while having the world's highest savings rate. Capital-rich regions or firms export capital to foreign countries via large trade surpluses because domestic investment opportunities are limited by regulations

[34]The data are from the 1995 industrial census. See Office of Third Industrial Census (1997).

and policies. Capital-poor provinces import capital from foreign countries to make up for the shortage. The overall effect is that foreign companies have come to play an arbitrage role that is lacking in the domestic financial market and thus have acquired a greater financing role in the Chinese economy, given the enormous financial market inefficiency of financial segmentation along regional lines.[35]

MNCs are not only multinational; they are, first and foremost, multiregional in China. Motorola, Schindler, Otis, Volkswagen, Ford, Nabisco, etc. have all established operations across the country, and, increasingly, Western MNCs are creating a holding company structure to coordinate their complex activities and interactions among their subsidiaries or affiliates and to economize on shared overhead costs. These cross-regional investments or acquisitions are not limited to *Fortune 500* corporations. A prominent example is Hong Kong–based China Strategic Investment Ltd. China Strategic Investment, with sale revenues of only $84 million in 1992, acquired 200 companies in China during a span of two years between 1992 and 1994. Its joint ventures are located in more than nine provinces, and its China Tires Holdings, via its acquisitions of tire plants in five provinces, emerged to be the largest tire producer in China in 1994 (Lim, 1994).

The second connection between economic decentralization and FDI demand is local protectionism. Chinese regional governments, in a way, all pursue a version of import substitution strategy analogous to the one pursued by Latin American countries in the 1970s, and this strategy has exactly the same effects on FDI. Because trade is restricted, either via implicit or explicit tariffs or quotas, market access is conditioned upon building and operating production facilities behind a protective wall. In this case, the interregional trade restrictions act exactly the same way as trade restrictions at a country level: They both raise returns from investments relative to trade and thus induce the type of investments that are designed to get behind trade protection to access the market. Because of the mobility of foreign

---

[35]There are specific examples of foreign companies playing this arbitrage role. China Strategic Investment's typical approach is to finance its acquisitions from the proceeds from revenues generated by previous acquisitions. This strategy enabled it to acquire some 200 companies between 1992 and 1994, even though its sales revenue in Hong Kong amounted to only $80 million.

equity capital relative to domestic equity capital, import substitution strategy at the regional level induces more *foreign* investment.

The second effect is less direct. Import substitution strategy, as is well-known in economics, creates rents and induces rent-capturing activities (Krueger, 1974). Rents accentuate domestic capital immobility; regional governments are not only loathe to export capital to other regions, they are also loathe to import capital from other regions, lest rents created in their regions accrue to other regions. This would mean that regional governments would demand something more than capital before agreeing to any rent-sharing arrangements without outsiders. Foreign companies are the beneficiaries of this preference because they possess know-how and technology and because FIE status itself commands a premium.

A Harvard Business School case on Otis in China provides a fascinating account of this dynamic. In 1984, Otis and Tianjing Elevator Company (TEC) entered an agreement to form a joint venture, China Tianjin Otis Elevator Company (CTOEC). As the business expanded, Otis felt increasing need to set up additional joint ventures in other parts of the country, because of the market segmentation. However, this attempt was frustrated by the Tianjin municipal government. The Tianjin municipal government viewed such an attempt by Otis as fostering competition, and in 1988, it rejected Otis' plan to set up another joint venture in Suzhou in Jiangsu province, even though CTOEC, in which TEC had a controlling stake at 65 percent, would have a 50 percent stake in the new venture.[36] In another deal, Otis tried to set up a joint venture in Guangzhou to capture the booming market there. This time, the Guangzhou government rejected the original proposal because it would involve equity participation from TEC.

Both of these episodes illustrate the extent of local protectionism in China. The Tianjin and Guangzhou governments viewed Otis' actions as shifting rents to other regions and as resulting in a pure financial redistribution. Neither government is averse to Otis' participation, but each wary of either benefiting competitors or allowing competitors to share a portion of its market growth. The Guangzhou

[36]The original agreement has given TEC approval power for business expansion plans in China. See Otis (1997).

episode illustrates how strong this consideration is. The Guangzhou government was willing to accept a minority stake in the joint venture with Otis on the condition that Otis would drop TEC's participation.

Thirdly, regionally based capital competition erodes barriers against FDI at the national level. It is well-known that Chinese localities compete with each other to attract FDI by reducing taxes and land-use fees and by provisions of infrastructure. To some extent, this is similar to the expensive bidding war among Ohio, Pennsylvania, and Ontario for a Honda plant in 1987. In the United States, this kind of bidding war changes the regional distribution of FDI without necessarily increasing the level of FDI in the country.[37] In China, this bidding does increase FDI inflows at the national level, because of two critical differences between China and the United States. One is that the policy resources under the command of the Chinese regional governments are much greater than those of American counterparts. Regional governments can offer far greater inducements compared with those of their counterparts in the United States. The other difference is that unlike the United States, China started from a position of tight restrictions and controls on FDI inflows. The effect of regional bidding for capital is that it brings down the nationwide barriers against FDI by equalizing policy and tax treatments to the level of the most liberal region. This is easily illustrated by the example of the four SEZs and the 14 coastal cities, which were initially given greater power to approve FDI projects at far higher dollar thresholds than other provinces. As these privileged regions began to attract large FDI inflows, other regions began to demand the same approval authority. Gradually, the central government extended the approval authority to other regions as well. It is also true that many of the FDI liberalization measures have been adopted by the central government after they have been implemented at the local level, such as permitting FDI in retail, telecommunications, and real estate.

---

[37]See Graham (1994) for an analysis of this episode.

Financial Market Inefficiency

One of the sources of financial market inefficiency has already been alluded to—segmentation of supply of capital along regional lines—and it induces a level of demand for foreign capital that would not materialize if domestic capital had been permitted to move more freely. Another source of financial market inefficiency has to do with the well-known failure of Chinese banks to channel credits to their most productive uses. The lending bias operates in two ways. One is that an overwhelming proportion of credits is directed toward SOEs; SOEs account for over 70 percent of bank lending, even though their output shares have declined to 40 percent. Nonstate firms, while more productive and profitable, were starved of credit financing during the entire reform era, until recently when the government removed credit quotas in late 1997.[38] Lending bias also means that banks are serving a heavily redistributional function across regions that the budget of the Chinese central government inadequately provides for. There is strong evidence that the central bank's refinancing—enforced via the reserve requirements on specialized banks—redistributes financial resources from deposit-surplus regions to deposit-deficit regions. Deposit-deficit regions—i.e., regions that lend more than they have deposits for—are northeastern provinces, which are the strongholds of large and heavily loss-making SOEs. Deposit-surplus regions are typically liberal southern provinces, such as Jiangsu, Zhejiang and Guangdong, that have a fast-growing nonstate sector.

One of the consequences associated with this lending bias is that efficient but private firms are denied access to China's vast savings pool and are too liquidity-constrained to finance their expansion. Spotting a potentially profitable opportunity, foreign firms, especially those from Hong Kong and Taiwan, become the suppliers of capital to the liquidity-constrained but fundamentally sound business operations. This is one of the most important reasons why FIEs dominate China's labor-intensive industries. In industries such as garment and shoe-making, Chinese private firms ought to have possessed strong competitive advantages, but poor allocative decisions of Chinese financial institutions imply that a severe mismatch be-

[38]See McKinnon (1994).

tween human and financial capital exists—i.e., efficient private firms cannot get financing, whereas inefficient SOEs are favored. The outcome of this allocative pattern is that private entrepreneurs access capital—sometimes short-term capital—by selling their own equity shares to MNCs based in Hong Kong and Taiwan.[39] Similarly, poor allocative decisions on foreign exchange lead to the same outcome. Because foreign exchange is allocated administratively, much of the official allocation has gone to SOEs to satisfy their import needs. Export-oriented private firms find it extremely difficult to access foreign exchange as a result. Foreign exchange is a critical resource for export-oriented firms because they need to source quality components and machinery from abroad to produce quality products. Hence, to access foreign exchange, domestic private entrepreneurs exchange their equity stakes with MNCs based in Hong Kong and Taiwan. In these two illustrations, the financing roles of MNCs arise not because China is short of capital but because its financial allocation is hugely inefficient. And it is this type of inefficiency that has prevented production linkages between Chinese and foreign firms based on a contractual arrangement. An equity arrangement—i.e., FDI—is favored not because it is intrinsically superior but because the contractual alternative is rendered unviable.

Policy Benefits

Probably the best understood institutional source of demand for foreign equity capital has to do with the policy benefits granted to FIEs in excess of those granted to SOEs. The most widely cited benefit is tax treatment. FIEs are granted tax exemptions and in general are taxed at a lower level than SOEs. In addition, FIEs are granted tariff exemptions on office and production equipment imports. Foreign observers believe that the tax regime is more liberal than similar regimes in other FDI host countries, and this has led to a high level of FDI inflows into China (Dean, 1988).

---

[39]One nonstate company I interviewed in Suzhou possessed very advanced know-how in making precision machinery, and its products were exported to many countries. Because of its nonstate status, it could not secure any credit financing from Chinese banks, and thus it formed a joint venture with a Hong Kong trading firm—which had marketed its products abroad but had little technical know-how—in order to secure the needed capital.

This account is plausible, but it is by no means complete, and it is even slightly misleading. For one thing, beginning in 1993, Chinese authorities have moved to equalize tax treatments of domestic firms and FIEs, and thus tax benefits have declined in importance as a driver of investment behavior. International evidence suggests that tax treatments in general have a weak effect on the distribution of FDI across countries. In the case of U.S. corporations, the U.S. government taxes their profits on a global basis, and thus the tax saving effect of investing in China will be offset by a tax increasing effect in the United States. It is worth emphasizing that the benefit of lower taxes primarily falls on the Chinese shareholders and thus increases their incentives for a corporate conversion into FIEs to qualify themselves for a better tax treatment. Thus demand for FDI is greater than otherwise would be the case, and it may result in a more accommodating stance toward demands made by foreign firms than otherwise would be the case. For example, it is plausible to imagine that without tax benefits, Chinese shareholders may resist foreign requests to take a controlling stake in joint ventures.

There are also less publicized policy benefits conferred on FIEs. During much of the reform period, foreign exchange constituted a valuable asset to firms in its possession in part because RMB was overvalued for many years and in part because, under a protectionist trade regime, access to imports was highly valued. Here there are critical differences between FIEs and domestic firms. First, exporting FIEs could retain 100 percent of their foreign exchange earnings, while domestic firms could retain only a portion and had to sell the balance to the central bank at the official rate. Thus, for each export transaction, FIEs made a surplus equivalent to the amount the RMB was overvalued. The foreign exchange premium began to decrease since the early 1990s as the scope of the foreign exchange market expanded.

Second, strictly speaking, what domestic exporting firms are allowed to retain is not foreign exchange but foreign exchange entitlements. FIEs, on the other hand, retain foreign exchange cash. This has subtle but important implications for the value of the foreign exchange retention. Converting entitlements into foreign exchange subjects the user firm to closer bureaucratic scrutiny and thus limits the "option" value of such a retention. In addition, converting entitlements into foreign exchange is by no means a certain process. In 1986 and, to a lesser extent, in 1993, authorities restricted such conversions because China ran a large foreign trade deficit. Thus, for domestic firms with foreign exchange entitlements, they bear some expropriation risks, from which FIEs are immune.

There are significant policy implications in this line of analysis. Our analysis of the significant and rising roles of FIEs in the Chinese economy raises a number of policy implications. It is generally the case that rising FDI is accompanied by rising intrafirm trade rather than interfirm trade. Intrafirm trade refers to trade between parent firms and their subsidiaries or affiliates abroad as opposed to the interfirm trade among unrelated entities at an arms-length distance. The rise in intrafirm trade has a number of pertinent policy implications.

For Chinese policymakers, intrafirm trade poses thorny challenges. One is the possibility that MNCs engage in transfer pricing to maximize profits on a global rather than a location-specific basis. Transfer pricing shuffles profits away from the taxing arm of the host governments, and therefore it reduces the tax base in the host country. Another effect is that transfer pricing reduces dividend shares of business partners in the host country. This is an especially important concern because most FIEs take the form of joint ventures.

The institutional benefits discussed above give rise to strong incentives for MNCs to engage in transfer pricing. Researchers in general have found strong evidence that MNCs are motivated by reduction of tax liabilities in the host country to engage in transfer pricing. Thus, relative tax rate differentials between home countries and China are a likely source of transfer pricing behavior. It ought to be noted, however, that the Chinese corporate income tax rate on FIEs is not inordinately high. In SEZs, the applicable rate is 15 percent; in economic and technological development zones, it is 24 percent, and in the rest of the country is 33 percent. Hong Kong's corporate income tax rate is 15 percent, and, given the fact that most FIEs originating in Hong Kong are located in SEZs, the apparent corporate tax rate equalization should have diminished such an incentive.

It is possible that the entire tax burden on FIEs located in China is still quite high. The value-added tax is 17 percent, and, in addition, local governments often impose discretionary levies. Most importantly, transfer pricing reduces profit shares accruing to the Chinese shareholder, and the Chinese tax allows FIEs to deduct their accumulated—rather than just current—losses for up to five years. These two motivations are probably stronger than income tax avoidance. Another facilitating condition is that China exempts FIEs from tariffs on imported inputs. Import duties often deter transfer pricing behavior since over-invoicing of the import bill would increase tariff liabilities.

The evidence on transfer pricing is limited and indirect. Its presence is suggested by a number of empirical anomalies rather than direct proof. One piece of evidence is that, despite putative operational efficiency, and managerial and technological know-how, there are in fact more loss-making FIEs than the supposedly moribund SOEs. In 1995, according to the Third Industry Census, 39.5 percent of FIEs reported losses, as compared with 34 percent of SOEs. Sun (1999) has reported some evidence for underinvoicing of Chinese exports to Hong Kong and overinvoicing of Chinese imports from China. In general, after taking into account freight and insurance costs, the average unit price of Chinese exports at Chinese customs was about 85 percent of the average unit price reported by Hong Kong customs. On the import side, again after deducting the freight and insurance costs, Chinese unit prices, on average, exceeded their Hong Kong prices by about 15 percent. Underinvoicing exports and overinvoicing imports are telltale signs of transfer pricing behavior.[40]

For U.S. policymakers, the rising prominence of FIEs in the Chinese economy also raises important policy questions. The significant and growing financing and economic roles of FIEs in the Chinese economy set China apart from Japan and Korea, which absorbed little FDI during their comparable stages of development. This has implications for U.S. economic policies toward East Asia. First, U.S. exports, to some extent, are not a full measure of U.S. companies' penetration of the Chinese market. US companies export directly to China but

[40]It is important to read this result with caution. The study does not break down trade between intrafirm and interfirm trade, and therefore it does not show that export underinvoicing and import overinvoicing are more pervasive among MNC affiliates than among unrelated entities, a logical inference from the transfer pricing logic. Another note of caution is that transfer pricing is only one of the explanations consistent with export/import misinvoicing. Capital controls and capital flight engaged in both by FIEs and domestic firms can also give rise to this phenomenon.

also produce inside China and sell locally produced goods there. The benefits from these sales are not reflected in the trade data but are reflected in the corporate earnings of U.S. corporations. In 1996, one FIE, Motorola (China) Electronics Co., Ltd., exported $690 million worth of goods, but the export value of the entire SOE sector came to $581 million. The export success of Motorola not only benefited Chinese employees but also Motorola's shareholders.

Second, U.S. trade policy is made on the assumption that political and economic boundaries coincide perfectly. This assumption is increasingly indefensible in light of shifts in industrial locations and of the associated changes in the direction of trade. The area where this assumption should be challenged to its core is Asia.[41] Kojima first put forward the hypothesis that some FDI activities are trade-oriented and others are anti-trade-oriented. [42]Trade-oriented FDI activities are in areas where the home economies are losing comparative advantage and the host economies are gaining comparative advantage. Anti-trade-oriented FDI activities are in areas where the host economies have a comparative disadvantage. Although this view has been challenged, especially the claim about anti-trade-oriented FDI,[43] the claim about trade-oriented FDI activities does seem to accord with the character of much of the FDI inflow into China.

Hong Kong is an extreme but highly illustrative example of trade-oriented FDI activities and of the effects of this kind of FDI on trade flows. By the early 1990s, four-fifths of Hong Kong manufacturing firms had relocated to China. Such investments have reoriented Hong Kong–China trade patterns: Most trade activities are directly related to the subcontracting investment activities undertaken by Hong Kong firms in China. In 1993, 74 percent of Hong Kong's domestic export to China was related to outward processing; of the import from China, it was 74 percent in 1993.[44] In effect, Hong Kong operates as a trading corporation that contracts out production units

[41]The best example is the emergence of so-called "Greater China," an area encompassing southern China, Taiwan, and Hong Kong, where economic integration has increasingly penetrated political divisions. See Jones, King, and Klein (1993).

[42]See Kojima (1973).

[43]See Dunning (1977).

[44]See Fung (1995).

in China—through the provision of production designs and materials—and purchases and distributes the finished goods worldwide.

The concentration of manufacturing locations in China has caused major changes in the direction of trade with the United States and has vastly complicated the management of trade deficits with the region. Briefly stated, labor-intensive goods that previously came from Korea, Taiwan, Hong Kong, and a number of Southeast Asian countries are now increasingly coming from China. This has produced a widening trade deficit between China and the United States and a dwindling trade deficit with the other two members of "Greater China." The U.S. trade deficit with China has risen concomitantly, with a sharp decline in its deficit with Taiwan and Hong Kong, at least until 1994. It is this rise in the trade deficit that has complicated an already fragile political relationship between China and the United States, for rather unnecessary reasons, because the U.S. deficit with "Greater China" rose by a far smaller margin. While the U.S. deficit with China rose by about sixfold between 1987 and 1992, its deficit with "Greater China" has risen by 9.6 percent. It is also difficult to argue that the rise in the deficit has been a result of China's import restrictions; China's imports from the United States have grown at a double-digit rate every year, except for 1987 and 1990. A far more plausible reason for the rising deficit with China is the trade reorientations that are associated with shifts in industrial locations in East Asia.

Given this production-trade link, an aggressive bilateral trade stance can lead to a number of undesirable outcomes. Reduced U.S. demand for goods from China can slow down the rapid capital integration between once politically hostile regions, such as Taiwan and Korea on the one hand and China on the other. It may also impede the process of import liberalization in China by creating a foreign exchange shortage and a regionwide slowdown of economic growth. These outcomes may not be consistent with U.S. long-run economic and political interests in the region. A subtle but important implication of the production-trade link is the possibility that U.S. investment and trade interests may be in conflict with each other. Since the 1992 Memorandum of Understanding, the United States has been pressuring the Chinese to liberalize further China's market access to U.S. goods and to phase out internal trade regulations and "onerous" import restrictions, such as import quotas and strict sanitary standards. However, domestically oriented investments depend on a high tariff structure to be profitable, as illustrated in the case of the automotive firms, and foreign investors typically request protection when they undertake protection-induced investments.[45] Thus, overly aggressive market-opening measures as demanded by the U.S. trade representative may in fact undermine the interests of U.S. MNCs with subsidiaries already established in China. This conflict between U.S. trade and investment interests will come into sharper focus if China agrees to the "fast-track" accession terms of the WTO.

REFERENCES

Amsden, Alice (1989). *Asia's Next Giant: South Korea and Late Industrialization.* New York: Oxford University Press.

Azis, Iwan J. (1994). "The Political Economy of Policy Reform." *Indonesia.* Washington, D.C.: Institute for International Economics, pp. 406–407.

Byrd, William A., Gene Tidrick (1987). Factor Allocation and Enterprise Incentives. *China's Industrial Reform.* New York: Oxford University Press, pp. 60-102.

Dean, Genevieve (1988). "Investment Incentives Throughout Asia." *China Business Review*, March–April, pp. 49–51.

Xiaoping, Deng (1993). *Banhao jingji teque zengjia duiwai kaifang zhengshi [Improving the Special Economic Zones and Increasing the Number of Open Cities*]. Beijing: Renmin chubanshe.

Dunning, John H. (1977). "Trade, Location of Economic Activity and the MNE: A Search for an Eclectic Approach." *International Allocation of Economic Activity.* London: Macmillan.

Fung, K.C. (1995). "Trade and Investment Relations among Hong Kong, China and Taiwan." *Unpublished Manuscript.* Santa Cruz: University of California.

---

[45]The Indonesian oil boom in the mid-1970s, which increased the attractiveness of the Indonesian domestic market and induced import-substituting FDI, coincided with an intensification of its infant industry phase. See Azis (1994), pp. 406–407.

Galenson, Walter (1985). "Direct Foreign Investment in Taiwan." *Foreign Trade and Investment: Economic Development in the Newly Industrializing Asian Countries.* The University of Wisconsin Press.

Graham, Edward M., Paul R. Krugman (1994). *Foreign Direct Investment in the United States.* Washington, D.C.: Institute for International Economics.

Huang, Yasheng (2000). Selling China: The Institutional Foundation of FDI During the Reform Era. Boston: Harvard Business School.

Huang, Yasheng (1998). Survey Team of Chinese Managers 1996. [Almanac of China's Economy]. Beijing, pp. 943–960.

Jones, Michael, King, Randall, and Robert E. Klein (1993). "Economic Integration between Hong Kong, Taiwan and the coastal provinces of China." *OECD Economic Studies,* Spring, Vol. 20, pp. 115–144.

Kamath, Shyam J. (1990). "Foreign Direct Investment in a Centrally Planned Developing Economy." *Economic Development and Cultural Change,* Vol. 39, No. 1, pp. 107–130.

Kojima, Kiyoshi (1973). "A Macro-Economic Approach to Foreign Direct Investment." *Hitotsubashi Journal of Economics,* June, Vol. 14.

Kornai, Janos (1992). *The Socialist System.* Princeton: Princeton University Press.

Kornai, Janos (1980). *The Economics of Shortage.* Amsterdam: North Holland.

Krueger, Anne O. (1974). "The Political Economy of the Rent-Seeking Society." *American Economic Review,* Vol. LXIV, No. 3, pp. 291–303.

Li, Lanqing (1995). *Zhongguo Liyun Waizi Jizhu Zhishi* [*Basic Knowledge on Utilizing Foreign Capital in China*]. Beijing: Zhonggong zhongyang dangxiao chubanshe and Zhongguo Duiwai Jingji Maoyi Chubanshe.

Lim, Soon Neo (1994). "China's Strategic Profit Surges to 138 Pc to Hk$ 153 M." *Business Times,* May 17.

McKinnon, Ronald I. (1994). "Financial Growth and Macroeconomic Stability in China, 1978-1992: Implications for Russia and Other Transitional Economies." *Journal of Comparative Economics,* Vol. 18, pp. 438–469.

Meier, Gerald M. (1995). *Leading Issues in Economic Development.* New York: Oxford University Press.

Office of Third Industrial Census (1997). *The Data of the Third National Industrial Census of the People's Republic of China in 1995.* Beijing: Zhongguo tongji chubanshe.

Otis Elevator Company (A): China Strategy (1997). Boston: Harvard Business School.

Pearson, Margaret M. (1991). *Joint Ventures in the People's*

Pomfret, Richard (1991). *Investing in China.* New York: Harvester Wheatsheaf.

Qian, Yingyi (1996). "Enterprise Reform in China: Agency Problems and Political Control." *Economics of Transition,* October, Vol. 4, pp. 427–447.

"Qiyejia Dui Hongguan Jingji Xinshi He Qiye Gaige De Panduan Yu Jianyi." ["Managers' Views on Macroeconomic Situation and Enterprise Reforms"] (1996). *Almanac of China's Economy 1996.* Beijing: Zhongguo Jingji Nianjianshe, pp. 943–960.

Republic of China. Princeton: Princeton University Press.

Shirk, Susan L. (1994). *How China Opened Its Door.* Washington, D.C.: The Brookings Institution.

Smith, Craig S. (1998). "Chinese Capital Helps Keep U.S. Rates Low." *Wall Street Journal.*

Stallings, Barbara (1990). "*The Role of Foreign Capital in Economic Development.*" *Paths of Industrialization in Latin American and East Asia,* in Gary Wyman and Donald L. Gereffi, eds. Princeton: Princeton University Press, pp. 55–89.

State Bureau of Machinery Industry (1998). *1997 Nian Jijian Gongye Zonghe Nianbao [Annual Report on the Machinery Industry, 1997].* Beijing: Zhonghua renmin gonghe guo guojia jijian gongye jue.

State Planning Commission (1994). "Woguo Liyong Waiguo Zhijie Touzi Wenti De Yanjiu Baogao" ["Report on the Problems in Utilizing Foreign Direct Investments in China"]. *Jingji yanjiu cankao [References on Economic Research]*, pp. 2–59.

State Statistical Bureau (1997). *Zhongguo Tongji Nianjian 1997 [China Statistical Yearbook 1997].* Beijing: Zhongguo tongji chubanshe.

State Statistical Bureau (1998). *A Statistical Survey of China 1998.* Beijing: Zhongguo tongji chubanshe.

Sun, Haishun (1999). "FDI, Trade and Transfer Pricing." *Foreign Direct Investment and Economic Growth in China.* Cheltenham, UK: in Yanrui Wu, ed. Edward Elgar, pp. 100–139.

United Nations Centre on Transnational Corporations (1992). *World Investment Directory 1992.* New York: United Nations.

Wade, Robert (1990). *Governing the Market: Economic Theory and the Role of Government in East Asian Industrialization.* Princeton: Princeton University Press.

World Bank (1997). *China's Management of Enterprise Assets: The State as Shareholder.* Washington, D.C.: The World Bank.

Wu Qiang (1996). "Ri Han Jishu Yinjin Zhengce Ji Zhongguo De Fazhan Zhanlie." ["Technology Import Policies of Korea and Japan and China's Development Strategy"]. *Jingji Guanli [Economic Management],* pp. 12–15.

Young, Stephen, and Lan Ping (1997). "Technology Transfer to China Through Foreign Direct Investment." *Regional Studies,* Vol. 31, No. 7, pp. 669–679.

Chapter Eight

CHINA'S MACROECONOMY: EXPANDING DOMESTIC DEMAND AND INTERIM REFORMS

Xiaomin Shi

INTRODUCTION

Currently, Chinese economic performance is characterized by the following trends: (1) the economic downslide has been checked somewhat as a result of governmental macroeconomic policies to expand domestic demand; (2) the strength of governmental fiscal and monetary policies is unprecedented, but the economy is not recovering as quickly as in the past, it is still adjusting with a weak upward tendency; (3) economic growth potential is enormous, but social investment and domestic consumption remain sluggish because of fairly strong structural restrictions. Chinese economic marketization has increased a lot during the more than 20-years of reform, and market mechanisms have increasingly been dominating economic performance, but the sticking point is that the government's management style and macroeconomic policymaking emphasis have not eliminated traditional government dominance and allowed the transformation into market dominance. At present, Chinese economic development is at a crossroads, where its operating mechanism, growth style, development strategy, and existing structure all need changing and adjusting, and the lag of the economic structure is more and more remarkable. This chapter attempts to illustrate some macroeconomic policies to deal with the current problems and difficulties. It points out that the keys to breaking through the current difficulties and realizing sustainable, stable and sound development are to perfect, reform, and renovate current government policymaking and management system selectively and gradually while continuing to implement short-term macro adjustment.

Pushing Forward Reform of Market Access, Investment, and Financing Systems, and Creating a Favorable Environment for Social Investment Growth

The centerpiece of investment and financing system reform is to restructure normal and canonical financing channels, lift some restrictions on market access of private enterprises, and create a favorable structural environment for improving social investment incentives. Quite a few specialists and scholars hold the opinion that structural barriers exist in almost any new economic growth. Outdated management styles, fairly strong administrative monopolies, excessive interference, and irrational fees can be found in infrastructure construction and management when cities are the centers of hi-tech industries, import and export agent business, and other basic and emerging service sectors such as education, medical care, public health, environmental protection, tourism, culture, publishing, network communications, community service, property management, and public transportation. Funds for social support are in short supply. The enormous potential demands in this area can bring about new economic growth. However, the precondition for fulfilling these needs is the government's determination to push forward financing system reform, break administrative monopolies on market access, improve protection of intellectual property, create an environment favorable to social investment, and shape a policy environment favorable to middle- and small-sized enterprises, social employment, enterprise management innovation, and strategic restructuring.

The first step in such a direction, would be government encouragement to open up pilot credit institutions mainly serving middle- and small-sized enterprises. While strengthening financial supervision and building necessary financial insurance systems, the Chinese government should allow and encourage a proportion of rural foundations, credit cooperatives, and branches of state banks and urban cooperative banks below the county level to be transformed into independent small commercial banks or small trust companies, which can take the form of shareholding systems, shareholding cooperative systems, partnerships or joint ventures, and which could adopt relatively flexible floating interest rates and take business risks independently.

Second, the Chinese government should expand exploration of and experiment with effective financing channels in capital market access for private enterprises. It should also push forward actively and cautiously with equity restructuring of listed companies, lifting some restrictions on acquisition of listed companies, encouraging capable private enterprises or naturalized citizens to make legal acquisitions in capital markets. Further, the government should carry out a complete summary of historical experiences and lessons in local property rights markets, while strengthening supervision and risk control, setting up local pilot capital markets in areas with developed economies and good market conditions, creating necessary conditions for middle- and small-sized enterprises to secure financing in capital markets.

Third, the Chinese government should relax market access restrictions on private enterprises, trying to reduce discrimination and improper interference in establishing, registration, and operation of private enterprises, prohibiting random fees. It should also speed up assigning and expanding private enterprises' import and export rights and proxy rights, properly reducing assigning qualification standards, and allowing these enterprises to enjoy the same rebate treatment and convenience as state-owned foreign trade companies. While perfecting governmental and social supervision, to break up monopolies, the government should introduce competition, lower costs and improve quality of services, encouraging private enterprises to enter traditional public services, such as real estate management, environment protection, garbage disposal, intermediary financial services, professional training and education, and small town construction.

Fourth, the government should safeguard private enterprises' legal interests. The new amendments to China's Constitution and to *The Law on Middle- and Small-Sized Enterprises* recently in deliberation undoubtedly provide strong legal protection for private enterprises' development. However, since Chinese private enterprises emerge from discrimination and repelling of traditional systems, the problem of undefined property rights as a result of the "Red-Cap" needs to be addressed. The Chinese government should accept entrepreneurs' deserved interests, including property rights and intellectual property rights. Resolving "left-over historical problems" properly would be of great significance in protecting private enterprises' incentives, promoting sustainable, stable development of private enterprises. The emphasis should be on trials and judgments in civil actions, justice and effectiveness of law enforcement activities.

And lastly, the government should encourage various industrial associations, research and consultation institutions, and intermediaries to provide comprehensive services to private enterprises, making them the link between government and private enterprises. Governmental support, service and supervision should also be carried out by these institutions. The government should improve its management style via various intermediary institutions and interest groups, weakening state-owned monopolies and introducing property social supervision and competition.

Promoting Stable Growth of Consumption Through Employment and Social Security, and Upgrading the Consumption Structure by Lowering Price Thresholds

Current sluggish consumption demand results from two factors. The first is that unstable revenue expectations deviate from expenditure expectations; the second is that price thresholds for upgrading consumer goods are excessively high (deep-rooted structural factors are behind these problems). Unstable revenue expectations result mostly from employment pressure and expected reform on social security, housing, and education. Affected groups are very extensive. Price thresholds are related to industrial monopoly and excessively high administrative charges. In contrast with market competition lowering prices, monopolistic product and service prices remain high, and groups with high social revenues are usually found in these industries. Thus, promoting stable growth and structural upgrading for consumption should begin with perfecting social security system, expanding employment, and reducing prices of monopolistic products and services. The government should take the following steps to effect such changes:

- Create jobs, providing good market access conditions for unemployed and laid-off workers. Currently in China, in the course of economic development, rural redundant laborers and state-owned enterprises' laid-off employees need to be gradually transferred and reemployed. The problem is a kind of reform cost, which is also related to social stability and improving social expectations. The important aspect of governmental employment reform should be placed on vigorously developing middle- and small-sized enterprises and on encouraging communities and individuals to establish small businesses. Meanwhile, the labor market should be developed and perfected, by setting up multilevel professional advisory agencies. Social security and social welfare programs should be separated based on professions and market competition employment systems oriented toward rural industrialization and urbanization. Nondiscriminative labor markets should come into being gradually.

- Accelerate the pace of perfecting social security system with elderly workers in state-owned sectors as the focus. It is an objective of market economies and an important component of system innovation during the course of transition to realize employment mechanisms and social security systems in which professions, social security, and welfare are separated. Recently, various welfare and security reform measures have been adopted because of revenue and employment instability, and the rising prices of medical care, education, and housing. People do not know how to calculate how much personal savings will satisfy a family's basic needs. This is the major reason behind current residential consumption "deflation" and savings growth. With respect to stabilizing expectations, the emphasis should be on ensuring social security reform in which historical contributions of retirees and some older worker should be recognized and their deserved benefit should be ensured. Living expenses for laid-off workers should be given to them in a timely fashion. The fiscal authorities should provide a floor for social security payments, begin to levy social security taxes, expand social security coverage to all enterprises and institutions, provide stable and reliable funding sources for social security of citizens, and shape a multilevel social security system that includes insurance, relief and welfare benefits.
- Upgrade the consumption structure by promoting competition and reducing administrative fees. Chinese residential consump-

tion of basic durable consumer goods has reached a saturation point; thus the emphasis of expanding consumption should be on cultivating new product trends and upgrading the consumption structure. Current sluggish demand results from high price thresholds. The major reason behind high prices is industrial administrative monopolies and excessive administrative taxes and charges in prices on monopolistic products and services. Houses and cars are believed to be new consumption "hot points," which can start overall consumption demand and consumption structure upgrading. However, as much as 30–70 percent of current commercial house prices is taxed by the government. The additional charges for a car purchased in China are as much as 25–40 percent of car prices (two times higher than that of a car of the same kind purchased elsewhere). Excessively high price thresholds have restrained purchasing and upgrading for many middle-income families, causing many consumers not to use credit for car and home purchases. In residential consumption hot points, some "structural deflation" of consumption may be unavoidable because of preparatory savings and accumulation by potential buyers. As a result, demand may fall into long-term sluggishness. To expand consumption, in addition to changing housing and consumer credit policies, administrative fees and taxes on housing, cars, and emerging hot points should be cut to lower price thresholds. Also, residential rents should be increased to a reasonable level. In the short run, the main purposes are to improve living conditions and reduce taxes. In the long run, a home investment market will eventually take shape.

- Develop new urban growth. The dual structure dividing the Chinese city and countryside is the basic contradiction impeding economic development. It is impossible to improve agricultural efficiency and realize agricultural industrialization and marketization if the majority of the rural population remains unchanged. Experience has shown that the rapid transformation of middle- and small-sized towns into developed areas is a vigorous new economic growth point. To gain the full benefit from middle- and small-sized towns, guidelines for urbanization should be made clear: emphasis should be placed on construction in middle- and small-sized towns near big and mid-sized cities and near developed regions. Such an effort requires not only coordination among fiscal, financial, household registry, and land management systems and infrastructure construction, but also examination of specific local conditions.

Speeding up the Shift of Governmental Functions, and Perfecting Macro Policymaking and a Macro Control System

The remarkable structural contradiction in current Chinese economic performance is the following: provincial and ministerial segmentation administrative management is in conflict with the operating mechanism of economic marketization. The interweaving of power and markets destroys market order and constricts market vigor; efforts at macro control are still limited to administrative measures only oriented toward the state-owned economy itself, not the society as a whole. Thus, acceleration of governmental administrative reform is not only the key to sustainable, stable, and healthy economic development, but also the central link of economic system's transition to a market economy.

To begin, the government should reaffirm the principles of "government controlling markets and markets guiding enterprises" put forward in the 13th Party Congress. The division between government and markets should be clearly defined. The shift of government functions should be speeded up. Based on the actual progress of economic marketization, the government should retreat from areas in which governmental interference is improper, and increase its presence where market power does not function well. The main purposes of governmental function shifting is to promote and perfect market mechanisms, reduce the government's direct administrative interference in the microeconomy, and to transfer some government functions to enterprises, and market and social intermediaries. Regarding the establishment and perfecting of market rules, while attaching importance to supervision of market players' behavior, more emphasis should be put on maintaining equal rights among market players, strengthening contractual relationships, and promoting market competition. Regarding the perfection of a macro control system, control capability should be strengthened, adequate and reliable public goods should be provided, and a favorable environment for economic development should be created. For example, the Shenzhen Municipal government on its own initiative discontinued many of its outdated examination and approval rights processes, and in doing so provided a good example for the whole country.

In addition, it is necessary to plot out the rational duties for each level of government, forming a highly efficient administrative management system with balanced obligations and rights. Government functions and budgetary expenditures at every level under market economy terms need to be defined. Overlapping of duties among government levels should be eliminated. On this basis, taxes, fees, and expenditures of every level of government should be standardized into a regular transfer payment system to offset necessary local expenditure shortfalls and to ease imbalances among various localities. The law and legal procedures should be defined clearly so that governmental decisionmaking can be more democratic and scientific, and legal, media and social oversight of government should be strengthened. A government responsibility system consistent with government functions should be established and perfected to coordinate government obligations, rights, interests, and available resources. Regular systems should be developed for examinations of and recruitment for civil servants, with hiring, firing, review, and promotion procedures. Civil servants' salary levels should be increased to optimize stimulation of government work and improve governmental efficiency. Overall, government should be streamlined, cutting out redundant positions and generally building an honest and clean system of government.

Furthermore, fiscal reforms should be deepened. Taxes and fees should be adjusted. Specifically, production VAT (value-added tax) should be changed into consumption VAT as quickly as possible. Tax policies should be adjusted. In particular, the restrictive taxes and charges in response to an "overheated" economy should be removed—such as the adjustment tax on fixed asset investment and the high level of "three-inspection" charges that are unfavorable to exports. Without increasing the overall social tax burden, the government should define a fiscal revenue level consistent with governmental functions by reducing large-scale charges outside of the budget and clearing up auxiliary banking activities of provincial governments. All these measures will result in greater transparency of fiscal expenditures and higher control capabilities of fiscal policies of the central government. Financial system reform should be pushed forward in a stable way, and the role and function of the central bank should be strengthened. While the central bank is relatively independent in making and implementing monetary policies, a supervision mechanism by which the People's Congress and its standing committee supervises the central bank should be established. Meanwhile, a financial market system should be completed, including marketization of state-owned commercial banks and interest rates that conform with the market. Monetary and capital markets should be developed and perfected. Monetary policy means and policy instruments should be diversified, shaping a pattern so that the central bank employs a cash reserve ratio, rediscount rate, and open market business to control economic performance effectively. of state-owned commercial banks and their interest rates should be sped up, monetary and capital market should be developed and perfected, monetary policy means and policy instruments should be diversified, shaping a pattern that the central bank employs cash reserve ratio, rediscount rate and open market business to control economic performance effectively.

Unswerving Continuation of Expanding the Effort to Open Trade

The opening-up effort must be continued unswervingly while implementing a macro policy for expanding domestic demand. Practice has shown that the open trade policy brings capital, technology and new consumption perceptions to China, promoting Chinese economic integration with the world economy, which is of great importance in promoting marketization of the Chinese economy and in improving economic performance.

The role of international capital and technology in renovating traditional industries is a key to opening trade. Since reform and the open trade policy was adopted, China's light manufacturing industry, which makes, for example, household electrical appliances, and the telecommunications industry have developed rapidly in recent years. The international competitive power of these industries has risen, showing a broad prospect for renovating domestic industries with international capital and technology. China should grab the favorable opportunity available now that the world economy is facing major restructuring. It should create conditions to attract foreign capital for domestic traditional industrial renovations. With the gradual surfacing of policy effects of expanding domestic demand, a relatively high economic growth rate will provide strong appeal for foreign capital's entry into China. Progress in this respect rests not only on such elements as good infrastructure but also on the legal system, market access, and fair competition.

Domestic enterprises should be encouraged to participate in international competition. Participating in international competition is an important way for domestic enterprises to gain technological innovations. At present, the emphasis should be on providing necessary policy environment and simple and high-quality services to domestic private enterprises. Meanwhile, the mutual open trade between Guandong province and Hongkong, and between Fujian province and Taiwan, is bringing about faster circulation of personnel, capital, technology and products, pushing mutual complementary relations between these regional economies to a new level.

Greater efforts should be made to enter the WTO. Although the current domestic and international situation leaves prospects for China's entry into WTO uncertain, the resolution to enter the WTO should not be shaken. Economic globalization is the major tendency of world economy. China will only lag far behind developed countries if isolated. Entry into the WTO is favorable not only to bettering China's foreign trade environment, but also for China's gaining insights about its shortcomings and the common rules of international trade, in addition to avoiding risks in international economic activities. The short-term shock to some domestic industries is not always negative. In fact, it is because of long-time protection that some industries continue to need protection. The automobile industry is a case in point. However, preparatory countermeasures are necessary in every sector.

Improving the Legal Basis of the Market Economy While Perfecting the Socialist Property and Credit Systems

The basis of a successful market economy system lies in an equal rights contractual relationship among market players safeguarded by complete legal and strict law enforcement systems. Legal systems should fit the basic framework of a market economy system and should be a driving force behind overall systematic innovation.

Efforts should be directed toward obvious problems in reform practices and current economic relations, formulating and perfecting relevant laws selectively and gradually. The principles behind legislation should aim to safeguard equal and legitimate rights of market players and to maintain a good market order as follows:

- While abiding by China's Constitution's stipulations for all kinds of ownership, China should effectively protect citizen's legal property, ensuring that all kinds of property rights are enjoyed equally in market transactions. Clauses in laws and regulations that go against basic principles of the constitution should be deleted; discrimination and violation of rights in law enforcement should be banned.
- The general rules of the civil code should be revised to protect potential litigant's legal rights and interests, to respect wills and similar codicils, and to provide a legal basis and rules for administrative policymaking and management. The civil code should also prevent too much administrative interference into the normal lives of ordinary citizens.
- Laws and regulations unsuitable for realistic economic relations should be revising and/or repealed. "Ministerial legislation" should be restricted, and contractual, credit, and property relationships in market economy conditions should be standardized. The judicial system should be reformed be removing local protectionism in jurisdiction and enforcement.
- Judicial supervision should be strengthened. Respecting legislative contradictions and problems in judicial practices, the following measures should be taken: revising and perfecting relevant laws according to legal procedure, perfecting open trial system; punishing those who bend the law to help their friends or relatives; and improving quality of law enforcement and officers.

CONCLUSIONS

The major problem in current economic performance is the structural contradiction that needs to be resolved by the Chinese government through conforming to reality and the requirements of economic marketization. Such conforming requires not only middle-

and long-term strategic planning, but also searching for transitional points. Presently, the transitional plan is to adjust corresponding policies and push forward relevant reforms with expansion of domestic demand and new economic growth at the center. These policies and reform measures must be effective in the short run, rational in the middle run, and favorable in the long run. At first, the major effort should be to avoid chaotic policy objectives that might cause serious contradictions for middle- and long-term development because of shortsighted policies.

COMMENTS ON XIAOMIN SHI'S CHAPTER

Alice Young

Xiaomin Shi's chapter conveys both the progress China has made over the past 20 years and the problems China faces in transitioning from a state economy to more of a market economy. He has made a number of excellent suggestions to reform government policy "selectively and gradually," such as stimulation of mid-sized and small enterprises through new credit and the capital markets, regional decentralization and encouragement of pilot projects, market access, and privatization of services. These are all important steps that should be taken, but I have several concerns.

First of all, it was difficult to ascertain how his "selected" suggestions differ in any major respect from the espoused Deng Xiaoping/Zhu Rongji policies of the Chinese government. The stimulation of mid-sized enterprises, regional decentralization, and the encouragement of experimental pilot projects have all already been described in various Chinese government directives.

Second, all of his suggestions first require the strengthening of financial oversight, risk management expertise, and judicial enforcement, none of which are readily available in China at the present time. The shift contemplated by the author is not only government to market control, but central to provincial control. Beijing is far away, as the famous Chinese proverb says, and although decentralization can better promote local economic growth, local institutions are inexperienced in risk management and capital markets, which are necessary ingredients for successful financial supervision and privatization. Although decentralization provides greater local flexibility, it can also result in local protectionism and restraints on capital flow movement from province to province. It was primarily through central government control that investment incentives could be shifted from the coastal economic trade zones to the interior zones to stimulate economic development in those less prosperous areas. Moreover, getting rid of the local protectionism that usually accompanies decentralization, and strengthening judicial supervision to ensure fairness, is viable if and only if the quality of law enforcers *improves*. It should be noted that 66 percent of the judges in China have no legal background whatsoever and are in fact mostly former Peoples' Liberation Army cadres.

Third, his recommendations do not appear to address Nicholas Lardy's concerns stated in his report to the Aspen Institute Congressional Forum in 1999, namely:

- the state-owned enterprises' (SOEs) oversupply of unsaleable products
- the overexposure of the government-owned banks to SOE debt
- the inadequacy of tax revenues to finance government expenditures for these reforms

For example, the author emphasizes creating employment opportunities for mid-sized, small private enterprises as a means of stimulating the economy, but he fails even to mention the elephant in the room—interim reform must also deal with the SOEs and the insolvent banking industry. Mid-sized and small private enterprises cannot begin to replace the previous government-subsidized SOE social insurance safety net, which provided medical and pension benefits to most of the working population. Moreover, the problems of the SOEs are exacerbated by the rapidly aging population, the one-child policy, increased longevity, lack of funded social insurance plans, and finally poor returns because of government restrictions and lack of asset management and risk management skills.

It should be noted that the author's proposal to reduce discrimination against private enterprises means not only the discrimination between SOEs and private enterprises, but also between foreign and domestic businesses, which China's entry to the WTO will in any case force it to address. Safeguarding private enterprises' legal interests is vitally important, but the key to a market economy in my mind is consistency, transparency, fairness, and evenhanded enforcement, whether it be private enterprises, SOEs or foreign enterprises.

Finally, in the interim period, must all measures by necessity be ad hoc? As a pragmatic lawyer rather than an economist, I would have preferred that Xiaomin Shi's chapter propose guidelines that attempt to create a balance between government control and market dominance, central control and localization, private enterprise stimulation and SOE reform, and to address unemployment and the bad debt of the banks.

Having said that, from my 20 years of transactional work in China, and if we take the long-term view of 5,000 years of Chinese history, the author's modest interim reform approach may have ample time to be further refined and implemented.

Part IV

U.S.-CHINA ECONOMIC AND SECURITY RELATIONS

Chapter Nine

CHINA AND THE WORLD ECONOMY: THE SHORT MARCH FROM ISOLATION TO MAJOR PLAYER

Henry S. Rowen

The decision taken by China's leaders in 1978 to restore some property rights to farmers was a pivotal event in China's modernization and the near-simultaneous beginning of the opening of its economy was of equal importance.

Openness is a crucial element in a strategy for successful development. According to Sachs and Warner, no country in a sample of 117 that pursued "appropriate" policies (involving a "property rights" test and an "openness" test) in 1970–1989 had less than 1.2 percent a year growth and not one of them having under $4,000 GDP per-capita grew at less than 2 percent.[1] They found that 37 countries acted to open trade and grew an average of 1 percent more per year in the first two years after liberalization and 1.3 percent more in the longer term by comparison with the decade before liberalization.

Openness has several positive effects: It limits the market power of domestic monopolies; rent-seeking opportunities are reduced; it is a

[1]Sachs, Jeffrey D., and Andrew M. Warner, "Economic Reform and the Process of Global Integration," *Brookings Papers on Economic Activity,* No. 1, Washington, D.C., 1995. Francisco Rodriquez and Dani Rodrik in "Trade Policy and Economic Growth: A Skeptic's Guide to the Cross-National Evidence," NBER Working Paper No. 7081, April 1999, and Ann Harrison and Gordon Hanson in "Who Gains from Trade Reform," NBER Working Paper No. 6915, New York, January 1999, have leveled criticisms against Sachs and Warner's paper principally on the grounds that some other factors than trade policy might have been responsible for the improved performance. The debate will go on.

means of learning technologies and organizational methods used in advanced countries, with foreign direct investment (FDI) being an especially efficient way to acquire them; and larger scales of production can be realized from exporting.

There are also potential disadvantages of openness, the main one being exposure to destabilizing shocks. The financial sector is especially prone to disturbances, as demonstrated in the financial crisis of 1997–1998. Governments are prudent in not opening their economies to short-term capital flows until their financial institutions are strong enough to cope with monetary surges. Openness also exposes a country to economic sanctions by trading partners. (However, that is a two-way street, because a trading partner that imposes sanctions hurts its own economy as well).

Openness has three components: trade in materials (raw and manufactured) and services, the movement of capital (financial and direct investment), and the movement of people. In 1977, China was the world's 30th largest trading nation, with total trade of less than $15 billion a year, while it played practically no role in international capital markets and its people were greatly restricted in their ability to move back and forth across its borders. Since then, China has freed substantially the movement of materials and services; it is selectively open to direct investment by foreigners but retains controls on financial capital; and it is much more permissive about its citizens moving across its borders.

TRADE

Deng Xiaoping's strategy at the beginning was to increase exports of raw materials, especially oil and coal, in order to cope with a rapidly growing trade deficit in the late 1970s. As a result, exports of oil more than tripled and, together with the rise in its price, oil export earnings increased almost seven-fold between 1977 and 1985 (shrinking thereafter). Overall trade doubled between 1978 and 1980—from a low level—and kept on growing rapidly thereafter.[2] Then greater market access was offered in 1992 to foreign investors, especially to

---

[2]Lardy, Nicholas R., *China in the World Economy,* Institute for International Economics, Washington, D.C., 1994.

those who would bring advanced technology. Exports grew at 14 percent a year during the 1990s, more than double the increase in world trade of 6 percent a year. In 1996, 60 percent of merchandise exports went to Asia and 19 percent and 16 percent, respectively, to North America and Europe; the pattern of imports was similar except that there were more from Europe and less from North America.[3] Exports of foreign-invested firms grew an average of 30 percent a year between 1990 and 1996, making it the tenth largest exporter in the world, while the output of these firms grew even faster. These firms were then responsible for 41 percent of China's exports.[4]

By 1997, its total trade (imports plus exports) was about $300 billion, about 3 percent of total world trade. To put this number in perspective, its share of world trade in 1928 was 2.3 percent; by 1977 it had fallen to 0.7 percent and only reached its earlier 1928 peak share in 1993.[5]

Exports of manufactured goods became dominant during the 1980s, growing from 1985 through 1993 at an average rate of 24 percent per year; by 1993 manufactured goods made up 80 percent of China's exports. These were labor-intensive goods: textiles, clothing, shoes, toys, sporting goods, TVs, radios, washing machines, and refrigerators. These were low-technology products made by low-cost labor that could for the most part no longer be made competitively in advanced countries. In 1999, exports still were labor intensive, but they were becoming more advanced technically.

China's exports could not have grown so much without a comparable growth in imports. Although there is much protection, most of it local, there already has been a substantial reduction in trade barriers. Tariffs have fallen by more than one-half since 1992 to below an av-

---

[3]Fung, K. C., and Lawrence J. Lau, *New Estimates of the United States-China Bilateral Trade Balances*, Asia/Pacific Research Center, Institute for International Studies, Stanford University, Stanford, Calif., April 1999.

[4]Naughton, Barry *China's Emergence and Prospect as a Trading Nation*, Brookings Papers on Economic Activity, Washington, D.C., Vol. 2, 1996.

[5]*The Economist*, November 20, 1999.

erage of 20 percent; a World Bank estimate of the average protective effect of nontariff barriers was only 9.3 percent for 1993.[6]

A key part of the process of expanding exports was the expansion of the number of foreign trade corporations and their decentralization to the provinces. They were allowed to retain increasing shares of the foreign exchange they earned, a powerful incentive to increase exports.[7] From having fewer than 20 monopoly trading corporations, China now has hundreds of thousands of trading firms.

The American share of merchandise exports from China grew from practically nothing in 1977 to about $21 billion in 1996—although there is a large difference in the numbers reported by the two governments. The U.S. government reports that the U.S. trade deficit with China in 1998 was $56.9 billion, while the Chinese government reports a trade surplus with the United States of $21 billion. (A bilateral trade balance in a multilateral trading world is not a very meaningful parameter economically but often is politically.) This gap of nearly $36 billion in the two official accounts requires an explanation, and Fung and Lau provide one.[8] They make four kinds of adjustments: (1) for freight and insurance; (2) for mark-ups for trade through Hong Kong; (3) for an estimated scale of smuggling autos, cigarettes, and oil; and (4) for the inclusion of services. The result of these adjustments is to reduce the estimated bilateral deficit in 1998 to about $35 billion, still a large number but much less than the $57 billion claimed by the United States. (Premier Zhu Ronghi cited this analysis in his speech at MIT in April 1999, as well he should have.) Fung and Lau also say that their adjustments do not alter the official estimates that the bilateral deficit has been rising at about $7 billion per year.

It is alleged by protectionists in the United States that imports from China are at the expense of domestic jobs. However, few of these products are being made in the United States any longer. In accordance with the familiar product cycle, they have migrated to coun-

---

[6]World Bank, *China 2020: Long Term Issues and Options for the 21st Century*, World Bank, Washington, D.C., 1997.

[7]Perkins, Dwight "Completing China's Move to the Market," *The Journal of Economic Perspectives*, Spring 1994.

[8]Fung and Lau, 1999.

tries with lower wage rates. China's competition in the making of such goods is mainly in Southeast Asia: Thailand, Indonesia, Malaysia, and the Philippines. One consequence of the fall in currency values in Southeast Asia in 1997 was the shifting of some work from China to that region (e.g., disk drive components) but hardly any work shifted from the United States.

China's imports grew about as rapidly as exports, and their composition also shifted away from commodities to industrial products, a move that was greatly helped by the increase in domestic agricultural output.

There is ample scope for continued rapid growth in China's trade, and World Trade Organization (WTO) membership will help to assure that. With world trade growing at about $300 billion each year, there should be room for an additional $20 billion worth of Chinese products annually. Assuming continued growth of world output and trade at past rates for the next decade, the rest of the world would have to absorb $550 billion of Chinese goods and services in 2009 out of world total trade then of about $9,000 billion. That would about double China's share of world trade to 6 percent, making it perhaps the world's fourth largest trading nation (after the United States, Japan, and Germany). If the increment in world trade value over the decade is $4,000 billion, it should not be seen as remarkable that China is the source of an incremental $400 billion. But there would be displacements, both in competing suppliers and, to a lesser extent, in importing countries and no doubt some protectionist opposition in them. Even so, it might not make a great deal of difference to China's development because, assuming sustained internal growth, the domestic market will be very large by then, perhaps $4,000 billion (in 1999 U.S. dollars).

FOREIGN DIRECT INVESTMENT

To attract direct foreign investment, China has offered substantial tax and customs duty exemptions in Special Economic Zones, Open Coastal Cities, Economic and Technology Districts, Open Economic Cities, and Open Economic Areas. The original incentives were highly successful, so much so that other provinces and cities wanted them, and they spread. In contrast, China has not opened itself much to financial capital, a prudent policy given the underdeveloped state of its financial institutions. The wisdom of having controls on capital flows was shown during the financial panic of 1997–1998, which left China relatively unscathed. (It is noteworthy that three of the four parts of "Greater China,"—the Mainland, Taiwan, and Singapore—did relatively well during the crisis; the fourth, Hong Kong, was hurt by a combination of a currency fixed to the dollar and the inability of domestic prices to fall rapidly enough to avoid a slump in output.) The Chinese also have not encouraged equity investment by foreigners in Chinese firms. As of 1999, many foreigners have had disappointing experiences and are pulling back. Many funds started in the early 1990s, and in 1995, at the peak, more than $1 billion was raised, but by 1998 the figure was halved. Profits have been poor, and there have been disputes over agreements.[9]

Direct investments are another story. China is now second after the United States as a destination for foreign direct investments, receiving 30 percent of all FDI going to developing countries—as conventionally reported. However, a large part of reported FDI, about 25 percent of the total, apparently has been capital recycled through Hong Kong (and elsewhere) and brought to China to take advantage of the benefits accorded capital labeled "foreign." Chinese enterprises exporting to Hong Kong understate the value of their exports relative to their market price; the difference is stripped off in Hong Kong when the goods are resold. This is a good way to move funds out of China altogether (and doubtless some of these funds have found their way to such places as Vancouver and California), but much of it comes back to China in the form of "foreign" investments that take advantage of tax and other benefits. (This maneuver, as discussed above, greatly distorts U.S.-China trade data.)

Nonetheless, since 1992, FDI has played a large role in China's rapid growth. In 1983, it was only 0.2 percent of GDP, and it did not go much over one percent until 1992. By 1997, FDI accounted for 7 percent of its gross industrial output, 11 percent of gross domestic investment in fixed assets, and, in 1998, 13 percent of gross domestic capital formation.[10]

---

[9] *Wall Street Journal*, October 11, 1999.

[10] Fung, K. C., Lawrence J. Lau, and Joseph S. Lee, *US Direct Investment in China*, unpublished manuscript.

There is a close connection between FDI and trade.[11] In 1998, foreign-invested enterprises were responsible for $81 billion out of a total of $184 billion in exports. If foreign-invested enterprises and processing and assembly exports are excluded, the average growth rate of Chinese exports from 1990 to 1998 would have fallen from 14.5 percent to 7.5 percent a year.[12] There is also a link between investments in China and exports to it via the propensity of investing firms to supply foreign affiliates from within the firm.

Lardy asks, Why has there been so much foreign direct investment given China's undeveloped legal structure, the nonconvertibility of currency, and corruption? The answers seem to be investments by ethnic Chinese throughout Southeast Asia and elsewhere and the fact that China kept liberalizing its foreign investment rules. The ethnic Chinese have a comparative advantage through their language competencies, family and clan ties, and a tradition of operating through personal connections. However, their potential for future growth in FDI is becoming smaller relative to that of other sources because the scale of foreign investments is growing larger and because advances in China's technological level implies a demand for more advanced technologies that can mainly be supplied by firms in advanced countries.

After a big increase in the early 1990s, "realized" (as distinct from "contracted") FDI has been on a plateau at about $40 billion a year. This is because the backlog of commitments made earlier had yet to move into reality and because of the slowdown in China's growth over the past five years. Also, some foreign investors have not made money, are investing less, or are pulling out.

The recent history of foreign investment in the electric power sector illustrates some of the uncertainties, risks, and promises in China.[13] From the early 1980s to the early 1990s, China was perceived as one of the best countries for direct investment in independent power projects, and many deals were made. Then problems arose in the

[11] Lardy, 1994.

[12] Fung, Lau, and Lee, unpublished.

[13] Thanks to Robert Crow, former chief economist of the Bechtel Corp, for these observations.

1990s over who among central and provincial administrators had authority to make deals. Also Prime Minister Li Peng decreed that foreign investors' could not get a rate of return higher than that in the United States. Because they perceived more risks in China, this cooled their interest—except in power plants of less than 300 megawatts that could be authorized at the provincial level without central government approval. Then in the late 1990s, several other events occurred to cool foreign investors' interest further: a slowdown in energy-intensive heavy industry and the raising of electricity prices toward market levels reduced demand for electricity; this left excess capacity. And the shift of some authority over such projects to the center from the provinces led to some cancellations.

A few big foreign-financed projects have, nevertheless, gone ahead, and as excess capacity is reduced over the next few years, and with institutional learning and reforms, there will likely be more foreign projects. There is a long-term demand for 10–15 gigawatts a year in generating capacity, an amount comparable to that being added in the United States. However, the capacity of Chinese equipment and engineering firms has grown, so foreign firms will be facing much more competition than in the past.

Although the creation of privileged zones for foreign investors has been a success, it has also created problems. One is the widened disparity in incomes between the favored areas in the south and along the coast and the less favored in the interior and north. To some extent, this regional income disparity reflects prior differences in human capital; for example, the Shanghai area was long more-advanced than other parts of the country, but the policy of selective openness to foreign investment widened existing differences. The income disparity has naturally led to large-scale migration of people to the fast-growing areas. The resulting huge "floating population" consists of people who are on the whole better off for having moved but who are denied various social benefits received by many of their settled coworkers. However, with the passage of time the privileges afforded foreign investors have become more widely distributed throughout the country.

Although it seems impossible to measure it with any precision, arguably the greatest effect of FDI is in transferring technology, management methods, business models, and the building of institutions.

(It is hard to argue that a country that saves 40 percent of its national income lacks financial capital.) There are many ways for less-developed countries to acquire technology: licensing, studying academic and trade journals, reverse engineering, learning from trading partners, inviting expatriates to come home, sending students abroad (hoping that they will return sooner or later), and FDI. The last of these is an especially effective way to get advanced technology because it comes via an institution: a multinational corporation that can bring tacit knowledge that is often crucial and that is not conveyed via arms-length techniques such as licensing. China's rapid progress must be due in substantial measure to FDI, and there is much more to come if it continues to make itself an attractive destination.

THE IMPORTANT ROLE OF HONG KONG

Throughout, China's outward-oriented strategy has had a special role for Hong Kong. The British colony had developed a sophisticated knowledge of how to operate in world markets. This knowledge, its role as a financial center, its management competencies, and its contacts proved valuable to Chinese enterprises trying to operate in the wider world with which they were unfamiliar.

Hong Kong has served in several ways to help the development of China, especially the bordering province of Guangdong. Hong Kong firms receive goods from China, sometimes add further value to them, and distribute them to customers around the world. Another role played by Hong Kong firms is to invest in Special Economic Zones such as nearby Shenzen. The pattern is one in which headquarters' functions, such as finance, product design, and marketing, are done in Hong Kong, and products are made, often nearby, in China. The scale of these operations has gotten quite large. Naughton observes that much of Hong Kong's investment in China represents the ordinary process of growth in a metropolitan region expanding outward in concentric circles and that the more liberal trade regime China has created space for Hong Kong and, ultimately, Taiwan to expand.[14]

---

[14]Naughton, 1996.

Although the general opening of China suggests that Hong Kong will play a less important role than in the past, Beijing has a strong incentive to sustain Hong Kong's competencies. These center on the rule of law and relatively little regulation and corruption, all attributes in short supply in China proper. The slogan of "one nation, two systems" refers to a political structure likely to be of continuing value. It still remains uncertain that this precious asset will not be depleted.

CHINA AND THE WORLD TRADE ORGANIZATION

The agreement between the American and Chinese governments on the terms of China's accession to the World Trade Organization is a signal event (although at this writing, the U.S. Senate has yet to confirm this agreement). Because it entails far-reaching concessions on China's part, it is not surprising that it took a long time to happen. Among many other consequences, China's accession means the end of the annual congressional vote on "normal trade" (formerly "most favored nation"). One might think of this as a U.S. concession, but it is a ritual the United States will be well rid of.

Viewed from an American perspective, three attributes of the WTO are paramount here: The first, of course, is its liberal content. The second is its multilateral character, one that should diminish the role of the United States as a nag in getting China to conform to market rules. And third is its potential for strengthening the hand of China's center versus local protectionism. This last point deserves comment.

Even before the reforms began, China was much less centralized than the Soviet Union, and with the reforms it has become a markedly decentralized one. As one scholar put it:

> [I]n a space of fifteen years or so, the Chinese political structure has been transformed from one that was once reputed for its high degree of centralization and effectiveness into one in which the center has difficulty coordinating its own agents' behavior. Because power and resources are dispersed, the exercise of central control now de-

> pends to a large extent upon the consent of the sub-national units whose actions are slipping from central control.[15]

Evidence on the fragmentation of power is extensive and local protectionism is rampant. Moreover, this dispersion of power coincides with a fundamental characteristic of the regime, which is that Communist Party interests—as interpreted though a vast bureaucratic apparatus—trump objective and public rules, i.e., laws. The system is both fractionated and obscure. Many laws, regulations, and rules are unpublished and inaccessible without personal connections. Recently China has agreed to publish trade and FDI-related measures (which in any case is called for under Article X of the General Agreement Tariffs and Trade (GATT) and incorporated in the WTO), and, although practice has improved, regulations are sometimes vague, arbitrary, and inconsistent. Bureaucrats still have much latitude in interpretation, and some rules are still not made public. Also provincial and local governments' actions often vary among each other and with the central government. There is much to be said for a federal system of government that allows for variation among the parts, and China exhibits federalist properties. However, a crucial attribute of federalism is an American type of constitution of interstate commerce clause, and China effectively lacks one.[16] Ironically, for a system that was founded on the principle of central control (a "command economy"), today China has too little of it in some ways.

Informed observers are skeptical of the capacity of the WTO dispute resolution system to secure Chinese compliance with agreed-upon goals and schedules and fear that the system could become seriously overloaded. Concerns have been expressed as to whether "even if the central government makes a commitment to develop Chinese legal

---

[15]Shaoguang Wang, "The Rise of the Regions: Fiscal Reform and the Decline of Central State Capacity in China," in *The Waning of the Communist State, Economic Origins of Political Decline in China and Hungary,* Andrew Walder, ed., Berkeley, University of California Press, 1995.

[16]Gabriella Montinola, Yingi-Yi Qian, and Barry Weingast, *Federalism, Chinese Style: The Political Basis for Economic Success in China*, Stanford University, Stanford, Calif., February 1994.

institutions in order to approach treaty standards, it would be able to carry out such a commitment."[17]

Accession has major implications for how the Chinese government handles a wide range of trade and investment topics. Its purpose is to lower barriers in several ways: tariffs, nontariff barriers such as quotas, import licenses, unwarranted inspections, and standards related to agriculture, health, investment, textiles, and dumping. Separate agreements are supposed to include intellectual property and services. The agreement with the United States includes foreigners being able to own 50 percent of telecommunication firms within two years and having management control, foreign banks being able to do local currency business with Chinese firms, and tariff cuts, including about a 75 percent reduction in those on autos. China has said that it will sign the global Information Technology Agreement on the occasion of its accession to the WTO; that would soon bring Chinese tariffs on many high-tech products to zero. China has made progress on intellectual property protection in recent years, but it will remain a contentious topic.

According to a World Bank report, China's full entry into the world trading system will lead to it more than tripling its share of world trade, to 10 percent by the year 2020, making it the world's second largest trading nation.[18] This probably will require annual growth in exports at 12 percent a year, modestly less than the growth rate of the 1990s. China might account for 40 percent of the increase in imports of less-developed countries between 1992 and 2020. This would not be entirely at the expense of such competitors as the Southeast Asian nations, but their terms of trade would suffer. Altogether, the benefits to China of membership have been estimated at $116 billion a year by 2005 (about 6 percent of its projected GDP).

THE EXCHANGE RATE

The Western financial press in the past three years has repeatedly carried stories to the effect that China was about to, or would within

[17]Stanley B. Lubman, "Dispute Resolution in China after Deng Xiaoping: "Mao and Mediation" Revisited," *Columbia Journal of Asian Law*, Vol. 11, No. 2, February 1999.

[18]World Bank, *China Engaged*, World Bank, Washington, D.C., 1997.

several months, or would early next year, devalue the yuan to offset the disadvantage from the depreciation of its competitors' currencies. These stories have lacked plausibility. Much has been made of the Chinese authorities' desire not to set off another round of devaluations, an explanation that has won them plaudits. This may be so, but there are more self-serving reasons. One is that they have lowered the value of the currency modestly by rebating the value added tax on exports (a common procedure elsewhere); another is that China's exports, except to countries whose economies were most hurt during the crisis, have held up well—notably to the United States. Yet another is that yuan devaluation would put further strain on the Hong Kong dollar and might lead to its link with the U.S. dollar being altered. Also, given the history of hyper-inflations in China, the government is sensitive to any moves that might cause people to flee its currency. This is not to say that the value of the yuan is forever fixed, but analysts would do well to consider the possibility that the yuan's next major move might be up rather than down.

It would also be a mistake to infer that American investment in China versus that in other less–developed countries is highly sensitive to exchange rates. It is not because most of it is aimed at serving the domestic market.

CHINA'S HIGH TECHNOLOGY FUTURE

A question of interest for several reasons is China's high technology future. Research-intensive products and services will become an increasing share of output; they will become increasingly important for trade, both ways; and they will play a large role in China's defense sector.

China is a large and growing market for computers and their components, telecommunication equipment, and aircraft and is a potentially large one for pharmaceuticals and many other research-intensive products. Its competencies to manufacture such products are growing. With over 1 million scientists and engineers and over 5,000 research institutes, its scientific and technological potential is great. Some of these research institutes are being restructured to become technology companies, some of them in collaboration with foreign investors or partners. The government has invested in 47 engineering centers with 11 so far operating as corporations.[19] About 100 high technology parks have been created (many of which so far display little activity).

The success of Taiwan in the computer industry serves as one model for the mainland. Its was a largely market-driven process, but with important help from the government's Industrial Technology Research Institute. Other features of the Taiwan model were the recruiting of engineers with experience from the United States; links with firms in Japan, the United States, and Europe to learn about technology and markets; favorable tax and securities laws; the emergence of private sources of finance in the form of individual and venture capital; and the development of good universities whose science and engineering faculty members have developed close ties with firms. A contributor to Taiwan's success (notably in the computer industry) is close links with the leading sources of technology and market know-how in Silicon Valley. There is much moving back and forth of data, ideas, and—despite the supposed "death of distance"—people on airplanes.

Taiwan serves not only as the best model of how to catch up in a fast-moving sector, but it is already serving as a bridge to help the mainland move ahead as firms in Taiwan out-source jobs to the mainland. But as the mainland develops, the task its aspiring high technology enterprises increasingly face will be one of creating intellectual property. Judging from the experience of Taiwan (as well as India, Israel, Ireland, and other places), this will be helped by close ties to the main centers of technology in developed countries.

An inevitable by-product of technologic advances for civil applications is advances for military applications. This is a switch from the situation several decades ago when advances in military technology often led to civilian ones, as happened, for instance, in jet aircraft, nuclear power, computers, and telecommunications. Now, for example in computers and telecommunications (whose technologies are converging), civil applications are often in the lead. There are, of course, important military sectors that have little or no significant

---

[19]World Bank, *World Development Report*, 1998/99, World Bank, Washington, D.C., 1999.

civilian counterparts, such as stealthy aircraft, but overall, countries that come to be advanced technologically in general, as will be true of China, will find the barrier to military uses of these technologies lower than in the past.

CONCLUSION

For those who recognize that openness promotes development and that a country's development, if it goes far enough, is a sufficient condition for its political evolution to political pluralism, China's increased involvement with the world economy should be welcomed not only for the familiar commercial reasons but for political ones as well.[20] According to this view, Deng Xiaoping's initial instinct to push exports, reinforced by his southern tour in 1992, has turned out to be fateful and highly beneficial for China's political as well as its economic development. Of course, this is not to maintain that all will be smooth sailing ahead on either front.

---

[20]Henry S. Rowen, "The Short March: China's Road to Democracy," *The National Interest,* Fall, 1996.

Chapter Ten

AMERICAN INTERESTS IN AND CONCERNS WITH CHINA

John Despres

America's main interests in China have been quite constant and largely consistent with China's own interests. But the American people's and their political representatives' concerns about China's current behavior and long-term intentions have waxed and waned. Since U.S.-Chinese relations were normalized two decades ago, Americans have both idealized and demonized the drive of China's leadership to preserve social stability and perpetuate its political power by raising the Chinese people's material living standards, the level of China's technology, and the strength of their security forces. Rose-tinted visions of China's early political reform have not materialized. Dire predictions of Chinese military expansion have also been discredited. Overly optimistic forecasts of profits from private U.S. investments in China remain unfulfilled. And a peaceful settlement between Taiwan and China does not appear imminent. As a result, Americans' views of China have become increasingly sober and stable since the thawing of the cold war.

Geopolitics have become more fluid in the 1990s. America's concerns with China's possible use of force against Taiwan have grown more serious and occasionally acute. Americans have also focused more sharply on China's acquisition, application, and export of strategic technologies. At the same time, popular opposition to freer trade with China in the absence of greater respect for human rights and religious freedom has grown, especially among lower-income Americans. Public opinion surveys even suggest that four out of five

Americans believe the United States should introduce environmental and labor standards into the World Trade Organization (WTO) when China joins this international rule-making and commercial dispute-settling body. Booming U.S. demand for imports from China have boosted trade deficits, reinforcing American frustrations with China's barriers to U.S. exports and investments. Indeed, China became a main focus for protests against globalization that disrupted Seattle in November 1999.

Still, China remains the world's most populous nation and, despite its recent slowdown, one of the fastest growing, with enormous potential for good or ill. To help realize the good and limit the ill, most Americans favor China's joining the WTO, assuming it lives by the rules. This is not just because prospective exporters and investors see great opportunities for themselves in China's growing market. Americans also expect China's participation in the WTO to accelerate the reform of its economic and legal institutions; to open the door for Taiwan's accession to the WTO and for direct, cross-straits trade links between Taiwan and China; and thus to lower political barriers to the movement of people, information, and ideas between them. Above all, they hope that China will refrain from provocative shows or coercive uses of force against its claimed compatriots on Taiwan, as when it fired missiles menacingly in the Taiwan Straits in 1996. For all these reasons, the United States will remain keenly interested in China's political as well as economic reform, its progressive integration into the global community, and the peaceful course of its cross-straits relations.

Strategic bonds between the United States and China weakened as the cold war thawed in the late 1980s and the Soviet Union expired in the early 1990s. There was no longer any need to contain Soviet expansion. Moreover, the eruption and repression of public protests in China in 1989 renewed American revulsion toward the Chinese leadership's harsh treatment of its critics and opponents, which had been largely dormant since the Cultural Revolution ended, Mao died, and U.S.-Chinese relations were officially "normalized" in the 1970s. The end of the cold war and China's violent crackdown changed the climate for U.S.-Chinese relations and opened American eyes to China's continuing lack of individual liberties and democratic practices.

Nevertheless, America's main interests in China have been quite constant, namely peace, security, prosperity, and a healthy environment. Chinese interests in the United States have also been quite constant and largely compatible, notwithstanding sharp differences over Taiwan, strategic technology transfers, trade, and human rights. Indeed, U.S.-Chinese relations have been consistently driven by strong common interests in preventing mutually damaging wars in Asia that could involve nuclear weapons; in ensuring that Taiwan's relations with the mainland remain peaceful; in sustaining the growth of the U.S., China, and other Asian-Pacific economies; and, in preserving natural environments that sustain healthy and productive lives.

What happens in China matters to Americans. It affects America's prosperity. China's growing economy is a valuable market to many workers, farmers, and businesses across America, not just to large multinational firms like Boeing, Microsoft, and Motorola, and it could become much more valuable by opening its markets further. China also affects America's security. It could either help to stabilize or destabilize currently peaceful but sometimes tense and dangerous situations in Korea, where U.S. troops are on the front line; in the Taiwan Straits, where U.S. democratic values and strategic credibility may be at stake; and in nuclear-armed South Asia, where renewed warfare could lead to terrible consequences. It also affects America's environment. Indeed, how China meets its rising energy needs and protects its dwindling habitats will affect the global atmosphere and currently endangered species.

China's economic growth has slowed, while its social and environmental challenges have continued to mount. It faces difficult choices. The gains from economic liberalization have been waning. Painful institutional and political changes will be needed to sustain growth. Most immediately, political leaders will need to dismantle their counterproductive controls over the allocation of scarce capital, particularly through the state banking system. To restrain corruption, reform the tax system, and raise the revenues needed to pay for essential public works and services, China's political leaders, lawmakers, regulators, and other officials will need to be made more openly and directly accountable to the people whose interests they claim to serve.

Yet, China's leadership, preoccupied with preserving its own power, lacks a convincing vision of China's future. While we do not know whether China will rise to the challenge and prosper, or stagnate and falter, Americans have a great stake in China's successful reform. That is why they have an interest in China's acceding to the WTO, opening it to the global economy, and strengthening its compliance with international rules and norms.

Even so, they expect potential conflicts of interests to recur. China would like the people of Taiwan to accept its view of Chinese sovereignty peacefully. But, when the people of Taiwan prepared to choose their next leader peacefully at the polls in 1996, and again in 2000, China asserted a right to impose its views on them forcefully, notwithstanding American insistence that it refrain from such violence. China also insists on its right to modernize its armed forces and to buy or sell strategic technologies, without disclosing how it does so and without conceding any allegations that it violated U.S. laws or its own treaty obligations. But Americans do not want it to acquire, deploy, or export strategic technologies that could be used against the United States or its allies in Northeast Asia, the Persian Gulf, or elsewhere.

China's self-perpetuating, one-party dictatorship also denies people's right to political speech, religious assembly, and labor or other organizations outside of state and party control. Openly criticizing such strict constraints on human rights will continue to be an essential expression of American ideals. Until China strengthens its property laws to meet international market standards, disputes over the intellectual, financial, and tangible property rights of Americans in China will also persist, and could rapidly escalate or proliferate.

Recent U.S. Presidents have made great efforts and had endless difficulties pursuing American interests in China. China was a source of troubles for President Clinton in 1998 and 1999. In particular, he seems to have let Chinese leaders expect more from him on Taiwan and the WTO than he was prepared to deliver. After announcing a new "strategic partnership" with China on his visit there in 1998, he neglected to reiterate America's overriding interest in peace when he articulated the Chinese leadership's "Three No's" policy toward the recognition of two Chinas, support for Taiwan's independence, and acceptance of applications by Taiwan to join international organizations, like the United Nation. At the time, this was reported to be the *quid pro quo* for letting President Clinton give a speech on Chinese TV, which was finally permitted without prior publicity when the viewing audience was predictably small.

While the president's recitation of the "Three No's" did not alter U.S. commitments, critics saw it as taking the Chinese side in the cross-straits dispute and Taiwan's President Lee took advantage of the ensuing controversy to assert special state-to-state relations between Taiwan and China. It is hard to know whether the cross-straits dialogue between the leaderships in Taiwan and China would have been renewed in the autumn of 1999, as planned, if President Clinton had not provoked President Lee into asserting Taiwan's statehood. It is also too soon to say whether serious or lasting damage was done by his rejection of Premier Zhu's unexpectedly bold and favorable offer in April 1999 for China's accession to the WTO. The damage has been limited and partially repaired already from the president's ill-advised hesitation to apologize for the unintended bombing of the Chinese Embassy in Belgrade and the Chinese leadership's hasty and mistaken decision that it was a deliberate attack that justified nationalist reprisals by students stoning the U.S. Embassy in Beijing. Whatever the ultimate verdicts may be on these episodes since the first meeting of the RAND-China Reform Forum conference in Beijing in June 1998, they illustrate the great stakes and instabilities in the vital relationship between the United States and China.

CONCLUSION

Great common interests and risks of serious conflicts between the United States and China will keep raising difficult new challenges. They will require new initiatives for mutually beneficial cooperation and continuous efforts to avoid potentially critical misunderstandings over unforeseeable events in Taiwan, Korea, Japan, the Persian Gulf, Yugoslavia, or elsewhere. Without doubt, sustaining China's economic growth and reinforcing its institutional reforms though greater openness is a winning prescription for both the United States and China. To pursue this course amid unexpected difficulties, both countries will need to pay close attention to many issues, conduct frank dialogues, and participate in constructive statesmanship. Ups and downs in U.S.-Chinese relations will likely recur, but they need not be as volatile as they have been in recent years. Assuming that the future will mirror the past, substantial changes in our situations and needs vis-à-vis each other will be unpredictable, inevitable, and hard to fathom. This puts a large premium on ensuring that there are clear communications between Chinese and Americans who are willing and able to keep the relationship on an even keel.

DISCUSSION ON JOHN DESPRES' CHAPTER

Shuxun Chen

I think that what interests and concerns in John's presentation is something in common and in difference between China and the United States. I basically agree with what he said in his presentation and in his outline. Both countries hope to seek to maintain a peaceful and stable security environment of the world, and wish to cooperate in limiting the potential conflicts and nuclear proliferation in Korea, South Asia, and the Persian Gulf; in protecting global environmental resources, in interdicting drug traffic; and in other areas of common interest. However, there are also many differences between China and the US, and some of them may present the obstacles to the development of the relations, and even may lead to the deterioration of the relations of the two countries, such as the Taiwan issue and the human rights issue mentioned by John.

It was an eventful year in 1999 for the Sino-U.S. relations, e.g. the Cox Report, the political donation, the bombing of the Chinese Embassy, the "State to State relations" by Li Denghui. Fortunately, China and the US finally reached the agreement on the WTO issue in November, otherwise, it should be said that it was the year that the Sino-US relation went backwards greatly. From Jiang Zemin's visit to the US in 1997 and Clinton's visit to China in 1998, both countries made a proposal to establish the "constructive strategic partnership relations", then to the backward of the Sino-US relations, especially after the bombing the Chinese Embassy in Belgrade in May of 1999, the relations between the two countries fell into the lowest point. Both sides are reconsidering the "constructive strategic partnership relations", and the mutual suspicious has been increased.

Why the Sino-US relations are fluctuated greatly? I think that the difference of cultural background is one of the most important reasons. Due to the different value and ideology, the Chinese differ greatly from the Americans for the perspectives on some events and issues, e.g. the Tian'anmen event, Li Denghui's visit to the US, human rights issue, Taiwan issue, and Tibet issue. Logically speaking, the fluctuation of the relations between the two countries should be even larger due to some serious differences, however, in the meantime, we have to notice the realistic elements in the Sino-US relations, such as the common interests mentioned above. Besides, China is a huge market, and the economic and trade cooperation between the two countries is mutual benefits to both sides. Thus, the Sino-US relations are relatively placid.

In the United States, generally speaking, the Administration is more realistic and advocates taking the "engagement" policy toward China, and the Congress and the media are more concerned about values and ideologies, and they prefer to take the "containment" policy toward China. When the relation is going on smoothly, the "engagement" and the "partnership" win an advantage, but whenever something happened, the "containment" is in the lead.

In 1950s and 1960s, China and the United States took each other as an enemy. At the end of 1960s, the two counties were facing a common enemy – the former Soviet Union. The leaders of the two countries made consideration from the strategic angle and decided to develop the relation between the two countries. Even though both sides had misgivings towards each other, held the completely different value and ideology, and had the superficial mutual knowledge and understanding, all differences between the two countries were laid aside for the time being in front of the threat of the Soviet Union, the other superpower of the world.

It should be recognized that, with the reform and opening-up in China and the more and more increased contacts between the two countries, the Sino-US relations have been moving straight forward and have eliminated some differences and misunderstandings, because many differences and misunderstandings were caused by the separation in the past. However, at the same time, we should also recognize the different value and ideology between the two countries, and both sides have its own interest and have its own perspectives. The threat of the Soviet Union was the "binder" of establishing and developing relations between China and the US. After the cold war, this "binder" has not existed any more, the elements of value and ideology are rising, and frictions and controversies are increasing. From the American side, the US has become the only superpower in the world, and some Americans have not broken away from the cold war thinking, especially some people from the various interest groups and the think tanks have put ideology into the position of the first importance to deal with the international affairs. These people constantly seek for the new enemy and look upon China as the new potential rivalry based on their cold war thinking. As the victor of the cold war, the Americans practice their democratic system as a model in the world and take the ideology as the basic lever of diplomacy. They peddle their value in developing the relations with China. From the Chinese side, China has a long historic cultural tradition, in which includes the strong nationalist spirit. The quintessence of the Chinese traditional culture is amiability to be the most importance. The Chinese are not aggressive and it has been approved in the Chinese history. In more than 100 years, China was under the invasions of the foreign powers, but the Chinese remained faithful and unyielding and maintained their dignity to fight against the invaders. At present, the Chinese are very vulnerable in facing the anti-Chinese groups of the world and the American hegemonism, for example, referring to the WTO negotiation between China and the US, many Chinese people were tired with the obstacles and conditions made by the Americans and unsatisfied with the concessions made by the Chinese government. The other example is that the nationalist sentiments of the Chinese people ran high after the Chinese embassy in Belgrade was bombed by the American. Although the top leaders of the two countries met in New Zealand and China and the US reached the agreement of the WTO negotiation, the mutual misgivings and the negative feelings prevailed.

Mr. Despres raised a question in his one page outline that candid Sino-American dialogues will be needed both to discover new possibilities for mutually beneficial cooperation and to avoid harmful misunderstandings of potentially critical differences between them. China is the largest developing country, the United States is the largest developed country and the only superpower in the world. To keep a smooth relation between the two countries is a good thing not only for these two countries, but also for the whole world.

There are many differences between China and the US, e.g. value and ideology, meanwhile, there are also some common interests, that is the realistic element, e.g. the economic interests and common interests in dealing with some international issues. In order to keep a smooth relation, both sides have to do their best to eliminate the differences, or to lay the differences aside, and seek for the common interests between them. The more the common interests, and the more smooth relations can be developed between the two countries. How can China and the US develop and keep such a smooth relation? Based on the experience in the nearly three decades after Nixon's first visit to China, it has been proved that strengthening contacts and exchanges is the effective way to develop the relations. These contacts and exchanges include the institutional and the individual, and the institutional includes the governmental and the nongovernmental. Through these contacts and exchanges, both sides are able to increase comprehensive and objective understandings to understand and forgive each other. After carefully analyzing the post-cold war situation and summing up the past experience and lessons, the Chinese government has pointed out the principles of eliminating conflict, reducing trouble, increasing understanding and strengthening cooperation to handle the international affairs and to deal with the international relations. I believe that if the US side takes the same or similar approach, the Sino-US relations will keep the development smoothly.

Chapter Eleven

SINO-U.S. ECONOMIC AND TRADE RELATIONS

Xianquan Xu

INTRODUCTION

Since the establishment of Sino-U.S. diplomatic relations, economic and trade relations between the two countries developed rapidly. Over the past ten years, trade volume between China and the United States has more than tripled. While differences and disputes in bilateral relations continue, the rapid growth of economic and trade relations between China and the United States cannot be stopped.

Two prominent issues exist in present Sino-U.S. economic and trade relations. One is trade balance. This chapter gives a multi-spectrum, in-depth analysis of this issue, identifying factors that have contributed to imbalances in Sino-U.S. trade. It also notes that the U.S. trade deficit with China has been exaggerated and overestimated and does not reflect the true economic and trade interests of the two countries. The United States should therefore not view the trade deficit with China as a serious issue. In fact, the deficit is a phenomenon stemming from the sustained growth of the U.S. economy and reflects the strength of the U.S. economy. The second issue is China's accession to the WTO. This chapter examines the reasons why Sino-U.S. negotiations on China's accession to the WTO has been such a prolonged process, finding that the United States has been the source of resistance. The deep-seated reason behind this resistance is that some Americans have not stepped out of the shadow of cold-war thinking. This chapter also points out that China's accession to the WTO is not merely a technical issue, but rather a political one and, therefore, requires that the final solution be sought from a political perspective. On November 15, 1999, China and the United States reached an agreement on China's accession to the WTO. This agreement has eliminated major obstacles in the development of Sino-U.S. economic and trade relations. It will also bring prosperity and stability to the world economy.

STATUS QUO

Since the establishment of Sino-U.S. diplomatic relations, economic and trade relations between the two countries have been developing rapidly, far beyond initial expectations. Particularly in the 1990s, when Sino-U.S. relations were at a low ebb, trade volume increased drastically despite frequent friction and disputes. According to Chinese Customs statistics, Sino-U.S. trade in 1998 was valued at $54.9 billion, 4.6 times that of 1990 ($11.8 billion).[1] The average annual rate of increase during that period was 21.19 percent. As recorded by U.S. Customs statistics, the 1998 trade volume between the two countries was $85.4 billion, which was 4.3 times that of 1990 ($20 billion). These statistics report the average annual rate of increase as 19.9 percent, which is much higher than the average rate of U.S. trade growth as a whole. China is the fourth largest trading partner of the United States (after Canada, Japan, and Mexico). The United States is China's second largest trading partner. China's exports to the United States account for over one-third of China's total exports. (See Table 11.1)

U.S. investments in China began in 1980 and experienced rapid growth in the 1990s. By the end of September 1999, there were 28,249 U.S. direct investment projects in China, with a total contracted investment of $50.9 billion and the actually invested value of $24.2 billion (MOFTEC, 1999). U.S. direct investments are distributed over 26 provinces, municipalities, and autonomous regions in China and cover a wide range of industries, including automobiles, pharmaceuticals, petrochemicals, chemicals, textiles, machinery, electronics, telecommunications, light industry, food, agriculture, and such

[1] All dollar amounts are U.S. dollars unless otherwise noted.

Table 11.1

Trade Statistics for China and the United States

	Chinese Customs Statistics (Billions of U.S. $)				U.S. Department of Commerce Statistics (Billions of U.S. $)			
Year	Total Imports and Exports	Imports from U.S.	Exports to U.S.	Trade Balance	Total Imports and Exports	Imports from China	Exports to China	Trade Balance
1979	2.45	1.86	0.59	-1.27	2.37	0.65	1.72	1.07
1980	4.78	3.82	0.96	-2.86	4.91	1.16	3.75	2.59
1981	5.89	4.38	1.51	-2.87	5.66	2.06	3.60	1.54
1982	5.34	3.72	1.62	-2.10	5.41	2.50	2.91	0.41
1983	4.03	2.32	1.71	-0.61	4.64	2.48	2.16	-0.32
1984	5.87	3.66	2.21	-1.45	6.38	3.38	3.00	-0.38
1985	6.99	4.37	2.62	-1.75	8.02	3.86	3.80	-0.06
1986	7.33	4.71	2.62	-2.09	8.35	4.77	3.11	-1.66
1987	7.86	4.83	3.03	-1.80	10.41	6.29	3.50	-2.79
1988	10.01	6.63	3.38	-3.25	14.31	8.51	5.04	-3.47
1989	12.25	7.86	4.39	-3.47	17.80	11.99	5.81	-6.18
1990	11.77	6.59	5.18	-1.41	20.03	15.22	4.81	-10.41
1991	14.20	8.01	6.19	-1.81	25.27	18.98	6.29	-12.69
1992	17.49	8.90	8.59	-.031	33.20	25.73	7.47	-18.26
1993	27.65	10.69	16.96	6.27	40.31	31.54	8.77	-22.77
1994	35.43	13.97	21.46	7.49	48.07	38.78	9.29	-29.49
1995	40.83	16.12	24.71	8.59	57.31	45.56	11.75	-33.81
1996	48.99	16.30	32.70	16.40	63.46	51.51	11.99	-39.52
1998	54.94	16.96	37.98	21.02	75.36	62.56	12.86	-49.70
					85.42	71.16	14.26	-56.90

NOTE: For U.S. statistics the figures for imports from the United States are from CIF for 1979–1984 and custom value from 1985.

service sectors as tourism, real estate, and financial services (see Table 11.2). An increasing number of American multinational corporations are showing optimism about China's markets. There are already more than 200 *Fortune* 500 companies investing in China, many of which are American conglomerates. The *Fortune* Global Forum '99 was convened in the Pudong Area of Shanghai on September 27. Among the executives of the more than 300 transnational corporations represented at the forum, many were entrepreneurs from American multinational corporations. The location of the *Fortune* Global Forum is usually based in an area of one of the most active and dynamic economies. The selection of Shanghai as the venue evidences the prevailing confidence in the great potential that Shanghai offers as well as the promising trend of China's economic development.

The achievements in the development of China-U.S. trade demonstrate the strong complementarity of trade and commonality of in-

Table 11.2

American Enterprise Investments in China (1982–1998)

Year	Number of Approved Projects	Contracted Value (millions of U.S. $)	Utilized Value (millions of U.S. $)
1982	23	247.00	118.68
1983	32	477.52	83.13
1984	62	165.18	256.25
1985	100	1152.02	357.19
1986	102	541.48	326.17
1987	104	342.19	262.80
1988	269	370.40	235.96
1989	276	640.52	284.27
1990	357	357.82	455.99
1991	694	548.08	323.20
1992	3265	3121.25	511.05
1993	6750	6812.75	2063.12
1994	4223	6010.18	2490.80
1995	3474	7471.13	3083.01
1996	2517	6915.76	3443.33
1997	2188	4936.55	3239.15
1998	2238	6483.73	3898.44
1999(1-9)	1575	4350.84	2791.62
total	28,249	5,094,440	2,422,416

SOURCE: MOFTEC, 1999.

terests between the two economies. Although some disputes have arisen in bilateral relations, the rapid development of China-U.S. trade and economic relations cannot be stopped.

Because of the differences in history, culture, social systems, ideology, and values, it is not strange that conflicts occur between China and the United States. Currently, the key issues giving rise to friction and disputes include trade balances, MFN, market access, protection of intellectual property, China's accession to the WTO, the textile trade, export of body parts from Chinese prisoners, antidumping laws, sanctions against China, and restrictions on the export of high-tech products. Below are my personal views on the two key issues mentioned at the beginning of the chapter.

THE CHINA-U.S. TRADE BALANCE ISSUE

China's statistics on exports to the United States exclude goods sold to Hong Kong or to a third country that are reexported to the United States, while U.S. statistics include such reexports as being from China. These variations in statistical methods have naturally led to divergent statistical results. An example of such statistical divergence can be seen in the trade surplus of $21 billion recorded by Chinese Customs in 1998, while that recorded by U.S. Customs was $57 billion. In addition, U.S. Customs calculations of imports from China ignore the value added from processing and repackaging of Chinese products in Hong Kong and in third countries for the purpose of re-export. Therefore, from the Chinese viewpoint, U.S. imports from China are overestimated.

One of the key reasons leading to exaggeration of the deficit suffered by the United States is the processing trade, which accounts for over 70 percent of the total trade between China and the United States. The materials, parts, components, and packaging materials needed for processed exports to the United States are supplied from the United States or other countries. The costs of the materials plus transportation and overhead expenses make up about 85 percent of the total product costs. The amount of the processing fee retained by China is a small percentage (only about 15 percent) of the total product costs. U.S. Customs then computes the total cost of such products as imports from China, which does not reflect the true picture and is therefore unreasonable.

The root of the problem is the statistical method based on the rules of origin. This method originated in the United States, gradually spreading to many other countries as a basic rule of statistical computation. In the past, since international trade was largely confined to inter-industry trading and there was limited foreign direct investment, statistical analysis based on the rules of origin could truly reflect the actual trade interest of each trading partner. However, against the current background of economic globalization and internationalization of manufacturing activities, where intra-industry and intra-multinational trading has increased substantially in volume and foreign direct investment has become increasingly pervasive, the conventional method of rules of origin cannot accurately reflect the trade interest of each trading partner. Rules of origin have given rise to two types of errors. First, multinationals have invested extensively in foreign countries. The raw materials, parts, and components associated with the manufacturing of these companies and trade of the finished products should be included in the statistics of the originating home country, but under the rules of origin, they are recorded in the trade statistics of the host country. Second, because the rules of origin emphasize merchandise trade and exclude service trade, the trade benefits of respective trading countries cannot be fully and accurately reflected.

In addition, the shift of production bases in the course of the processing trade has given rise to a "trade-balance-transfer" effect. Companies that were originally engaged in the processing trade in their home countries, such as Hong Kong, Taiwan, and South Korea, have moved their factories to mainland China. With that move, the value of the export products processed on mainland China are then transferred to China's account of export, thereby increasing the U.S. deficit with China. According to U.S. Department of Commerce statistics, the U.S. trade deficit with the four "tigers" of East Asia dropped from $34 billion to $7.8 billion from 1987 to 1995, while the trade deficit with China in the same period showed an increase, from $2.8 billion to $33.8 billion.

Also, the United States exercises stringent controls over exports of high-tech products to China, in effect restraining exports by American enterprises. This constitutes another reason for a trade imbalance between China and the United States.

Moreover, there are reasons to believe that U.S. export statistics have been underestimated. According to a report by *Business Week* (June 7, 1999), U.S. export statistics are inaccurate, leaving out tens of billions of export dollars, in addition to overestimating deficits. The U.S. Department of Commerce estimated that about 10 percent of the merchandise exported per annum were unreported. If all of these discrepancies are taken into consideration, the total deficit suffered by the United States was only $101 billion instead of $169 billion. This includes the overestimation of the U.S. deficit with China.

To summarize, the errors caused by origin determination are the key factors of statistical divergence. In the context of internationalization of production and economic globalization, economic and trade interests between countries cannot be viewed from only the single perspective of merchandise trade. Instead, merchandise trade, service trade, and direct investment should be taken into consideration together in assessing trade interests. The service trade in the United States, for example, is the most developed in the world and has been enjoying increasing surpluses. In 1997, the United States had a total of $85.2 billion surplus in its service trade, which was not reflected in the current account. Particularly noteworthy is the fast-growing revenue from foreign direct investment. U.S. multinationals invest in manufacturing facilities in host countries, thereby gaining access to locally produced products in the host countries' domestic markets. The sales of locally produced products have virtually substituted exports from the home country to the host countries. Moreover, such sales, which save transportation expenses and reduce operating costs, are more advantageous than direct export.

According to data from China's Ministry of Foreign Trade and Economic Cooperation (MOFTEC, 1999), the total sales of U.S. invested enterprises in 1998 was RMB 197.5 billion, which is equivalent to $23.8 billion. Deducting $5.4 billion for exports, the sales in China's domestic market amounts to about $18.3 billion. These domestic sales have in fact substituted part of what would have otherwise been U.S. exports to China (see Table 11.3). Moreover, some of the products produced by those U.S. invested enterprises have had very high rates of penetration in the Chinese market. For example, Kodak has over 70 percent of China's film market, Motorola occupies

Table 11.3

Total and Export Sales Income from American-Funded Enterprises in China (1998)

Sector	Number of projects (thousands)	Total sales income (millions of RMB)	Exports (millions of U.S.$)	Sales income in China[a] (millions of U.S.$)
Farming, forestry, animal husbandry, and fisheries	1,850	773.27	20.71	72.68
Exploitation and mining	610	171.12	6.84	13.82
Manufacturing	75,910	152,036.67	5,140.06	13,221.85
Electric power, gas, and water production and supply	700	12,243.37	1.29	1,477.37
Construction	2,850	2,202.42	3.23	262.76
Geological prospecting and water conservancy	70	82.83	4.85	5.15
Transportation, warehousing, postal, and telecommunications services	1,130	2,628.79	7.64	309.84
Wholesale and retail trade and catering services	6,740	5,682.55	41.20	645.09
Banking and insurance	40	108.94	0	13.15
Real estate	4,360	4097.18	17.41	477.41
Social services	9,640	6,861.24	9.73	818.92
Health care, sports, and social welfare	500	286.05	5.36	29.15
Education, culture and arts, radio, film, and television	170	325.15	0	39.27
Scientific research and polytechnical services	910	373.80	1.19	43.95
Other sectors	4,020	8,447.15	123.89	896.29
Total	110,440	197,485.05	5,397.88	18,452.97

SOURCE: MOFTEC, 1999.

NOTE: The above table may be incomplete because of possible omissions of unreported figures.

[a]$1 = 8.28 RMB.

30 percent of China's mobile phone market, and Coca-Cola and Pepsi-Cola have a combined share of over 50 percent in China's carbonated soft drink market.

Let's take a look at the profitability of the multinational-invested enterprises in foreign countries. According to a report by *Business Week* (March 1, 1999), the money made by American enterprises from the sales of overseas operations is three times that from the export sales of their plants in the United States. Data from China's Ministry of Foreign Trade and Economic Cooperation (MOFTEC, 1999) reveal that the total gross profits made by American-invested enterprises in China in 1998 was RMB 7.985 billion (about $960 million), with the net profits being RMB 3.5 billion (about $423.9 million) (see Table 11.4).

The data in the tables above indicate that the benefits generated from investments are more important to the Chinese economy than exports. The U.S. trade deficit with China, as recorded in U.S. Customs statistics, do not reflect the true trade interests between the two countries and are obviously exaggerated and overestimated. As a result, the United States should not view its trade deficits with China as a serious problem. It is in fact beneficial to the U.S. economy if service trade and the benefits from direct investment are taken into consideration. It is worth it to mention here that trade deficits go hand in hand with the strong growth of the U.S. economy, reflecting the strengths of the U.S. economic power and strong consumption boosted by increases in domestic demand. Importation of large quantities of low-cost, high-quality labor-intensive consumer products is to the advantage of American consumers in general, saving about $20 billion in consumer expenditures, and such importation will benefit the U.S. economy in particular as a supplement to the U.S. economic structure in terms of economic structural adjustment and upgrading. It will also help the United States control inflation and maintain low interest rates, thereby boosting fast-growing income. However, there is no direct and natural correlation between trade deficit and the rate of unemployment.

Table 11.4

Total and Net Profits from American-Funded Enterprises in China (1998)

Sector	Number of Projects (thousands)	Total Profits (millions of RMB)	Net Profits (millions of RMB)
Farming, forestry, animal husbandry, and fisheries	1,850	74.11	67.52
Exploitation and mining	610	46.77	47.46
Manufacturing	75910	4,904.90	2,349.88
Electric power, gas, and water production and supply	700	3,331.76	2,644.22
Construction	2,850	54.24	37.01
Geological prospecting and water conservancy	70	11.61	7.51
Transportation, warehousing, postal, and telecommunications services	1,130	109.48	79.36
Wholesale and retail trade and catering services	6,740	348.87	381.54
Banking and insurance	40	1.19	1.19
Real estate	4,360	85.98	16.12
Social services	9,640	187.06	902.00
Health care, sports, and social welfare	500	15.91	21.81
Education, culture and arts, radio, film, and television	170	0.13	10.16
Scientific research and polytechnical services	910	25.66	14.32
Other sectors	4,020	142.31	131.06
Total	110,440	7,985.13	3,518.26

SOURCE: MOFTEC, 1999.

NOTE: The above table may be incomplete because of possible omissions of unreported figures.

CHINA'S ACCESSION TO THE WTO

Thirteen years have elapsed since China commenced negotiations on its resumption of GATT membership and entry into the WTO. Why were negotiations protracted for such a long period? In my view, the main barrier came from the United States. On a number of public occasions, the United States expressed its support of China's bid to join the WTO. However, during less-public negotiations, the United States expressed concerns about China as a developing country, repeatedly exerting pressure on China to accept high and demanding terms and forcing China to open more markets in an attempt to gain dominance over important industries and wring more benefits from the mainland. These pressures have hindered China's efforts to join the WTO.

China's economic strength and international competitiveness have been weak and are far from being a contending force against developed countries. China will not accept demanding terms that are inappropriate for China's level of economic development and could harm the national economy. China's economic opening is a gradual process that needs appropriate time for transition. There should be no doubt that China's position is appropriate for joining the WTO as a developing country. China's stance on WTO accession has always been clear.

China's entry into the WTO will not constitute a threat to the United States or any other countries; instead, it will only bring benefits. In my opinion, some Americans continue to harbor "cold-war thinking," which prevents them from seeing China's economic situation as it truly is. Some rigid-minded people both within and outside of the U.S. Congress think that China will constitute a major threat to the United States once it becomes a strong economic power, and therefore they take China as a hypothetical enemy. They oppose China's accession to the WTO and advocate a containment policy toward China. In fact, China's development as an economic power is in the best interests of the United States. China and the United States have recently established mutually dependent, complementary, and supportive relations. Chinese workers are producing a variety of low-cost quality consumer products for millions of Americans. These products, in effect, help the United States control inflation and create necessary conditions for sustained development of the U.S. economy. At the same time, the United States has created a lot of employment opportunities in China, which are conducive to China's economic development. How is it that this mutually dependent and close partnership can so easily be seen as belligerent? The several-thousand-year-old Chinese cultural tradition culture favors "turning enemies into friends," rather than "turning friends into enemies."

Based on my many years of research, I think that China's WTO accession is not only an issue of a technical nature. More important, it is an issue of a political nature. Discussions on technical details will only lead to prolonged bargaining and endless debate, and it will be very difficult to achieve common ground amid these differences and to eventually strike a decisive agreement. It is more important that politicians from both sides consider the long-term fundamental interests of both countries and resolve the problem.

The time has finally come. China and the United States have decided to move forward with the basic interests of both countries in mind. On November 15, 1999, they reached an agreement on China's accession to the WTO. This was an historic moment, beneficial to China, the United States, and the rest of the world. It has eliminated a major obstacle in Sino-U.S. economic and trade relations, symbolizing the beginning of a new era for Sino-U.S. relations. The agreement will further promote Sino-U.S. relations, assuring stability and paving the way for future improvements and developments in Sino-U.S. relations.

The signing of this agreement on China's accession to the WTO has received strong responses, and the American business community is particularly enthusiastic. It is widely believed that the agreement represents great opportunities for entering Chinese markets, bringing substantial business benefits, and opening unlimited business opportunities for American investors and business people.

The further opening of China's markets, lowering tariffs, eliminating quantity restrictions, and expanding market access will create necessary conditions for the entry of American goods and services into China, which will lead to significant increases in American exports to China, thereby expanding domestic employment in the United States. According to a report by the U.S. International Trade Commission (*Assessment of the Economic Effects on the United States of China's Accession to the WTO*), following China's accession, U.S. exports to China will increase by 10 percent, or $2.7 billion a year, in light of China's April tariff offer. The U.S. Department of Agriculture also predicted an increase of U.S. agricultural exports to China of $2.2 billion per annum.

The opening of China's service sector, which will be even more beneficial to the United States, includes access to telecommunications, banking, insurance, securities, tourism, and professional services. All of these will provide new opportunities for American service providers. Permission given to foreign investors to enter China's Internet and telecommunications market will offer American telecommunications companies and related service providers a great deal of benefits. In this way, American hi-tech companies and service providers are the biggest winners in the Sino-U.S. bilateral agreement.

China has also made commitments to grant foreign companies foreign trade and distribution rights, which include wholesaling, retailing, maintenance, after-sale services, and transportation. American businesses can distribute imported products and products that are made in China, which will in turn provide export opportunities for American products.

After China joins the WTO, the investment environment will be further improved. Foreign investment in China is expected to increase as a result of the increased attractiveness of the vast market. It is projected that foreign direct investment will increase to $100 billion by 2005, and it is likely that American investments will take the number one position in this increase. At the same time, American multinationals will strengthen their presence, making China their production base. Investments in the service sector and high technology are also expected to increase. American investors will see considerable returns.

For China, entry into the WTO conforms to the long-term and fundamental interests of the Chinese people and corresponds to the needs of China's reform and opening to foreign trade. It will also benefit China to achieve a sufficient, stable, and rapid economic development. In the short run, however, most of China's industries, particularly some state-owned enterprises, will experience many repercussions in being subjected to severe challenges.

China's accession to the WTO will also propel China along in its economic reforms, accelerating the shift to a market economy, facilitating the adjustment of its economic structure and reform of the enterprise system, and optimizing resource allocations in all directions. Introduction of the mechanism of competition will lead to increased efficiency and compliance with international norms and will accelerate China's integration into the mainstream of the international economy, thereby allowing China to reap the benefits of economic globalization and gaining more markets for China's economic development. Particularly, China's WTO accession will create a better external environment for Chinese enterprises, ensuring that they will enjoy nondiscriminative economic treatment and providing more market opportunities in their efforts to expand into international markets and exports. According to estimates by the World Bank, five years after China accedes to the WTO, the country's total import and export volume is likely to double, to $600 billion.

China's efforts to strengthen the rule of law and perfect its legal system may be reinforced by its accession to the WTO, resulting in increased transparency and an improved investment environment, which will attract more foreign investors and ultimately benefit China's economic development.

However, China's accession to the WTO will undoubtedly pose severe challenges to Chinese industries. The short-term effects are likely to result in more bankruptcies and worker layoffs, all of which may lead to social instability. These were the justifications for China's entering the WTO as a developing country, which will allow China to have an appropriate transition period for its nascent industries to mitigate these negative effects.

The above demonstrates that the agreement between China and the United States is a win-win situation, with American benefits being more direct. Therefore, the United States should support permanent trade relations with China. At the same time, the United States should also utilize China's WTO accession as a turning point to resolve remaining disagreements in Sino-U.S. economic and trade relations.

China is the largest developing country in the world. The United States is the most developed country in the world. Both countries have vast territories and abundant natural and human resources. Both countries have huge domestic markets of great potential. Through trade and economic cooperation, both countries can achieve resource complementarity and market sharing. Combining U.S. capital, technology, and management expertise with China's low-cost labor and huge domestic market will bring enormous opportunities of common interest to both countries. Therefore, improving Sino-U.S. relations and dissolving differences will help both countries forge benign and interactive relations and will have significant bearing on the economies of both China and the United States, as well as far-reaching implications for world prosperity in the 21st century.

CONCLUSIONS

When we examine the two major issues in Sino-U.S. economic and trade relations, the American deficit with China is in fact not a serious issue. An analysis on the basis of the facts clearly demonstrates that the statistical method based on the rules of origin has exaggerated the deficit, which does not reflect the true trade interests between the two countries. Processing trade is the key cause behind the deficit. A correct view of the deficit can be arrived at only when we take into consideration merchandise and service trade and foreign direct investment. Imports of low-cost, good-quality consumer products from China to the United States have supported structural economic adjustments and promoted upgrades in American industries, while also satisfying consumer demand, helping control inflation, and playing a facilitating role in the sustained economic development of the United States. With China's WTO accession, there will be a noteworthy increase in American exports to China, which will gradually decrease the U.S. deficit with China.

China's WTO accession has experienced over 13 years of prolonged and difficult negotiations. China and the United States reached a bilateral agreement on China's accession to the WTO on November 15, 1999. This mutually beneficial agreement has eliminated a major obstacle in Sino-U.S. relations, creating the necessary conditions for stable development of economic and trade cooperation between the two countries. It will also bring the world economy prosperity and stability. For this reason, the United States should take further steps in approving permanent normal trade relations with China.

REFERENCES

China Customs Statistics, Beijing, 1991–1999.

China Statistical Yearbook, Beijing, 1999.

Chinese Academy of International Trade and Economic Cooperation, *Research on the Economic Benefits of American Investment in China,* Beijing, 1999.

Clinton, William, *Speech on U.S. Government Policy Toward China,* U.S. News Agency, Beijing, April 7, 1999.

Ministry of Foreign Trade and Economic Cooperation (MOFTEC), *Statistics on Foreign Investment in China,* Beijing, 1999.

Noland, Marcus, *The U.S.-China Economic Relations,* Institute of International Economics, Beijing, 1996.

Sheng, Lijun, "China and the U.S.: Asymmetrical Strategic Partners," *Washington Post,* Summer Quarterly, 1999.

Tian, Shitang, "A Perspective on the U.S. Deficit," *China Economic Times,* March 29, 1999.

U.S. Department of Commerce, "Bureau of Economic Analysis," *Statistics,* Washington, D.C., 1991–1998.

U.S. Presidential Economic Report, U.S. Government Printing Office, Washington, D.C., 1998.

Wang, Zhile, *American Corporations' Investment in China,* China Economic Publishing House, Beijing, January 1999.

Xu, Xianquan, and Smith, *China and the World Trade Organization,* China Foreign Economic and Trade Publishing House, Beijing, December 1996.

Xue, Rongjiu, *Economic Globalization and Issues of Rules-of-Origin Statistics,* University of International Business and Economics, Beijing, 1999.

COMMENTS ON XIANQUAN XU'S CHAPTER

Hang-Sheng Cheng

My talk consists of two parts: First, I shall comment on Mr. Xu's paper; then, I shall present my own views on the subject.

To start, I wish to compliment Mr. Xu on his well-researched and tightly-argued paper. The data he presents are very useful, especially those in the tables at the end of the paper, which I believe are not available elsewhere. I have no doubt that this paper will be an important contribution to any conference volume the sponsors of this conference may wish to publish.

I also applaud Mr. Xu's judicious selection of the two topics: the U.S.–China bilateral trade balance and China's WTO accession. They are indeed key issues in U.S.–China economic relations. Resolution of these two issues would help solve most of the others, including the MFN (now called NTR, or normal trade relations), market access, intellectual property rights, textile trade, etc.

On these two, I have little to add to what Mr. Xu has said in his paper. The bilateral trade balance is a hot issue in official discussions and news media. However, to economists it is a non-issue. A country's total trade deficit reflects the excess of its national spending over its domestic savings, and bilateral trade balances reflect international comparative advantage and consumer preference. They are topics in different areas of economics. Mixing them is a common mistake based on misunderstanding, with unfortunate policy consequences. For instance, applying political pressure on a foreign country to ease trade restrictions may help alter bilateral trade balance, but will do nothing to change a nation's total trade balance. We have to ask ourselves whether it is total or bilateral trade balance that we care about. More basically, for an international–currency country such as the U.S., one needs to ask why we should care about either at all.

On China's accession to the WTO, even the White House now admits that it made a mistake in April 1999 in not accepting Premier Zhu Rongji's offer of concessions, including breakthroughs on industrial tariffs, telecommunications, financial services, as well as increased market access for U.S. agricultural products. An even greater blunder was committed by the White House to publish Zhu's list of offers, which should have been a matter for discreet negotiation between the two governments. As we know, as a consequence Zhu took on much criticism in China for having made the offers and gone home empty-handed.

Mr. Xu also states that China's accession to the WTO is in both countries' national interest. This leads me to ask, What is the U.S. national interest in its economic relations with China? I believe that for too long we have been bogged down on technical issues and failed to focus on this fundamental question of our long-run national interest. I believe that many of the flip-flops in our policy towards China and conflicts in our economic relations have their roots in this short-sighted, fragmented approach in dealings with China. It is high time that we begin a national debate on this question and determine where our long-run national interest lies. Then and only then could we avoid protracted and fruitless negotiations on partial, sectoral issues and work towards the formulation of a strategy for pursuing our national interest.

My position on this question can be summarized, without elaboration, in the following four propositions:

a. Given China's abundant labor supply and U.S. superiority in technology and capital, the two economies are complementary to each other. Both can reap large benefits from open trading. That is to say, restrictions on trade between the two are against the national interests of both countries.

b. Economic reform is the top policy priority in China. Over the last two decades, reform has had impressive success, but is now entering the most difficult stage. Outside help in terms of technical expertise in many areas—such as engineering, enterprise management, banking, capital market development, accounting, law—is much needed and would be greatly appreciated by both the government and the people. When offered with sensitivity and discretion, it would help dispel much of the mutual suspicion and hostility that now exist between our two countries.

c. It is in the long-run U.S. national interest to assist China in its economic reform. Properly conceived and executed, not only would it help win goodwill and thus help resolve many existing conflicts, but also would help gain access for U.S. businesses in a wide spectrum of functional areas and geographic regions in China.

d. There already exist many official or unofficial channels through which technical assistance is rendered. They need to be expanded and integrated into a coordinated national program with proclaimed, and sustained official backing. The program could be run by a non-government organization, but should be funded by Congress to demonstrate national policy commitment. Additional funding would be minuscule. It would be a most cost-effective way to promote long-run U.S. national interest in its economic relations with China.

Chapter Twelve

U.S.-CHINA: BONDS AND TENSIONS

Hui Wang[1]

It is almost certain that the world in the new millennium will see more interactions between the United States and China and also their growing effects on their and the world's prosperity. It is uncertain, however, how the interactions will develop. Recently, both sides have been puzzled in their interactions.

When U.S.-China relations became strained after the Tiananmen Square incident, Deng confirmed his conviction that China and the United States required a long-term, cooperative, and more trustful relationship, which would be in China's best interest.[2] During the last decade of the 20th century, however, a concert of historic events unfolded and complicated the earlier relatively simple tones of U.S.-China interactions. Along with other critical events, the collapse of the Soviet Union shook the fundamental bonds of the U.S.-China relationship as much as President Nixon's visit to China did in the past. China's "rising" and Taiwan's change in international status have also affected the U.S.-China relationship. From the view of dynamic equilibrium, although U.S.-China relations from the early

---

[1]Hui Wang is President of First China Capital, Inc. and a consultant at RAND. Tel. 310 383-3780. E-mail: fcc888@hotmail.com.

[2]In the early 1990s, Deng Xiaoping issued a mandate for relations with the United States: Increase trust, reduce tensions, develop cooperation, and avoid confrontation. It appeared publicly for first time on December 1, 1992, in *The People's Daily* in a report of President Jiang Zemin's meeting with a U.S. House of Representatives delegation and Ambassador James Sassor. On February 26, 1989, in a meeting with then President Bush, Deng Xiaoping was quoted as saying, "Increase trust and reduce tensions."

1970s had their ups and downs, the common fear of the USSR often generated enough mutual interest, tending to draw the two sides together. As Nixon explained it:, "During the Cold War, the United States and China were brought together and held together by our fears."[3] However, the end of the USSR and the cold war essentially eliminated that immediate motivation to remedy any problems in U.S.-China relations.

Prospectively, growing mutual economic benefits and potential mutual interests in maintaining peace and prosperity underline a possible structure for the U.S.-China relationship. The end of prolonged negotiations between the United States and China on China's entrance into the WTO and illustrates that both sides recognize broad mutual shared interests even though profound differences exist. As the United States is leading the world economy, the potential global impact of China for decades to come, from economic to environmental, should not be overestimated. Particularly, if China continues on its course of economic reform and accelerates broader social and political reforms, interactions between the United States and China could be profoundly more beneficial and productive.

Now, although no new terms have officially replaced the "constructive strategic partnership" initiated and advocated by the U.S.-China Summit in 1997 and 1998, both face challenges to the goal of a mutually beneficial relationship. China appears to be more suspicious of U.S. intentions regarding China's emergence than at any other time in the last three decades. China has become more confused about the already seemingly elusive U.S. decisionmaking process and at times has been reluctant to communicate with the United States. In addition, President Clinton's policy of engaging China was never an easy sell, and the American public, including the media and the Congress, often finds it difficult to accept China as a partner. However, many politicians and experts in international policy warn of the strategic danger in possibly misunderstanding and treating China badly and the potentially enormous costs of deterioration of the U.S.-China relationship.

---

[3]Richard Nixon, *Beyond Peace,* Random House, New York, 1994, p. 131.

The colorful history of over two decades generally attests that both the United States and China have strategically and pragmatically benefited from their cooperative relationship and mutual good will. History also shows the high price for mistakes in relations with China as shown by two wars near China, and the additional cost to China was forced isolation. The lessons and experiences are rich. In addition, one of legacy of the U.S.-China relationship is a tremendous improvement in and diversified channels of communication between the two countries since rapprochement. These should allow easier avoidance of problems.

Where is the U.S.-China relationship heading and what is driving it? An examination of bonds and tensions between the United States and China is intended to help address this question.

INTRODUCTION

Bonds and tensions between the United States and China are like a matrix of vectors, pulling or push the relationship. Certain elements that cause each side to receive what is expected and justified contribute to the equilibrium. Bonds between the United States and China stem from shared economic, security, and political interests and goals. Tensions between the United States and China arise from differences in and conflicts about economic, political, and security interests and goals. Even the most cynical agree that the United States and China share and respect many interests, rules, laws, and norms. At the same time, even those most optimistic about the relationship recognize the existence of vast differences in interests and in underlying culture, history, political structure, values, social and economic preferences, and recent experience. Additionally, vision and capabilities of leaders and domestic political conditions may from time to time become an important factor in shaping the relationship.

In this chapter, we will discuss bonds and tensions, focusing on world peace and stability, regional security and prosperity, Taiwan, business and trade, the environment, the ideological divide, and domestic factors and debates.

Even through some of the forces that previously drove the United States and China to equilibrium and cooperation do not exist any more, changes in the dynamic world also factor new elements and incidents into the relationship. As the collapse of the Soviet Union had different effects on the United States and China, so are their views of mutual interests, needs for each other, tensions, and related tolerance of each other. We have seen a continuous swing in the relationship and some erosion in public support on both sides. While the United States looks for a direction in its China policies, China guesses at the American's intentions. Particularly, the political rhetoric of presidential election years sends confusing signals and extreme messages to the Chinese. However, new bonds are growing, too, and some of them are not sufficiently appreciated. For example, one of areas in which the United States and China has a growing and long-term interest is the economy. The Chinese economy is still rapidly growing and is more integrated into the world economy than it was ten years ago. The United States and China have more interrelated economic interests than ten years ago, and their economic bond seems likely to continue well into the future.

For discussion, Figure 12.1 is used to illustrate movement of equilibrium of the U.S.-China relationship as determined by bonds and tensions between the two sides. Particularly, the figure illustrates interaction between the two sides in determining equilibrium of the relationship. The vertical axis shows factors of the U.S. side. The higher in the direction of arrowhead, the stronger bonds and the weaker tensions. The horizontal axis shows factors of the China side. From left to right, bonds get stronger and tensions weaker. Conversely, from high to low, or from right to left, tensions get stronger and bonds get weaker. The diagonal represents a collection of equilibrium of the U.S.-China relationship. At equilibrium, interactions of the two sides are reciprocal and the relationship between the sides is considered stable. The diagonal represents the rule of reciprocity in development of the bilateral relationship. The relationship may from time to time fall into the area between the two arches, centered around the diagonal. Departing from the origin along the diagonal, it moves in the direction of a warmer and more cooperative relationship. Theoretically, the closer to the diagonal, the more stable the relationship. Conversely, the further apart from the diagonal, the less stable the relationship. There is a tendency for the relationship to move toward the diagonal one way or the other. If one side

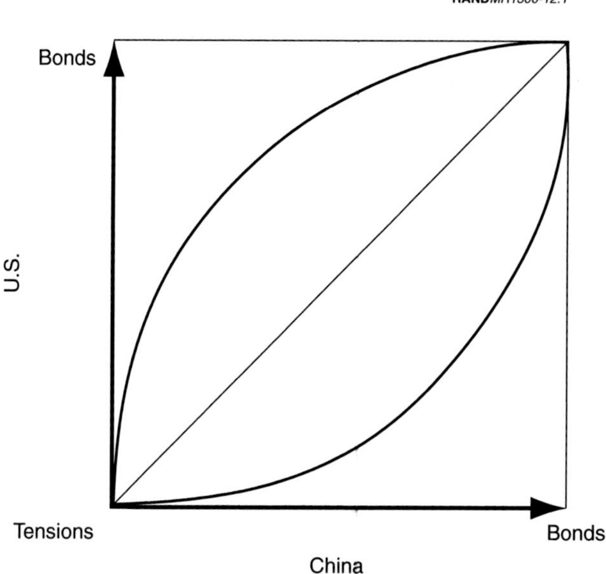

Figure 12.1—The U.S.–China Relationship

considers it treats the other side better than it receives in kind from the other side for a sufficient time, then it will adjust the relationship based on the reciprocity rule. The area beyond the two arches has only a small chance of occurring. In other words, a relationship would be very unlikely to exist beyond the two arches. We apply this figure to the U.S.-China relationship. The star in the figure indicates where the relationship stands, for example, in 1988.

When the relationship falls into the area between the upper arch and the diagonal, two types of situations can occur. First, the United States considers that there are more bonds and less tension than in the Chinese viewpoint. In this area, the United States tends to initiate actions to improve the relationship. Second, China considers more tension and fewer bonds than in the U.S. viewpoint. In this area, China sees the United States as causing more harm, either existing or potential, to the relationship. While the relationship is in this area, the United States would expect China to respond favorably to its signals and actions that are positive to the relationship. If China responds as expected, the relationship tends to move horizontally to equilibrium, which reflects a warmer relationship. However, if China does not respond for a period of time as expected, the United States would tend to move downward in equilibrium, meaning a colder relationship.

When the relationship falls into the area between the lower arch and the diagonal, there are also two types of situations. First, China considers more bonds and less tension than does the United States. In this area, China would tend to initiate actions to improve the relationship. Second, the United States considers more tension and fewer bonds than China does. In this area, the United States sees China as causing more harm, existing or potential, to the relationship. While the relationship is in this area, China would expect the United States to respond favorably to its signals and actions that are positive to the relationship. If the United States responds as expected, the relationship tends to move upward to equilibrium, which reflects a warmer relationship. If the United States does not respond for a period of time as expected, China would tend to move horizontally to equilibrium, meaning a colder relationship.

For example, Figure 12.2 shows the relative positions of the United States and China in 1988 and 1990. Many observers agree that the cooperation between the United States and China reached its peak in the late years of the Reagan administration, and the relationship went on well through the first few months of the Bush administration, before the Tiananmen Square incident. Both saw each other more as an asset than as a threat. In Figure 12.2, the star for 1988 shows the U.S.-China relationship, basically in equilibrium, located in the area of strong bonds and less tension. Cooperation between the United States and China broadened and deepened. Some cooperation, such as in jet fighter testing and design improvement, was intended to improve the Chinese capability to counter threats from the Soviet Union. Other cooperation indirectly helped raise Chinese technology and skills, such as the financing for over two dozens satellite launches by Chinese rockets, which enhanced Chinese space capabilities.[4]

---

[4]Jonathan Pollack provides a lucid account of these developments in his article: "The Cox Report's 'Dirty Little Secret," *Arms Control Today,* April/May 1999, pp. 26–27. See also, Bates Gill, "Limited Engagement," *Foreign Affairs,* July/August 1999, pp. 65–76.

As compared to the relationship in 1988, the one in 1990, represented by the 1990 star in Figure 12.2, was sharply lower and a bit leftward. As Secretary James A. Baker observed in 1995:

> The Tiananmen Incident shattered the bipartisan consensus in the United States that had been carefully constructed over two decades by five administrations for engagement with China.[5]

This explains the fall of the U.S.-China relationship in 1990 from that in 1988. Understandably, China's perception of the relationship descended but not as much as the change in U.S. perception, as illustrated by the leftward movement of the 1990 star in the figure.

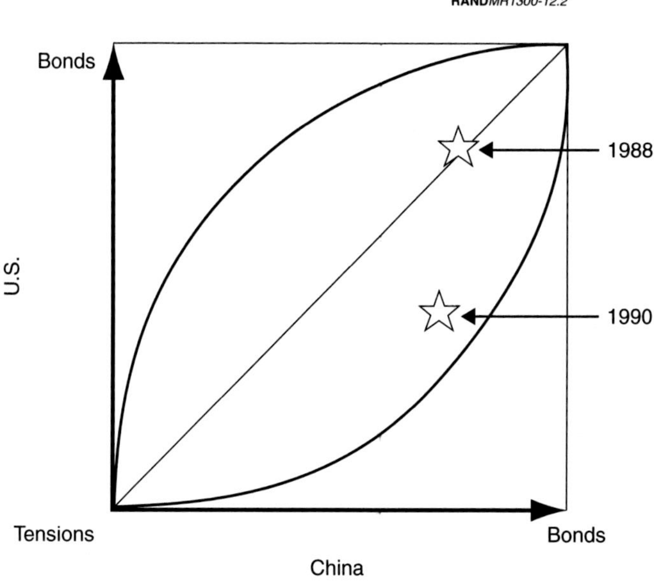

Figure 12.2—The U.S.–China Relationship, 1988 and 1990

---

[5]James A. Baker, III, *The Politics of Diplomacy,* G. P. Putnam's Sons, 1995.

WORLD PEACE AND STABILITY

The United States has profound interest in promoting a peaceful, stable, and prosperous world. China, to a large extent, shares this interest, and its cooperation and participation could make the American task easier. While the United States maintains dominant power in the world, China remains an East Asian regional power with several elements of global significance. Following are a few of these elements. As a permanent member of the United Nations Security Council, China provides crucial support for carrying out international mandates, peacekeeping, and humanitarian relief and assistance. With its 1.2 billion people, China represents over one-fifth of the world population. China is a member of the world club of nuclear weapons. China set a record for enduring development and growth and bears yet greater market potential for decades to come.

As signatories to such international agreements as the Comprehensive Test Ban Treaty, the Nuclear Nonproliferation Treaty, and the Chemical Weapons Convention, the United States and China share a mutual interest in their viability. Moreover, the United States would benefit from a China that not only accepts international norms but is also involved in crafting, monitoring, and implementing them.

The United States has a strong interest in keeping weapons of mass destruction and other sophisticated weapons out of unstable regions and away from terrorists. The United States understands that many of the threats today and in the decade to come will come not from conflicts between great powers but from states that defy existing rules and from violent nongovernmental groups. China is already a nuclear power with increasingly sophisticated weapon capabilities. The United States needs China's cooperation in preventing dangerous weapons from falling into the wrong hands.

China has been adjusting its arms sales practices and export of unsafeguarded nuclear facilities. But the United States seems to want China to limit or end some of its weapon sale programs and relationships with troubled clients. In recent years, mostly in response to U.S. requests, China has made efforts in controlling and preventing proliferation of missile and nuclear technologies. However, while the United States takes a lion's share of the world arms and weapons market, including selling advanced weapons to Taiwan, which troubles China deeply, China is not immune to its own domestic opposition to current policies of cooperation with the United States. Although a peaceful and stable world is in the interest of both the United States and China, differentiated economic interests have to be addressed, and in fairness, China can be expected to respond only to appropriate incentives. Not without costs, not without opposition, and not without second thoughts, China has managed to demonstrate improving compliance with prevailing rules. The United States needs to have a closer relationship with China to convince and motivate China to cooperate further on arm sales issues. In addition, China has cooperated with U.S. and international organizations in campaigns against drug trafficking and smuggling.

The United States and China also share an interest in limiting the spread of Islamic fundamentalism. For many years, the United States has been combating Islamic fundamentalist terrorists, whose anti-U.S. activities range from kidnapping to embassy bombing. Recently, China has become more concerned with its own terrorist related-problems, having suffered bombings on city buses and in busy shopping areas in cities of Xingjiang and other areas. Some of these terrorists have been trained in traditionally anti-U.S. and anti-West terrorist camps in central and southwest Asia. Although China has traditionally had good relations with Muslim countries, it has become more alarmed by the destructive activities of Islamic fundamentalists. When U.S.-China relations are stable, the United States may find China more willing to cooperate in limiting the spread of Islamic fundamentalism, given China's recent terrorist experiences.

Moreover, both countries would benefit if China had a greater stake in the success of institutions and regimes that foster economic growth. That would mean China's cooperation in supporting, in addition to the United Nations, the World Trade Organization, the International Monetary Fund, the Asia-Pacific Economic Cooperation group, the International Atomic Energy Agency, and others. When the worst financial crisis since World War II hit Asia and subsequently spread to other parts of the world, China's responses earned broad praise. By deciding and openly announcing it would not devaluate the yuan, China offered much needed stabilization during spiraling currency devaluation and a financial system meltdown.

Both the United States and China want to see a stable South Asia and prevent conflicts between nuclear-equipped India and Pakistan from getting out of control. Recently, the high-profile race for nuclear weapons tests between the two in 1998 and the Kashmir conflict in 1999 alerted the world to the instability in this region and confirmed the possible use of the ultimate threat. These incidents further remind the world of how disturbing their profound distrust could be to the region specifically and the world in general if a hostile game of threatened nuclear weapons use abruptly escalated. The United States is expected to continue to play a role in cooling down crises between India and Pakistan. China, although historically inclined to favor Pakistan, would be the last to want to see relations between the two escalate, both of which share borders with China. Since China has increasingly neutralized its position in such conflicts, both countries will try to garner China's favor, as indicated by both India and Pakistan sending top envoys to Beijing during their most recent confrontation. China, thus, could provide strong support to the United States in preventing any such crises from becoming extreme.

REGIONAL SECURITY AND PROSPERITY

The United States and China have strong mutual interests for peace and security in East Asia and the West Pacific Ring. With bitter experience of being invaded not too long ago and enjoying the rich rewards of economic reform and opening in the last two peaceful decades, China craves a continuing peaceful and stable domestic and surrounding environment. China sees itself fighting an uphill battle against growing challenges and dissatisfaction generated from its economic and social transformation and economic opening. China wants to avoid any chaos and loss of control. Any major disruption, such as a war, could put a halt to the current process of reform and structural change. The United States has broad commitments and strong interests in this area of the world largest population and economic block, from military to business ties. On the one hand, China sees the United States as the single force that can change the environment for its economic growth and further modernization, forcing China to choose very different approaches of development if it does so. On the other hand, the United States recognizes that China has the greatest potential to support or disrupt U.S. interests in this dynamic area of the world.

From the prospective of U.S. national security in this region and Asia at large, winning China's understanding, cooperation, and support has proven rewarding, while China has found the same with the United States as its ally. After Nixon's visit to Beijing in 1972, China cooperated with the United States in ending the Indochina wars and in keeping peace there, in driving the Soviet Union out of Afghanistan, in maintaining North East Asian peace and stability, in addition to other more global issues. In the 1970s and 1980s, respect and cooperation prevailed. In fact, since rapprochement with China, the United States has not entered any ground wars in Asia. In the 1950s and 1960s, hostility between the United States and China tragically cost the United States over 100,000 lives in Korea and Vietnam, and resulted in an even greater number of deaths for China.

Unforgettably, China, mostly by siding strategically with the United States in countering the threat from the Soviet Union since the early 1970s, contributed to and benefited from the ending of the cold war as did the United States. During the 1970s and 1980s, the United States and China cooperated militarily, from personnel training, intelligence sharing, and weapons testing, to weapon sales and weapon manufacturing equipment sales. In addition to military and diplomatic cooperation with the United States, China challenged the whole centrally planned Soviet economic model by its then-risky but tremendously successful reform and transition to a market-oriented economy. China, having suffered from the Soviet-style economic system itself, boldly dissolved the commune agricultural system and encouraged free enterprises across industries in the 1980s. Reform helped China achieve a high degree of economic growth and dramatically raised the quality of life of the Chinese people. China presented a strong and convincing case for economic decentralization and liberalization. China's economic success fundamentally shook confidence in the Soviet economic system and enlightened the thinking of officials and people of centrally planned economies, including those in the Soviet Union.

In terms of security and stability in Northeast Asia, outstanding is North Korea and its nuclear weapon and ballistic missile capabilities. Moreover, North Korea is heavily armed with over one million troops and has also developed other weapons of mass destruction, such as chemical weapons. North Korea's ideological isolation and economic failure heighten the risk for a military miscalculation. Although dialogue and negotiations with North Korea have increased in recent years, North Korea in general remains one of the most uncertain and explosive regimes in the world. While having much less influence over Pyongyang than most of Kim II Sung's time, China has been critical in averting a second conflict on the Peninsula. China explicitly opposes any military action from the south against the north, and China still holds the most influence over North Korea in any major crisis. Therefore, although the United States has been making the most initiatives on security issues with North Korea, China's support and cooperation remains crucial to any lasting success. Such joint diplomacy should include resolving questions about Pyongyang's nuclear program, persuading North Korea to halt further missile testing, and coordinating humanitarian relief. As members of the Four Party Talks on Korean security, the United States and China should continue their cooperation in dissuading North Korea from obstructing progress or from bolting from the process altogether. The talks remain one of the most important channels to diffuse tensions between North and South Korea—a near-term interest that Washington and Beijing share.

Even if there were a potentially dramatic change in North Korea, even beyond the point of North Korea being a threat, the United States needs to cooperate with China regarding the Korea Peninsula. Preparation for a wide range of possible challenges and events of new conflicts or lasting peace requires, at the minimum, the United States to closely consult with China. Likely, the Chinese influence on a unified Korea could grow substantially. Certainly any postunification arrangement in which Washington maintains a military presence in Korea will require some clear understanding with Beijing. Otherwise, China can be expected to exert tremendous, albeit subtle, pressure on the government of a unified Korea to forego any continuing U.S. military presence, leaving Japan domestically vulnerable as the only country in Asia with troops. After all, understanding and cooperation from China on any such security issues require a reasonably good relationship between the United States and China.

However, U.S. moves to proceed with theater missile defense in cooperation with Japan, South Korea, and Taiwan are understood in China as politically and strategically motivated efforts to confront and contain China. China increasingly considers the proposed development of theater missile defense in Japan, South Korea, and Taiwan a major shift, if not outright reversal, of U.S. policy and strategy toward China. By feeding Chinese fears of "being surrounded," the U.S. alliance in East Asia may do more harm than good. If the North Korean ballistic missile threat disappears, there will be no excuses for American military presence in the area. The extension of theater missile defense to Taiwan would constitute an extremely serious and high-stake turning point of U.S. security strategy in the region. Reactionary adjustments and long-term changes in China's strategy should be expected, and costs to everyone involved would be high. Before such plans for theater missile defense permanently set back U.S.-China relations, it would be helpful for the United States to reflect on the lengths it has gone to over three decades to open China's door and how easily such policies could close it.

It is in both U.S. and China's interests to maintain stability in the countries of Central Asian members of the former Soviet Union, including Mongolia, Kazakstan, Kyrgyzstan, Uzbekistan, Tajikistan, and Turkmenistan. Most of these newly independent countries suffer to different degrees from economic decline and social unrest. The United States wants to see a continuing orderly transition in these countries to a market economy and a democratic political system. Moreover, given the geographic location, the United States wants to assimilate the new Central Asian states into the international community and avoid any adverse changes in relation to the American-dominated security of the Persian Gulf. Meanwhile, as its economic reach rapidly extends, China is enjoying growing interactions in this area. China wants to increase its trade and economic ties with this area and to develop a local partnership for stability and development near its western border. It was in Central Asia that the United States and China once successfully cooperated against invasion by the Soviet Union in Afghanistan and made a classic example for Sino-U.S. cooperation by combining the most advantageous resources from each. However, if the relationship deteriorates, China could be displeased by U.S. strengthening ties in the region—China may perceive such a move as a new potential threat to its western border.

Neither the United States nor China want Russia to lose its remaining social and economic order. Since Russia possesses thousands of nuclear warheads and sophisticated missiles, further deterioration in Russia could potentially make world security uncertain and the already costly efforts at stabilization more costly. At the same time, both the United States and China do not want to see an expansionist Russia again but a cooperative and restrained Russia. In a long run, the United States and China potentially have more ground regarding Russia to cooperate on than to compete about. Russia is deeply suspicious about the United States and recent NATO developments. The unexpected Russian occupation of Pristina airport in Kosovo and firing of antimissile rockets are clear signs of this suspicion. Russian leaders were explicitly aggravated by the U.S. antimissile plan and implied that there would be consequences if the United States resigns from the 1972 Antiballistic Missile Treaty. In addition, Russia does not want to degrade economically into a third-world country, and although Russia has been accepting U.S. support, its understanding of U.S.-Russian relations are very different from that of the United States. As Russia's status as a world power continues to fall, its complaints and distrust will deepen. Even if Russia should become strong again someday, it will present uncertainties to its neighbors and to world powers, no matter whether it is capitalist or communist. Russia is no doubt less threatening than it was 15 years ago. And only ten years' experience of the "new" Russia has not contested the memory of the "Great Russian imperial consciousness" of the hundred previous years.[6] As long as China possess little military projection power, Russia will view China more as a counter balance to the U.S. superpower and less as a rival. Nevertheless, because of the long shared border, Russia and China's vigilance of and hedging against each other will reappear when Russia becomes stabilized. From a geopolitical point of view, the United States and China have common interests in preventing a reemergence of an expansionist Russia. But if U.S.-China relations deteriorate, a Russia-China alliance would likely emerge to counter U.S. dominance, which is the last thing that the United States would want to see.[7]

Both the United States and China want Japan to remain a world center of economic prosperity, extending the influence of peace and stability far beyond the region. Japan is another geopolitical factor keeping the United States and China together. Any emergence of Japanese militarism would not be in the interests of either the United

---

[6]Zbigniew Brzezinski, *The Grand Chessboard*, 1996, and *Game Plan*, 1986.

[7]See *The Grand Chessboard* by Zbigniew Brzezinski.

States or China. Even though Japan is a major ally of the United States in Asia, China will likely continue to consider a U.S. military presence in Japan a good exchange for keeping Japan from rearming.

TAIWAN

U.S. support of Taiwan, through arms sales and political commitments, continually provokes Chinese suspicions and distrust. The Taiwan issue also occasionally creates opportunities for the United States to strengthen bonds between itself and China, such as the Clinton administration's responsive reassurance to Beijing of the U.S. "One-China" policy in the wake of Lee Tenghui's state-to-state talk. Essentially, China sees the United States as the only real foreign obstacle to the long-dreamed of unification of Taiwan and China.

Taiwan stands out as the source of the most damaging tensions and distrust in the U.S.-China relationship. Taiwan could even cause a war between the United States and China. Taiwan has enjoyed broad sympathy and support from the United States, including formal U.S. congressional commitment to the Taiwan Relations Act and a wide range of personal contacts. In fact, several presidential candidates have promised to involve the United States if China attacks Taiwan. However, as China has indicated, and history demonstrated, it would be a deadly serious mistake to underestimate China's willingness to defend its interests—and Taiwan is foremost among them.

China views Taiwan as its territory and considers that separation occurred as a result of a combination of civil war and U.S. military involvement. As far back as the 1970s, the Chinese government made it clear that U.S. recognition of Taiwan as part of China was a critical condition to normalized relations. The United States has repeatedly acknowledged that there is one China and that Taiwan is part of China. To mainland Chinese, Taiwan is part of China, and it is inconceivable that it should be separated from China. Concession of Taiwan as separate from China could strip the Chinese government of its legitimacy and the Chinese people's faith. Regarding issues of territory and sovereignty, the Chinese believe Taiwan is to China as Hawaii is to the United States. The Chinese government simply cannot afford to lose Taiwan without exhausting all means to stop it. Growing up with both pride in its civilization of a thousand years and sorrow about cruel humiliations, the Chinese consider unification with Taiwan as the final milestone to ending its "Century of Shame." This national sentiment is deeply rooted in China's sufferings. It is worth pointing out that this sentiment may restrict China's view of the dynamically changing world and cause it too much prejudice to deal appropriately with other members of the international community.

Tensions about Taiwan are best reflected in contradictions of U.S. Taiwan policies. To begin, U.S. policy on Taiwan is governed by the Taiwan Relations Act. However, U.S.-China relations regarding Taiwan were initiated, developed, promoted, and institutionalized more on the basis of bilateral treaties, commitments, public statements, and private promises by and between the administration offices of the six consecutive U.S. presidents since Nixon and the Chinese government than by the Taiwan Relations Act. Fundamental contradictions in U.S. signed treaties together with commitments to China and the Taiwan Relations Act are increasingly viewed by China as U.S. violations of pledges to the Chinese. One of the contradictions, for example, is that the Taiwan Relations Act obliges the United States to sell arms to Taiwan while the United States publicly committed to China to reduce the quality and quantity of arms sales to Taiwan.

At the same time, the United States sees itself as obligated to keeping Taiwan's peace. To the mainland Chinese, U.S. obligations to Taiwan can be better understood as the result of more than two decades of confrontation under the cloud of the cold war. The American obligation toward Taiwan in general cannot be easily dismissed. The United States, however, does not have the same obligations to Taiwan as it has to Japan and South Korea. It also appears not to be in the best interests of Japan or South Korea to allow U.S.-China military confrontations over Taiwan. Japan and South Korea would much prefer to see the United States use its skill, rather than arms, to manage conflicts of interest in the face of dynamic changes in the region. It is also in the United States' best interests to reduce tensions with China regarding Taiwan and avoid a potential arms race in the region.

Two critically important changes occurred since the late 1970s, when normalization of relations between the United States and China took place and the Congress passed the Taiwan Relations Act. First, China became a market-oriented economy, and China, although still not democratic, is significantly more economically open and integrated with the rest of the world than at any time before. Second, China has abandoned the goal of "liberating Taiwan"[8] and, instead, proposes a multiple system under one state. Specifically, China proposes that Taiwan keep its own political, legal, military, and financial systems, independent of mainland China. China's proposal grants Taiwan more autonomy than Hong Kong has. The proposed Taiwan model critically differs from the Hong Kong model in that Taiwan would maintain its own military and own democratic selection of top political officials. It is understandable that Taiwan views the unification of mainland China and Taiwan very differently from the way that China views it, from the fundamentals of the relationship to the position of negotiation, given the gap between the political and economic development of the two. Even though Taiwan has very different designs for its future and its relationship with mainland China, China at least has adjusted itself to a more reasonable and open approach in seeking unification.

The Taiwan issue is not one of freedom and democracy. The U.S. military involvement in defending Taiwan began when there were not even democratic elections in Taiwan. Today, Taiwan's democratic election system is a huge asset for its future development and prosperity. China's proposal acknowledges the value of Taiwan's political system. In fact, in the not-too-distant future, China may want to learn how Taiwan managed its political transition to a more democratic system, as Hong Kong set the example of an efficient civil system and a highly free-market economic system.

The Taiwan issue could push China to become a strong sponsor of the otherwise rapidly declining Russian weapons production facilities. China would view itself as being forced to spend billions of dollars to support both defensive and offensive Russian weapons capabilities. Many signs already indicate that such support would not be just a remote possibility. Allowing the Taiwan issue to corner

---

[8]This was initially introduced by Deng Xiaoping on a visit to the United States. See *People's Daily,* February 1, 1979. For the evolution on unification with Taiwan, see Deng's instructions in 1984 ("Deng Xiaoping on Unification," pp. 35–38) and Jiang's eight points of 1995 ("Continue Striking to Complete Unification of the Motherland," January 30).

China and motivate it to go to Russia for military capabilities definitely contradicts the simplest strategic thinking of the United States. Any sort of Russia-China alliance would disturb the current security balance in the region, and none of the U.S. allies would want to see this happen.

The United States has much more to lose than gain by keeping the Taiwan issue hanging and its Taiwan policy as it is. If there were a civil war, no matter how the United States enters it, it will only can only look bad for the United States, simply because it would be a "Chinese" war. The United States would be viewed as an instigator because, without U.S. support, conciliation and compromise would replace war in the search for a solution. U.S. military involvement in defending Taiwan could cost the United States loss of both Taiwan and China. First, China is stronger today than it was 30 or 40 years ago, and the interests in Taiwan of the United States and China are not symmetric. Second, to China, Taiwan is a life and death issue. To the United States, Taiwan is one of problems in the world that the United States has an interest in. If Taiwan seeks independence, and the United States becomes involved in a war in Taiwan, Taiwan will be destroyed. China and Taiwan will both blame the United States, and the United States will likely gain nothing positive from the situation. Furthermore, the Chinese would believe that without the United States, Taiwan simply would not chose independence from China. In addition, Taiwan would not appreciate U.S. support if it ends with war and devastation of the island. Some independence advocates may even complain that the United States did not give enough support in a war or that it did not endorse Taiwan independence clearly and firmly enough.

Regarding hedging policies, there are various schools of thought. U.S. hedging on China with Taiwan sounds logical but is seriously flawed.[9] One of the theories is that the United States should help Taiwan preserve the status quo, and that if China evolves into a democratic and friendly nation, U.S. policy could shift to encourage unification. Otherwise, the United States could support strengthening of Taiwan's de facto independence. The flaw is obvious: This is by

[9]Gilbert Rozman also provides a thought on hedging: in a world in which China stands alone, though respected and unthreatened, the United States leads a coalition of regional powers as a hedge against possible threats from China.

and large a hedging of taking hostages. When hostage hedging happens, hostilities have already taken place, and therefore no other side for hedging exists. Even Taiwan, similar to a hostage, would hardly be happy with this situation for long either.

On the one hand, Taiwan could block China's view over the United States and, similarly, it could block American's view over China. China could not take U.S. intentions to defend Taiwan more hostile to China. If such similar problem happens to the United States, the United States would understandably very much does the same. It would do both the United States and China good if such a source of negative feelings and distrust could be eliminated. A separate Taiwan was, in general, a result of "century of shame" in history and, more specifically, civil war. The United States and China should find way to step across this slippery pool of water and look at larger issues with longer views to enhance the interest of both. The issue of the United States defending Taiwan keeps provoking doubts, suspicions, and distrust among the Chinese about the intention of the United States. In the last few years, the Chinese increasingly doubt their inclined assessment of economic and political values that the United States advocates. They become more suspicious of the U.S. purpose of engaging China and ask themselves if the U.S. stance on Taiwan is part of its new containment policy. Further, distrust arises that the United States wants, if possible by any means, to see a weak China because the United States takes a strong China as a challenger.

On the other hand, with the Taiwan issue lingering, Americans could get the impression that China is threatening a much smaller Taiwan, which has a democratically elected government. Americans sometimes become incensed when a communist country tries to deprive a democratic nation of its freedom. Because of potential military confrontation and the fact that China is nuclear weapon equipped, Americans may consider China as an even bigger threat.

However, fighting a war to solve the Taiwan issue is not in China's best interests either. China could win such a war. But the war would cost both Taiwan and China years of savings and investments. Chinese would be taking Chinese lives. Such a war would subordinate many of the urgent tasks for modernizing China, leaving millions of people below the poverty level in Ganshu and Guizhou to suffer much longer. If China resorts to war, with or without U.S. military invention, China will pay a dear price with extremely high interest for decades to come. Recent history clearly shows how important and how much value a good image is to China and to China's dream of modernization. In general, war on Taiwan would inevitably contradict China's interests in economic development, regional security, and integration with the world community. A war would not only cost China tremendously and immediately but also hurt its critical international relations and image for a long time to come. China should want to play the role of sophisticated and respected dealmaker rather than orthodox knight. China needs to be seen as a country that the region can rely on for safety and stability. China does not want to make its neighbors feel safer only if they have a force to counter and balance it. China should want to deepen economic integration in the East Asian region rather interrupt the current process with a war.

Regarding the people of Taiwan, China should want to earn and establish more trust after 50 years of separation. China needs to learn to listen to Taiwan. China needs to constantly examine what it offers Taiwan. Further, China should examine what it can do to improve itself to better embrace Taiwan. China may have to admit that there are things needed to accomplish the patching of some important gaps. It is likely beyond question that China should go further with its economic and political reform. In addition to many of Taiwan's concerns, there is suspicion or a lack of assurance or institutionalized guarantees for China's promises. This lack remains a basic obstacle to unification in the hearts of some Taiwanese.[10] The freedom that mainland Chinese enjoy and the institutions behind this freedom will be the most convincing evidence in Taiwan's verdict.

If war is China's only means of effective communication with Taiwan, this is telling of at least poverty of wisdom, considering all the pride of China's past and in the face of developments in the age of communication. Both sides of the Taiwan Strait came from a similar culture of the art of war and philosophy of peace. According to Sun-tzu: "To win without fighting is the acme of skill." If wisdom,

[10]Taiwan's President, Jiang Jinguo, discussed unification in 1982 with a *Newsweek* reporter.

confidence, and patience can combine properly, a win-win outcome is still possible.

China needs to search for vision and wisdom in resolving the Taiwan issue. The vision is looking forward 30 to 40 years, when broader economic integration, deeper cultural exchanges, and more rational reasoning based on human respect will eventually set the background for political decisions. Wisdom should be reflected in China's offers to Taiwan. Particularly, these offers should reward Taiwan for voluntary unification.

In addition, any war with Taiwan will cause China to lose the foreign investments that China's growth increasingly relies on. China relies more than ever before on long-term partners in its trade and investments. A war would cast a lingering shadow over the heart of business planners and investors. A war would also distance China from the world business community if not ruin its hard-earned relations with this community.

As the common ground on which the U.S.-China relationship prospered in the 1970s and 1980s continues to face erosion, the two sides need to think more openly, patiently, and creatively to reach an appropriate approach to Taiwan. A peaceful solution regarding Taiwan will eventually rest on the economic interests, well-being, and the development of rational thinking on both sides of the Taiwan Strait. The United States

and China need to look beyond Taiwan in search for a new relationship on the basis of long-term strategic interests in the 21st century.

BUSINESS TIES AND TRADE IMBALANCE

Business and economic bonds between the United States and China have been steadily strengthening since the rapprochement of the early 1970s. Still, more economic opportunities continue to arise and unfold. The growing economic bonds between the United States and China can be attributed to economic resources and mutually attractive business opportunities. On the one hand, China can offer an enormous market of people with fast-rising incomes and an almost unlimited supply of labor. The United States, on the other hand, offers the leaders in technology and development of competitive business organizations. However, tensions regarding trade imbalances became noticeable in the early 1990s and have turned political.

Since the first U.S. joint-venture started in Beijing in April 1980, investments from the United States have bloomed in China, from McDonald's fast food, to Motorola cellular phones, to GM's Buick cars. American direct investments in China mounted to $25 billion by the end of 1998, while another $20–25 billion was committed toward future investments, with nearly $4 billion committed for investments in 1998 alone (see Table 12.1).[11]

U.S.-China trade experienced steady growth since the early 1970s and particularly since China began its economic reforms in the late 1970s and early 1980s. In 1972, direct trade between the United States and China was less than $13 million (or, according to American statistics, which include trade through third countries, trade was less than $100 million). U.S.-China annual trade rose to nearly $5 billion in 1980 according to both American and Chinese statistics. It further increased to $20 billion in 1990 (according to U.S. statistics) or $12 billion (according to Chinese statistics), and more recently stood at over $80 billion (U.S. statistics) or $55 billion (Chinese statistics) (see Table 12.1).

While the U.S.-China trade volume grows, the share of trade with the United States in the overall foreign trade of China has been rising. According to Chinese statistics, the share of Sino-U.S. trade of total Chinese foreign trade increased from 12.6 percent in 1980 to about 15 percent in 1995, and to an estimated 20 percent in 1998. According to U.S. statistics, the share rose from 12.9 percent in 1980 to 17.3 percent in 1990, to 20.4 percent in 1995, to 21.9 percent in 1996, to 23.2 percent in 1997, and to an estimated 25 percent in 1998.

At the same time, the share of trade with China in the overall foreign trade of the United States rose from an insignificant figure in the 1970s and early 1980s to about 5 percent in 1998. From 1996 to 1998, China was among the top five trade partners of the United States, after Canada, Japan, and Mexico.

---

[11]All dollar amounts are U.S. dollars unless otherwise noted.

Table 12.1

U.S. and China Total Trade Volume and Balance (in billions of unadjusted U.S. dollars)

Year	Chinese Statistics: Total	Chinese Statistics: Balance	U.S. Statistics: Total	U.S. Statistics: Balance
1972	0.013	0	0.10	0.03
1973	0.26	–0.18	0.80	0.67
1974	0.48	–0.27	0.93	0.70
1975	0.47	–0.21	0.46	0.14
1976	0.32	0	0.33	–0.07
1977	0.29	0.065	0.33	–0.03
1978	0.99	–0.45	1.1	5.0
1979	2.4	–1.3	2.4	1.07
1980	4.8	–2.8	4.9	2.6
1981	5.9	–2.9	5.5	1.7
1982	5.3	–2.1	5.4	0.41
1983	4.0	–0.6	4.6	–0.30
1984	6.0	–1.4	6.3	0.38
1985	7.0	–1.7	8.1	–0.37
1986	7.3	–2.1	8.3	–2.1
1987	7.8	–1.8	10.4	–3.4
1988	10.0	–3.3	13.5	–3.5
1989	12.3	–3.5	17.8	–6.2
1990	11.8	–1.4	20.0	–10.2
1991	14.2	–1.8	25.3	–12.7
1992	16.7	0.5	33.2	–18.2
1993	27.7	6.3	40.3	–22.8
1994	35.4	7.5	48.1	–29.5
1995	40.8	8.6	57.3	–33.8
1996	42.8	10.5	63.5	–39.5
1997	48.9	17.4	75.4	–49.5
1998	54.9	21.0		

SOURCES: *The World Almanac and Book of Facts*, 1995–1999; *Almanac of China's Foreign Trade 1998; Almanac of China's Statistics*, 1995–1998; *A Statistical Survey of China 1999*, Beijing, China Statistics Press, 1999.

NOTE: The data on China do not include those for Hong Kong.

While both countries enjoyed economic benefits from this trade, the U.S. trade deficit with China has become a major economic and political issue. The U.S. trade deficit with China ranks number two after Japan. If the trend continues, the U.S. trade deficit with China could in the near future surpass that of the United States with Japan.

Regarding the trade imbalance issue, the first and the most important factor is the openness of the Chinese market. China should make its markets more open, allowing more American goods and services to have access to the Chinese market. China should act more quickly to remove market barriers and entry restrictions designed to limit competition from foreign businesses. At the same time, the United States should look more closely and specifically at the trade deficit issue. Some specific factors in trade balance measurement and assessment should be considered carefully: After two decades of foreign investment and economic reform, for every dollar of Chinese export in 1998, 45 cents accrues to foreign investors.[12] In the last decade or so, Hong Kong and Taiwan businesses moved to China a massive amount of labor-intensive industries, such as shoes, apparel, toys, electrical and electronics, and computer parts and components. Moreover, the United States needs to further lift restrictions on exports and allow more U.S. technologically advanced products to be exported to China. The current rigid restriction system deprives American businesses of hard-earned opportunities and chokes a potentially enormous market and development of business interests. This is particularly true for technology industries given the extremely fast pace of technology development and innovation. Given that the United States and China reached an agreement in November 1999 on China's entrance into the WTO, it is ever more promising that the Chinese market will be more open to U.S. business and investment. Once China enters the WTO, implementation of China's commitments will be overwhelming, but, as the Chinese economic transition for entrance into the WTO proceeds and succeeds, enormous opportunities will emerge for China and the United States.

With proven benefits and rewards from economic opening and market-oriented reform, China has to more firmly embrace globalization and integration with the world economy. Fear of foreign economic dominance, overprotection of the national economy, and more time for economic transition are unceasing dragging on the reform process since the very first day China took the path of reform. Although appropriate planning and careful timing is always a good idea for major policies, experience suggests that China should worry more about being slow to open up and reform than being too fast. Even assuming China moves faster in opening up its markets, a large American trade deficit with China is likely to remain.

---

[12]China Statistics Press, *A Statistical Survey of China 1999*, 1999.

Another area in which China needs to improve is to make its market more open and attractive to U.S. investment. China receives less than 0.5 percent of U.S. investment from abroad, in sharp contrast to 5 percent share of trade. China attracts less investment from the United States than do Taiwan or Singapore, where economies enjoy much more freedom and easy access for foreign investors under the rule of law. Specifically, China should expedite reducing barriers for foreign investment in infrastructure and the service, retail, and financial sectors.

China also needs to focus on improving the investment environment regarding the rule of law. Although there is no doubt that China has moved far and fast in developing a market-oriented economy, China lags way behind in terms of the investment environment as compared with competing economies in such East Asian countries as South Korea, Taiwan, and Singapore. In China, uncertainties about business transaction costs are high, while legal protection of property and business is low. Currently, China attracts most of its foreign investment from overseas Chinese. China also needs to make itself more attractive to multinational corporations, which rely on the rule of law for both protection and establishment of expectations. For long-term or short-term benefits, there is nothing more beneficial to China than spending resources on accelerating development of the legal system for a market-oriented economy.

Currently, the United States and China should focus on reaching a fair, commercially viable, and practically accountable agreement for China on WTO entry. Once an agreement is reached, the next task will be for the United States to work with China to fully implement China's WTO commitments, which may require much more political and economic resources than can currently be understood, given the diversity of the Chinese economy.

In other economic and business areas, depending on overall relations, the United States can cooperate with China by applying its experiences and resources. Specific areas include fixing problems of state-owned enterprises, industrial restructuring, banking system reform, efforts against corruption, development of the rule of law, development of social and economic policies for unemployment and social security, and ongoing career education.

THE ENVIRONMENT AND NATURAL RESOURCES

China is a major partner with the United States in the global effort to protect the environment. Although China's per-capita production is very low, with one-fifth of the world's population, China should expect to cooperate more on and contribute more than it has in the past to pollution control and environmental protection. Currently, China is the world's number one producer of steel, coal, cement, fertilizer, and similar products. And two-decade's economic growth, which has lifted millions out of poverty, has caused serious environmental damage that will be felt for many years to come.

Some of this damage is already devastating. A survey in 1997 shows more than one-third of monitored urban river sections are seriously polluted and that they do not even meet the lowest standards necessary for irrigation water, not to mention drinking water. In many major cities, such as Hangzhou and Yibin, over 70 percent of rainfall is acid rain. The frequency of acid rainfall in some cities, such as Changsha and Zhuengyi, reaches 90 percent.

Although China has taken many measures to prevent environmental damage, it will likely see its environment get worse before it gets before. The United States and China are both among the top polluting countries in the world. The principal pollutants include carbon monoxide, lead, nitrogen oxide, and sulfur oxide. China is the world's second largest greenhouse gas producer, trailing behind only the United States.

Although it has a long way to go, China has voluntarily devoted substantial financial and human resources, in addition to regulation efforts, to clean air and water and to preserving the ecological system. China's increasing market orientation requires a strategy for future environmental protection that goes beyond the measures of the past. Achieving environmental protection goals will require sacrifices in the near term and experience to make the battle more effective.

The United States and China, together with other countries, need to cooperatively work out incentive programs for China and other less-developed countries to shorten the process of cutting down emission rates to the level of more-developed countries. China remains a poor country, with half the population subsisting on under $2 a day. As Mark Hertsgaard observed, although being a big source of pollutant emissions, "China emits a far smaller amount of greenhouse gases per capita than the rich nations whose earlier industrialization has already condemned the world to climate change."[13] The fact is that the per-capita income of China is still well below the world average, and the Chinese in most of the inland areas have basic and urgent needs still to be met. Given this, future benefits and costs are subject to a higher discount rate in calculations and decisionmaking. Controlling pollution and improving the environment may involve near-term sacrifices and disproportional allocations of the benefits. Environmental protection could be an extra or unfair burden for certain generations. On top of that, it requires understanding, cooperation, investment, and conscious action from all of the people. Although determined, China is facing an uphill battle in this ambitious environmental war—to reduce emissions in 2020 below today's levels, improve air and water quality, and lower pollution-related health costs by 75 percent—while at the same time China will again quadruple its output. As for the United States, it needs to work with China on the environment. Absent a radical shift in world policies, the greenhouse effect, for example, and other environmental damage will accelerate global climate change, melting polar ice caps, and causing more and nastier hurricanes, droughts, and blizzards. The United States, China, and the rest of the world will suffer from such changes. The United States also has the resources and experience to assist China. This is a potential a major bond for the United States and China. Although China has realized the benefits of preserving the earth and protecting the environment, China undoubtedly has its own agenda, which may be far from that of the United States on this score. Given the huge differences in social and economic development, both the United States and China can see a clear common interest in working closely on accelerating China's environmental efforts.

IDEOLOGICAL DIVIDE AND DOMESTIC FACTORS

Tensions arise between the United States and China on such issues as the structure of the world order and how to maintain it, interna-

---

[13]Mark Hertsgaard, "Our Real China Problem" (originally published in *Atlantic Monthly*, November 1997), in Orville Schell and David Shambaugh (eds.), *The China Reader*, Vintage Books, New York, 1999, p. 388.

tional interference in human rights issues versus state sovereignty, democratization and government-citizen relations, abortion and family policies, freedom of religion, and the rule of law. When there was a common threat, tensions in these areas did not prevent the two countries from developing strategic cooperation against the Soviet Union in the 1980s and part of the 1970s. Since the early 1990, however, there has been a consistently increasing level of difficulty in consensus building on almost all of these issues. The difficulty for the U.S. administration in reaching consensus with the Congress cannot be better illustrated in terms of its potential damage to the U.S.-China relations as in the case of President Clinton's reluctance to proceed with a WTO agreement when Premier Zhu took a great risk in making unexpected concessions in Washington.

China differs with the United States on the structure of the future world order. Beijing opposes what it sees as Washington's troubling tendencies toward unilateral action. Like many other countries, China does not support U.S.-led military interventions in such hot spots as Kosovo and has expressed grave concern about the possibility of U.S. military action in North Korea. However, on the developments in East Timor and the subsequent sending of UN peacekeeping forces, China and the United States stood together throughout, with early opposition from Russia.

The issue of human rights in China causes constant tensions between Washington and Beijing. The Chinese leadership strictly limits any organization's ability to challenge the ruling party. The Chinese government considers criticism of China's human rights record as interference in its state sovereignty. The Chinese leadership argues that it has improved economically human conditions and living standards, lifting more Chinese out of poverty than at anytime before. It often points to decentralization and liberalization of the economy as development of freedom for individuals. The Chinese government further views human rights issues as having been used against it in the way of blackening its image and introducing unstable factors. Chinese leaders have repeated from time to time that stability overrides everything.[14] The Western conviction is that state power stems

[14]Even before the Tiananmen Square incident, Deng Xiaoping told visiting U.S. President Bush: "Stability overrides everything. Without stability, nothing can be

from the people rather than the people's strength emerging from the state. Yet, in the past, American administrations have seen human rights as a Chinese domestic issue, secondary to fundamental U.S. interests. More recently, however, humanitarian and security interests have become increasingly intertwined for the United States.

Both the United States and China involve multiple domestic forces in shaping their relationship. In the United States, as a result of democracy, interest groups, the media, and various governmental branches all attempt to affect the relationship. Sometimes, domestic feelings can choke new initiatives that may carry strategic merits for fundamental U.S. interests. Cultural and ideological differences may also intrude in U.S. policies on China. For example, according to Kenneth Lieberthal, 120 congressmen voted against China's most-favored-nation trade status in 1996 because of their opposition to China's birth control policies.[15]

U.S. labor unions have also been criticizing China's trade policy, considering China a threat to their interests. Growing imports from China and the large U.S. trade deficit with China has been a regular target of many U.S. interest groups. Conservative presidential candidate Pat Buchanan also joined in the fray with his strong rhetoric on protectionism. The voices could get very loud, particularly when the U.S. economy was in trouble and unemployment rates were high.

Human rights and antiabortion groups represent two of the strongest voices against China. Considering that the abortion issue has caused serious violence in America, it is not surprising that this group has taken a stand against China's mandatory birth control policy. These two groups are sometimes highly political and influential in domestic policy. Human rights groups have become more powerful in international policymaking than ever before, in terms of their influence both over the government and corporations. They regularly publish human rights reports and comment on government and corporate policies. It is interesting to note that these groups, while often critical

---

done, and we could lose what we've achieved" (Shu Ge, *American China Policy and the Taiwan Issue,* p. 590, 1998) .

[15]Kenneth Lieberthal, "Domestic Factors in U.S.-Sino Relationship," in Zhao Baoxi (ed.), *Sino-American Relations,* 1997.

of China's behavior, work hard with Chinese authorities and agencies to keep dialogue and communications open.

The U.S. Congress, by and large, has also been difficult in reaching consensus with the administration on China policies since 1990. With the Tiananmen Square incident lingering, the Congress has been critical of both Presidents Bush and Clinton. Although partisan factors are undeniable, the Congress appears to view China differently at present than it did in most of the 1980s. The Congress has been particularly alert to the issue and potential threat of a rising China.

China has sometimes found it difficult to comprehend that political forces, other than the administration, have sway in the formation of U.S. policy on China. The Bush and Clinton administrations have borne a heavy burden of criticism over their China policies. While U.S. administrations should develop clearer and more persuasive thinking on China policy in efforts to build consensus with Congress, both the United States and China would be better off if China had a better understanding of the mechanisms involved in U.S. politics and reflect this understanding in its policies and dealings with regard to the U.S.-China relationship.

As for China's U.S. policymaking process, it is no longer the same as what it was in Deng's or Mao's time. Interest groups are playing a greater role. The reactions in the bureaucracy to Premier Zhu's concessions and failure clearly implied this change. Given governmental decentralization and the development of industrial representation in government since the early 1980s, economic and political interests have driven ministries, provinces, and industrial associations to voice their demands and protect their interests. It is noticeable that economic liberalization in China does not stop at the corporate and individual level, but penetrates into all levels of the economic hierarchy and the thinking of citizens and officials.

Nationalism appears to be rising in China and could become an important domestic factor the Chinese leadership will need to carefully consider in dealing with the United States. In addition, the dispatch of two U.S. Navy carriers to the Taiwan Strait and the accidental bombing of the Chinese Embassy aroused broad resentment in China.

CONCLUDING REMARKS

There are many bonds and tensions between the United States and China arising from their own deep interests and perception of the interests. Development of the relationship is subject to these opposed forces.

The equilibrium of U.S.-China relations moves as a result of constantly shifting actions and interactions. The relationship is a high-stakes game. At present, the United States has greater strength and influence. China has its vast fast-learning populace. The United States has more international interests to manage. China has more domestic problems of social and economic transformation to resolve. Both benefit from their trust in each other and suffer from confrontations with each other. The United States has many forces contributing in the shaping its policy toward China. China is beginning to see different groups voicing opinions about China-U.S. policy

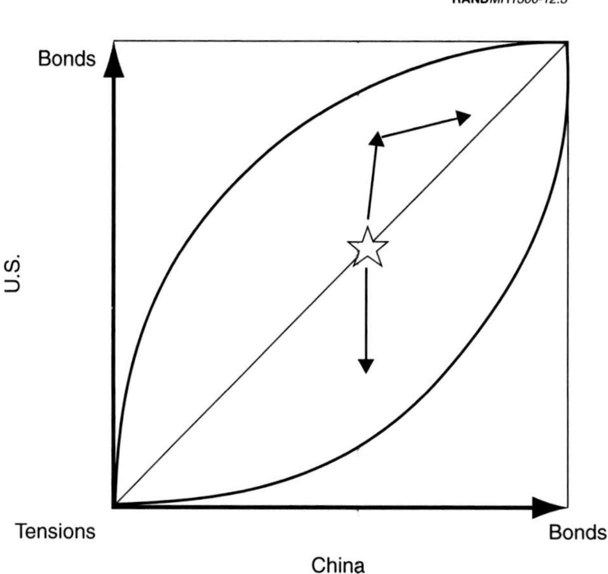

Figure 12.3

as a result of economic and social progress. The United States, in dealing with China, seems to need more political patience, cultural tolerance, understanding of China's social diversity, and even broader media coverage of social and economic developments in China. China, in dealing with the United States and the world at large, seems to need to challenge itself more with market competition, development of legal and democratic institutions, social openness, and adaptation to international norms. In general, both need show each other more respect and to improve their understanding of the other for a constructive relationship to develop between these two vastly different countries. It is hoped that the United States and China can learn to develop good will and mutually beneficial cooperation.

At this time and in the near future, the United States is in the better position for initiating and leading the development of the U.S.-China relationship. China will respond, as confirmed by the history of the last half century. As David Shambaugh elegantly put it: "If the United States treats China as an adversary, it will become one."[16] With all the common bonds and interests of the United States and China, if the United States treats China as an friend, China is likely to act like one.

---

[16]David Shambaugh, "China's Military: Real or Paper Tiger?" in Orville Schell and David Shambaugh (eds.), *The China Reader,* Vintage Books, New York, 1999, p. 446.

CONFERENCE AGENDA

RAND–China Reform Forum Conference
China, the U.S., and the Global Economy
Santa Monica, California
November 9-10, 1999

AGENDA

TUESDAY, NOVEMBER 9
RAND, North Conference Facility

8:30 a.m. **Continental Breakfast**

9:00 a.m. **Welcome**
James A. Thomson, RAND

Opening Remarks
Charles Wolf, RAND
Shuxun Chen, China Reform Forum

9:15 a.m. **Session One: Outlook for the Global Economy (moderator: Charles Wolf)**

- ***TRENDS AND PROSPECTS IN THE GLOBAL ECONOMY***
Gary Hufbauer, Institute for International Economics

9:30 a.m. *World Economic Restructuring and China's Economic Transformation*
Yuanzheng Cao, BOC International Holdings Ltd.

9:45 a.m. Discussants: Angang Hu, Chinese Academy of Sciences; Benjamin Zycher, RAND

10:15 a.m. General discussion

10:45 a.m. Break

11:00 a.m. Session Two: Outlook for the U.S. Economy

\- *Can the United States' Economic Success Continue?*
Gail Fosler, The Conference Board

11:15 a.m. Discussant: Ren Wei Huang, Shanghai/Pudong Center for American Economic Studies

11:30 a.m. General discussion

12:00 p.m. Lunch

1:30 p.m. Session Three: Trends and Prospects in the Chinese Economy (moderator: Shuxun Chen)

\- *Chinese Economy in Prospect*
Angang Hu

1:45 p.m. *China's Economic Growth: Recent Trends and Prospects*
K.C. Yeh, RAND

2:00 p.m. Discussants: Charles Wolf, Angang Hu

2:30 p.m. General discussion

3:00 p.m. Break

3:15 p.m. Session Three resumes

\- *The Role of Foreign-Invested Enterprises in the Chinese Economy: An Institutional and Policy Perspective*
Yasheng Huang, Harvard Business School

3:30 p.m. *Chinese Macro Economy: Expanding Domestic Demands and the Interim Reform*
Xiaomin Shi, China Society for Research on Economic System Reform

3:45 p.m. Discussants:Xianquan Xu; Alice Young, Kaye, Scholer, Fierman, Hays & Handler

4:15 p.m. General discussion

5:00 p.m. Adjourn

6:00 p.m. Dinner

WEDNESDAY, NOVEMBER 10
DoubleTree Guest Suites, Santa Monica, Carousel C

8:30 a.m. Continental Breakfast

9:00 a.m. Session Four: US-China Economic and Security Relations (moderator: Shuxun Chen)

\- *Situations and Trends of Arms Development in the East Asian Region*
Bin Yin, China Reform Forum

9:15 a.m. *The Importance of an Open China*
Harry Rowen, Asia Pacific Research Center, Stanford

9:30 a.m. Discussants: Michael Swaine, RAND, Xianquan Xu

10:00 a.m. General discussion

10:30 a.m. Break

10:45 a.m. *American Interests In and Concerns with China*
John Despres

11:00 a.m. *Sino-US Economic Relations*
Xianquan Xu, MOFTEC

11:15 a.m. Discussants: Shuxun Chen; Hang-Sheng Cheng, 1990 Institute; Roy Doumani

11:45 a.m. General discussion

12:15 p.m. Lunch

1:45 p.m. Session Four resumes (moderator: Charles Wolf)

- *US-China Relationship In Danger: Bonds and Tensions Between the Two*
Hui Wang, First China Capital

2:00 p.m. Discussants: Bin Yin, Charles Wolf

2:30 p.m. General discussion

3:00 p.m. Break

3:15 p.m. Concluding Discussion

4:30 p.m. Adjourn

6:00 p.m. Closing Reception and Dinner

CONFERENCE PARTICIPANTS

RAND–China Reform Forum Conference
China, the U.S., and the Global Economy
Santa Monica, California
November 9-10, 1999

Participant List

Conference Sponsors

Committee of 100

The Capital Group Companies · Lombard Investments · Overland Group · UCLA Center for International Studies · Zhejiang Gateway International Investment Company

Conference Participants

MR. JAMES V. BITONTI, JR., *Zhejiang Gateway International Investment Company, USA*

MR. HUAYIN CAO, *Interpreter, CHINA*

DR. YUANGZHENG CAO, *BOC International Holdings Ltd., CHINA*

DR. SHUXUN CHEN, *China Reform Forum, CHINA*

DR. HANG SHENG CHENG, *The 1990 Institute, USA*

MR. JOSEPH CHULICK, JR., *Lombard Investments, Inc., USA*

GINA DESPRES, ESQ., *The Capital Group Companies, USA*

MR. JOHN DESPRES, *USA*

MR. ROY DOUMANI, *USA*

MATT FONG, ESQ., *Sheppard, Mullin, Ricter & Hampton, USA*

DR. GAIL FOSLER, *The Conference Board, USA*

DR. ANGANG HU, *Chinese Academy of Sciences, CHINA*

DR. REN WEI HUANG, *Shanghai/Pudong Center for American Economic Studies, CHINA*

PROFESSOR YASHENG HUANG, *Harvard Business School, USA*

DR. GARY HUFBAUER, *Institute for International Economics, USA*

MR. H. LAWRENCE HULL, JR., *Lombard Investments, Inc., USA*

MR. FRED LIAO, *Overland Group, USA*

MR. WEIMING LU, *Committee of 100, USA*

PROFESSOR RICHARD ROSECRANCE, *UCLA, USA*

PROFESSOR HARRY ROWEN, *Asia Pacific Research Center, Stanford, USA*

DR. XIAOMIN SHI, *China Society for Research on Economic System Reform, CHINA*

DR. CHARLES SIE, *Committee of 100, USA*

MR. C. B. SUNG, *Committee of 100, USA*

DR. MICHAEL SWAINE, *RAND, USA*

MR. HENRY TANG, *Committee of 100, USA*

DR. HUI WANG, *First China Capital, USA*

DR. CHARLES WOLF, JR., *RAND, USA*

PROFESSOR XIANQUAN XU, *MOFTEC, CHINA*

DR. K. C. YEH, *RAND, USA*

DR. BIN YIN, *China Reform Forum, CHINA*

ALICE YOUNG, ESQ., *Kaye, Scholer, Fierman, Hays & Handler, LLP, USA*

DR. JOHN YOUNG, *Committee of 100, USA*

DR. BENJAMIN ZYCHER, *RAND, USA*

BIOGRAPHICAL SUMMARIES OF CHAPTER AUTHORS

Dr. Yuangzheng Cao is the Deputy CEO and Chief Economist of the Bank of China International Holdings, Ltd. , and has served as economic adviser to several transitional countries including Vietnam, Mongolia, and the Czech Republic.

Dr. Shuxun Chen is the former Secretary General of the China Reform Forum.

Mr. John Despres is a private consultant, and former Assistant Secretary of Commerce.

Dr. Gail Fosler is senior vice president and chief economist at the Conference Board.

Dr. Angang Hu is a professor at the Research Center for Chinese Study, Hsinghua University, and adviser to the Chinese government on economic and public policies including tax reform, reduction of regional disparities, and stabilization of economic growth.

Dr. Yasheng Huang is a professor at the Harvard Business School.

Dr. Gary Hufbauer is a senior fellow at the Institute for International Economics, and a former vice president and director of studies at the Council on Foreign Relations.

Mr. Xiaomin Shi is Secretary General of the China Institute of Economic System Reform, and participated in designing the program for reform of the Chinese economic system.

Mr. Henry Rowen is codirector of the Asia-Pacific Research Center at Stanford University, professor emeritus at the Stanford Business School, and a former assistant secretary of defense.

Dr. Hui Wang is president of First China Capital, Inc., and a consultant to RAND.

Dr. Charles Wolf, Jr., is senior economic adviser and corporate fellow in international economics at RAND, and a senior fellow at the Hoover Institution.

Mr. Xianquan Xu is a senior research fellow at the Chinese Academy of International Trade and Economic Cooperation, and a senior advisor on WTO issues at the Ministry of Foreign Trade and Economic Cooperation.

Dr. K. C. Yeh is a senior economic consultant, and former senior economist at RAND.